OFF THE BEATEN PATH® SE

TWELFTH EDITION

GEORGIA

OFF THE BEATEN PATH®

DISCOVER YOUR FUN

JANICE McDONALD

Globe
Pequot
Guilford, Connecticut

All the information in this guidebook is subject to change. We recommend that you call ahead to obtain current information before traveling.

Globe Pequot

An imprint of Globe Pequot, the trade division of
The Rowman & Littlefield Publishing Group, Inc.
4501 Forbes Blvd., Ste. 200
Lanham, MD 20706
GlobePequot.com

Distributed by NATIONAL BOOK NETWORK

British Library Cataloguing in Publication Information available

Library of Congress Cataloging-in-Publication Data available

ISBN 978-1-4930-5353-7 (paper : alk. paper)
ISBN 978-1-4930-5354-4 (electronic)

♾™ The paper used in this publication meets the minimum requirements of American National Standard for Information Sciences—Permanence of Paper for Printed Library Materials, ANSI/NISO Z39.48-1992.

To those who love exploring and have learned how
to step out of their comfort zones to do so.

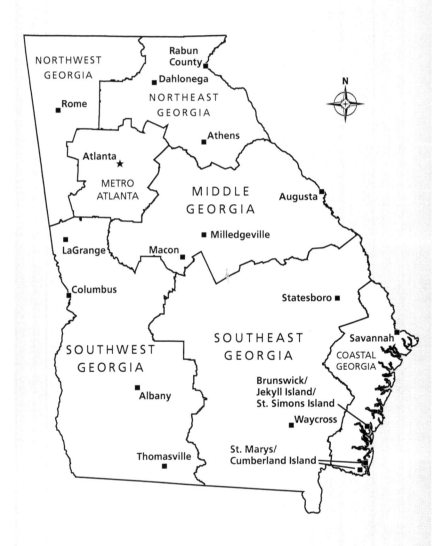

Contents

About the Author

Any new travel find is a new adventure! Traveling isn't just a pastime for Janice McDonald, it's a lifestyle. She has traveled to all seven continents, producing videos, writing books and articles, and just simply exploring. Yet, she still gets a kick out of what she discovers in her own backyard in Georgia. A native of Myrtle Beach, South Carolina, Janice has called the Atlanta area home for more than half her life. She enjoys nothing more than discovering new places to see in her adopted state. A favorite rule of hers in any country is to avoid the main roads and take the road less traveled. She invites you to do the same as you get Off the Beaten Path in Georgia with her.

Acknowledgments

Updating a book about travel in the midst of a pandemic can be daunting. I found myself on the road when no one else was, at times peering into windows. This book is about discovering new places and getting reacquainted with old familiar ones. A lot of people went with me on these journeys, both physically and figuratively. Some went along simply through the phone calls on the way. I would like to thank my sisters, Paula Miles and Anna Boyce, who are always great to travel with. Offering suggestions and companionship were Barbara Lynn Howell, Steve Green, Sheila and Ed Hula, Karen Rosen, Sandee LaMotte, Kathleen Saal, Sandra Holmes, and Kristal Baker. There isn't enough space to list all of the convention and visitor bureau personnel in various towns and counties who were willing to talk me through and to guide me. Dear Vivian Walker, who owns a few bed and breakfasts in the little town of Washington, was incredibly helpful in making sure I knew history and favorite places in her hometown. As always, I also want to thank the Georgia Department of Natural Resources and the Georgia Department of Economic Development for their insight and guidance.

Introduction

I grew up a Carolina Girl and wasn't sure I could love a place as much as I loved my home state. But Georgia has not just won me over; it has exposed me to an incredible state with spectacular sights, hidden wonders, and an amazing diversity in its natural habitats.

Getting off-the-beaten-path to explore and discover those out of the way treasures has opened my eyes and many doors. It was a blast, and I would share each new discovery with friends and family. I have become a de facto tour guide, getting calls from complete strangers who were referred to me by friends. The thing I encourage each of them to do is to be open to something new. Trust the person who is sending you. The places you think you may not be interested in may turn out to be the places that leave the best lasting impressions.

Georgia is blessed to have such history and such vastly different and unique places to discover within its borders. Its coastal beaches, islands, and marshes take me back to my Coastal Carolina roots, but no amount of describing can prepare you for the beauty. The Spanish moss–laden trees are hauntingly beautiful, and the saltwater marshes change color with the sun. Passing through the midlands while farmers were plowing their fields caused me to pull over and watch them turn the red Georgia clay. Driving white-knuckled on the winding highways north of Helen during a foggy morning paid off as the sun burst through to reveal the mountains ahead. Georgia's State Park system throughout is amazing, but the scenery in those parks in North Georgia can be breathtaking. If you can go one place, make it Anna Ruby Falls, especially after a rain.

As you get away from the main highways, you will see that every stop on the road has a story and offers a unique draw. A covered bridge may offer a great photograph, but what if you learned it was built by a freed slave who taught his craft to four sons who also built bridges across the state? Or the large mound of earth you're looking at holds the key to an ancient Indian tribe? Even a trail or stream is connected to the people who came through centuries ago and holds some sort of natural wonder worth diverting from the main road.

But not all there is to see deals with the past. There are people to meet who are currently making their mark on Georgia and there's much to see and do for the active. From kayaking or canoeing down the Suwannee River to hiking the Appalachian Trail, combing the beaches of barrier islands, or just kicking back and fishing. Try it all!

Since many of the updates were made during the COVID-19 pandemic, many businesses, parks, museums, etc. were/are adjusting hours and openings based on what was going on in their communities, so be sure to check their websites or call before going.

In this book's listings, restaurant cost categories refer to the price of entrees without beverages, desserts, taxes, or tips. Those listed as inexpensive are $10 to $12 or less; moderate, between $12 and $19; and expensive, $20 and over. Places to stay listed as inexpensive are up to $100 per double per night; moderate, $101 to $200 per night; and expensive, $201 and up per night.

Before you launch your off-the-beaten-path adventures, you'll be able to gather information from these sources: **Georgia Dept. of Economic Development, Tourist Division** (75 5th St. Northwest, Suite 1200, Atlanta; 404-962-4000; georgia.org) and **Georgia Department of Natural Resources, Parks and Historic Sites Division** (2 Martin Luther King Jr. Dr., Atlanta; 800-366-2661; gadnr.org).

The Parks Division's Reservation Resource lets you make one toll-free call for campsites, cottages, picnic shelters, and lodge rooms throughout the system. Rates vary at different parks. Campsites, with electrical and water hookups, range from $23 to $50 a night. Completely furnished 1-, 2-, and 3-bedroom cottages are $75 to $250. There are even yurts for $50 to $100. Rates are higher on weekends and in certain seasons. Double rooms at state park lodges are $75 to $225. Call individual parks for exact rates. In metro Atlanta call (770) 389-PARK; anywhere else in the United States call (800) 864-PARK or go to gastateparks.org.

An easy reference in exploring highways in Georgia is that exits are based on mile markers and will help you know how far you are from borders and towns. For instance, exit 2, on I-75 in southeastern Georgia, is 2 miles from the Florida border. Exit 353, near the Tennessee border in northwestern Georgia, is 353 miles from the Florida border. For a brochure of the numbers, contact Georgia Department of Transportation (500 W. Peachtree St. NW, Atlanta; 404-631-1990; dot.ga.gov).

If you're interested in a particular area, contact the local convention and visitors bureau or chamber of commerce.

FACTS ABOUT GEORGIA

State tourism toll-free phone number: (800) VISIT-GA (847-4852). Free brochures for many locations are located at exploregeorgia.com/brochures.

MAJOR NEWSPAPERS

Atlanta Journal-Constitution, Augusta Chronicle, Macon Telegraph, Savannah Morning News, Columbus Enquirer, Athens Banner Herald, Rome News Tribune

Famous People

39th president Jimmy Carter

Juliette Gordon Low, founder of the Girl Scouts

Dr. Martin Luther King Jr.

Gone with the Wind author Margaret Mitchell

Television and radio host Ryan Seacrest, from Dunwoody

Tyler Perry set up his studio empire in College Park

Spike Lee and Kanye West were both born in Atlanta

Media mogul Ted Turner

Singing Legend Gladys Knight

Golfing legend Bobby Jones

Rock bands Widespread Panic, R.E.M., and the B-52s, all from Athens

T.L.C., the Black Crowes, and OutKast are from Atlanta

Rappers Childish Gambino, Jermaine Dupri, Jeezy, Ludacris, T.I., 21-Savage, Gucci Mane, 2 Chainz, and Lil Baby

Country bands Lady A, Sugarland, The Zach Brown Band, and Florida-Georgia Line are all from Georgia as are country singers Jason Aldean, Travis Tritt, Alan Jackson, Trisha Yearwood, and Luke Bryan

Academy Award–winning actress Julia Roberts, born in Atlanta and raised in Smyrna

The Help author Kathryn Stockett lives in Atlanta

Milledgeville novelist Flannery O'Connor *(The Violent Bear It Away, Wise Blood)*

Columbus novelist Carson McCullers *(The Member of the Wedding, The Heart Is a Lonely Hunter)*

Eatonton Pulitzer Prize–winning novelist Alice Walker *(The Color Purple)*

Eatonton folk story author and humorist Joel Chandler Harris *(Uncle Remus: Tales, Uncle Remus: His Songs & His Sayings)*

Moreland novelist Erskine Caldwell *(God's Little Acre, Tobacco Road)*

Ray Charles, Lena Horne, Otis Redding, "Little Richard" Penniman, bandleader Harry James, opera superstar Jessye Norman, songwriter Johnny Mercer, comedian Oliver Hardy

Danielsville's Dr. Crawford W. Long, who performed the world's first painless surgery with ether in 1842

Baseball's "Georgia Peach" Ty Cobb, from Royston

Actor Burt Reynolds, born in Waycross

Actresses Dakota and Elle Fanning are from Conyers

Actress Kim Basinger is from Braselton

Comedian Jeff Foxworthy

Dwayne "The Rock" Johnson lives in Powder Springs

Western legend John "Doc" Holliday, born in Griffin

POPULATION

Georgia has 10.8 million people and is the nation's eighth most populous state.

MAJOR METRO AREAS

Atlanta, 6.1 million
Augusta, 600,200
Savannah, 393,400
Macon, 229,000
Columbus, 322,100

Size

With 57,513 square miles, it is the largest state east of the Mississippi, 21st in the nation.

PUBLIC TRANSPORTATION

Atlanta has a rapid rail and public bus system, Metropolitan Atlanta Rapid Transit Authority (MARTA). Other cities with public transportation systems are Macon, Savannah, Augusta, Athens, and Columbus.

CLIMATE

Summers are hot and humid, especially in the southern half of the state and the coast; spring is beautiful and balmy; winters are usually mild, with some snow accumulation in the northern mountains; fall, especially in the northern areas and the mountains, is brisk and cool, with colorful foliage.

GEORGIA TRIVIA

Georgia has 159 counties, more than any other state except Texas (which is four times larger), and more than twice as many as almost-the-same-size Florida and Alabama. There'd be even more, but two counties went bankrupt in the 1920s and merged with Atlanta's Fulton County.

ELEVATIONS

Georgia's highest point is Brasstown Bald Mountain, 4,784 feet above sea level; lowest point is sea level on the Atlantic coast.

Georgia's hottest recorded temperature was 112 degrees Fahrenheit on August 20, 1983, at Greenville; the coldest was 17 degrees below zero in Chatsworth on January 27, 1940.

INTERESTING INFORMATION

You can travel around the world and never leave Georgia. Towns include Vienna (called VIE-enna), Cairo (KAY-ro), Berlin, Boston, Bremen, Hamburg, Rome, Milan, Athens, Arabic, and Sparta. You can shop at Bloomingdale and try to solve the secret of Enigma. Like Scarlett O'Hara, you'll never be hungry in Peach, Bacon, Baker, and Coffee Counties. Don't stub your toe on The Rock, and don't Bogart that joint, my friend.

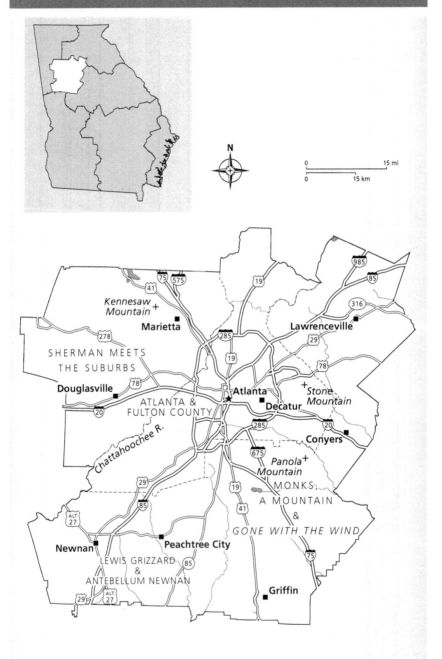

N

0   15 mi
0   15 km

Kennesaw Mountain +

■ **Marietta**

Lawrenceville ■

SHERMAN MEETS
THE SUBURBS

Douglasville ■

ATLANTA &
FULTON COUNTY

★ **Atlanta**

Decatur ■

+ *Stone Mountain*

Chattahoochee R.

■ **Conyers**

Panola + *Mountain*

M·O·N·K·S
A MOUNTAIN
&
GONE WITH THE WIND

Newnan ■

■ **Peachtree City**

LEWIS GRIZZARD
&
ANTEBELLUM NEWNAN

■ **Griffin**

Metro Atlanta

Atlanta & Fulton County

With a population of 6.1 million, **Metro Atlanta** is one of the nation's fastest-growing and most diverse urban centers. New suburbs with cookie-cutter subdivisions and shopping malls, threaded by busy freeways, sprawl in all directions. In the city of Atlanta—population 524,000—an energetic young population is busily reviving many older neighborhoods. Downtown is a bustling center of activity which was largely sparked by the 1996 Atlanta Summer Olympic Games.

Centennial Olympic Park was created for the Olympic Games, transforming a blighted area into the centerpiece of new tourist activity. The park is now surrounded by new high-rise condos, hotels, retail shops, restaurants, and major new visitor attractions. In the 22-acre park, at Marietta Street and Andrew Young International Boulevard, you can sit in the sunshine and admire downtown's striking skyline. If the weather's warm, shuck your shoes and splash in the park's *Fountain of Rings* and perhaps look for your name on the 500,000 bricks that pave the walkways. The *Quilt of Dreams,* made of brick and marble, tells the story of the largest games in Olympics history. *The Southern Company Amphitheater* has a stage that has regular performances. *Unity Plaza* on the northeastern corner includes a water feature and a sculpture called *Androgyne Planet* which stands as a tribute to the Olympic spirit.

Attractions include the massive *Georgia Aquarium.* Built by one of the co-founders of The Home Depot, Bernie Marcus, the Georgia Aquarium's tanks hold more than 10 million gallons of water. One tank alone is 6.3 million gallons. It's home to the world's largest fish, whale sharks destined to reach the size of school buses, and a supporting cast of over 120,000 fish and mammals from around the world. The ark-shaped aquarium is at 225 Baker St. (404-581-4000; georgiaaquarium.org). Open daily. Tickets are $35.95 for general admission. Children under 3 are free.

The nearby *Imagine It! The Children's Museum of Atlanta* (275 Centennial Olympic Park Dr.; 404-659-5437; childrensmuseumatlanta.org) has scores of interactive ways to keep energetic youngsters busy. The museum was redesigned and reopened in 2015. Open daily. Age 3 and up $18.95, 2 and under free.

The *World of Coca-Cola* attraction opened in summer 2007. For details, see the "I'll Have a Co-Coler" sidebar, page 24. Get information on area attractions at the Atlanta Chamber of Commerce on the edge of the park (235 Andrew Young International Blvd.; 404-880-9000; worldofcoca-cola.com). General admission is $14.

The *National Center for Civil and Human Rights* (100 Ivan Allen Jr. Blvd.; 678-999-8990; civilandhumanrights.org) pays homage not just to Atlanta's countless contributions to the Civil Rights Movement, but to human rights struggles around the world. It shares the plaza with the Georgia Aquarium and World of Coke. Open Tues through Sat. Adults $19.99; seniors, military, and students $17.99; children ages 7 to 12 $15.99; and children 6 and under free.

For quick eats, step across Marietta Street to the food court and sit-down restaurants in the *CNN Center* atrium. You can take the *Inside CNN Tour* of the Cable News Network Studios and Turner Broadcasting Network and see news broadcasts around the world. Fifty-five-minute tours begin every ten minutes. Adults, $16.50; seniors and ages 12 to 18, $15.25; ages 4 to 12, $14; under age 4 admitted free. For information and reservations phone (404) 827-2300 or visit tours.cnn.com.

A block from CNN is the football shaped *College Football Hall of Fame* (250 Marietta St.; 404-880-4800; cfbhall.com). An interactive experience, this tribute to all things college football is open daily. Adults are $22.99; kids 3 to 12, $17.99; 3 and under are free.

The best way to view it all may be from **Skyview Atlanta** (168 Luckie St. NW; 678-949-9023; skyviewatlanta.com). This giant Ferris wheel towers 20 stories high and is across the street from Centennial Park. Tickets for those 13 and older are $14.50; ages 3 to 12, $9.50; 3 and under free. Groups can get discounts. Rides last between 7 and 12 minutes.

West Midtown is one of the "happening" neighborhoods in the heart of Atlanta. Spurred by the rebirth of downtown after the success of Centennial Park and the Georgia Aquarium growth, a once almost abandoned area of old warehouses and vacant lots has been reborn. Located just west of the park, bordered by Marietta Street and stretching as far as 8th Street NW, West Midtown, it is now the location for many of Atlanta's hottest restaurants, trendy shops, coffee shops, galleries, and cool loft residential complexes.

The **King Plow Arts Center** (887 W. Marietta St.; 404-885-9933; kingplow .com) is housed in a factory built in 1890 and is the anchor in what is called the Marietta Street Arts Corridor. It was followed by the ever-popular **Goat Farm Arts Center** (1200 Foster St.) which has become a destination for people wanting to experience art in the making through visual and performance art. The Arts Corridor includes theaters, galleries, and designer as well as architectural firms.

Galleries in West Midtown include the **Sandler Hudson Gallery** (1000 Marietta St., #116; 404-817-3300; sandlerhudson.com), and the **Jennifer Schwartz Gallery** (675 Drewry St.; 404-885-1080). They host an art crawl on the third Saturday of each month.

The restaurant scene includes the hard-to-get-into-but-always-awesome **Bacchanalia** and its side kick **Star Provisions** (1460 Ellsworth Industrial Blvd. NW; 404-365-0410), upscale Southern fare at **JCT Kitchen** (1198 Howell Mill Rd.; 404-355-2252), inexpensive but good tacos at **Taqueria del Sol** (1200 Howell Mill Rd.; 404-352-5811), or amazing seafood with signature cocktails at **The Optimist** (914 Howell Mill Rd.; 404-477-6260). The brick oven pizza at **Antico** (1093 Hemphill Ave. NW; 404-724-2333) is consistently rated the best in Atlanta and you can BYOB.

Castleberry Hill is an arts district, downtown off-the-beaten-path, but only a short walk west of Centennial Olympic Park and its numerous attractions. The neighborhood, a pie-shaped wedge bounded by Peters, Walker, and Nelson Streets, was once a bustling industrial area with packing plants, warehouses, and livery stables. In the early 1980s artists and other urban pioneers discovered the rundown buildings and commercial storefronts and began converting them into galleries and spacious loft apartments.

Now almost a dozen art galleries and studios call Castleberry home. Loft conversions and new residential buildings are home to more than 600 permanent residences. Among the galleries that keep regular hours are **Besharat**

Gallery (175 Peters St.; 404-524-3660; besharatgallery.com), **Blu Bisque** (323 Nelson St. NW; 404-593-1431; blubisque.com), **Liana Delgado Art Studio/ Gallery** (161 Mangum St.; 770-366-5893; lianadelgado.com), and **ZuCot Gallery** (100 Centennial Olympic Park Dr.; 404-380-1040; zucotgallery.com). It's best to call in advance. The **2nd Friday Art Strolls** held each month from 7 to 10 p.m. are the best way to take in all the galleries, including ones opened only for the stroll. Check the website, castleberryhill.org.

There are a few restaurants which have become mainstays in the neighborhood. **The Elliott Street Deli and Pub** at 51 Elliott St. (404-523-2174; elliott street.com), has become a local hangout and often hosts events like the annual Chili Cook-off or hot dog eating contest. Other restaurants and bars include **No Mas! Cantina,** a spacious 2-level Mexican eatery with loads of art and handicrafts and a big outdoor patio. An adjoining store with the same name sells handmade Mexican furniture and quality crafts (180 Walker St.; 404-574-5624; nomascantina.com).

If you are a baseball fan, it's worth a jaunt across I-20 towards **Center Parc Credit Union Stadium** (755 Hank Aaron Dr.). Now the home to the Georgia State Panthers, this was also formerly the home of the Atlanta Braves Baseball team and before that, the 1996 Atlanta Olympic Stadium. The Fulton County Stadium where Brave player Hank Aaron hit his 755th home run was directly across Hank Aaron Drive. When the stadium was torn down, the Braves used GPS to layout an outline of the field and the baseball diamond in the parking lot that replaced the stadium. The **Hank Aaron Wall** marks the spot where the homerun that soared Aaron into the record books went over the wall. Despite massive development, that marker remains and you can see it in the Green parking lot for the stadium, accessed off Pollard Boulevard behind the Aspen Heights condos.

Directly across Capital Avenue from the **Georgia State Capitol** (Capitol Avenue SW) is the understated, but beautiful, **Liberty Plaza**. With replicas of both the Liberty Bell and the Statue of Liberty, the plaza has become a prime spot for press conferences, as well as social and political gatherings.

Downtown Atlanta's **Woodruff Park** doesn't have a lot of greenery, but on weekdays this open space at Peachtree, Marietta, and Decatur Streets is a prime people-watching location. At weekday lunch, the benches and small patches of grass fill up with Georgia State University students, office workers, street preachers, politicians, freelance musicians, and entertainers. Pick up a sack lunch at one of the numerous eateries around the park and sit back and watch the water wall and fountain at the north end of the park. *Phoenix Rising*, the large bronze sculpture at the park's south end, symbolizes Atlanta's rebirth after its Civil War destruction.

If you are looking for the legendary **Underground Atlanta** (50 Central Ave. near the Five Points MARTA station; underground-atlanta.com), you may want to wait. The underground portion closed in 2018 and while above ground shops are open, the "city beneath the city" is undergoing a major transformation.

The Historic Fourth Ward Neighborhood just east of downtown is one of the city's trendiest places to visit. It helps that the **Martin Luther King, Jr. National Historic District** and the **Martin Luther King, Jr. Center for Nonviolent Social Change** are both located at its heart at Auburn Avenue and Boulevard. The Fourth Ward was Dr. King's neighborhood, and no doubt he'd be surprised to see the host of new restaurants and bars that now line Edgewood Avenue. The National Historic Site is run by the National Park Service and is open daily 9 a.m. to 5 p.m. and is free to the public. The King Center is independent of the historic site and operated by the King family, but it is across the street at 449 Auburn Ave. (404-526-8900; thekingcenter.org). It is also open daily from 9 a.m. to 5 p.m. and is free to the public.

The Center is the meeting spot for the insightful **Civil Rights Tour** which takes you on a visit to some of the best and least known venues of the Civil Rights Movement. Conducted by Tom Houck, who was Dr. King's driver, each tour gives a personal insight as to the events of that era. Because Houck is friends with many of the key players, it is not unusual to have someone who was involved in the movement to come along. Tours are every Sat at 10 a.m. and are $39 (404-816-1766; civilrightstour.com).

The **Historic Fourth Ward Park** at the eastern edge of the neighborhood offers a great place for kids and adults to play. It is part of the internationally acclaimed **Atlanta Beltline** (beltline.org) development, which was conceived to connect all of Atlanta using old railroad paths. There are trails in all parts of the city which intra-connect and have spurred the building of several live-work-play developments. The Eastside Trail is the busiest and connects Piedmont Park to the Historic Fourth Ward and on to Cabbagetown. It runs adjacent to the popular **Ponce City Market**. Opened in 2015 in the 1926 Sears and Roebuck building, it is now home to shops and trendy restaurants as well as residential and office space (675 Ponce de Leon Ave. NE; 404-900-7900; poncecitymarket.com). Up top is the **Skyline Park,** a rooftop amusement center that has great views of the city, some vintage rides, skee ball, mini golf, and chances for adult beverages (poncecityroof.com).

Billiards, pool, and ping-pong have become hot activities in Atlanta. A favorite haunt is **Sister Louisa's Church of the Living Room & Ping Pong Emporium** (466 Edgewood Ave. SE; 404-522-8275; sisterlouisaschurch.com). No televisions, no internet, just fun activities to make people interact with one

METRO ATLANTA'S TOP HITS

Ansley Park

Antebellum and Victorian Newnan Driving Tour of Homes

Atlanta Botanical Garden

Atlanta Braves Baseball

Atlanta History Center

Atlanta Preservation Center

The Big Chicken

Centennial Olympic Park

Center for Puppetry Arts

Chattahoochee Nature Center

Chattahoochee River National Recreation Area

CNN Center studio tours

College Football Hall of Fame

Decatur Court Square

Fernbank Museum of Natural History

Fernbank Science Center

The Fourth Ward

Georgia Aquarium

Herndon Home

High Museum of Art

Imagine It! The Children's Museum

Kennesaw Mountain National Battlefield Park

Lawrenceville Courthouse Square

Lewis Grizzard Memorial Museum

Marietta Town Square

Martin Luther King, Jr. National Historic District

Michael C. Carlos Emory University Museum of Art and Archaeology

National Center for Civil and Human Rights

Norcross's Historic Old Town

Oakland Cemetery

Panola Mountain State Conservation Park

Pickett's Mill Battlefield Historic Site

Piedmont Park

Roswell

Southern Museum of Civil War and Locomotive History

Stone Mountain Village

Virginia-Highlands

World of Coca-Cola

Wren's Nest

Yellow River Wildlife Sanctuary

Zoo Atlanta

another. Theme nights include tarot card readings and karaoke. Grant Henry, aka Sister Louisa, is there most nights to take you on in ping-pong.

North of downtown, the ***Midtown neighborhood,*** along Peachtree Street between Ponce de Leon Avenue and 16th Street, is one of Atlanta's liveliest and most eclectic areas. Straight, metrosexual, and gay bars and dance clubs, restaurants of every stripe, hotels, shops, live theaters, and sleek high-rise condos line Peachtree, Tenth, and Juniper Streets and Piedmont Avenue. You'll know you have arrived by the giant rainbow crosswalks at Piedmont and Tenth.

The **Woodruff Arts Center** (home of the **Atlanta Symphony Orchestra** and **Alliance Theater**) and **High Museum of Art**, at 1280 Peachtree St., are the city's cultural temples. The High's distinctive white building was designed by architect Richard Meier and will no doubt be recognized as a backdrop from countless movies and television shows. Its own collection includes more than 14,000 works of art across all disciplines. But make sure to check the schedule because the museum's collections in general are world class and the limited-engagement exhibits draw large crowds. Past exhibits included one featuring hundreds of pieces of art from the Louvre, previously never seen outside of France. The High is open Tues to Sat 10 a.m. to 5 p.m.; Thurs 10 a.m. to 8 p.m.; Sun noon to 8 p.m. Closed Mon and holidays. Adults $14.50. Contact the museum at (404) 733-4400 or high.org.

The **Margaret Mitchell House and Museum** (999 Peachtree St.; 404-249-7015; gwtw.org) highlights the Atlanta native's life and gives background to her best-selling novel, *Gone with the Wind*, and the 1939 movie. Mitchell wrote her novel on the battered typewriter in her basement apartment in the restored Victorian boardinghouse she called "The Dump." There's a video about her life and her book, as well as letters, photos, and memorabilia. Opened in 1999, the GWTW Museum adjacent to the house is devoted to the movie, which premiered in Atlanta in 1939. Exhibits include movie scripts, props, costumes, set design sketches, the front door of the O'Hara family's fictional Tara plantation house, and a portrait of Scarlett O'Hara (Vivien Leigh) in a blue dress, still showing a stain from a whiskey glass an angry Rhett Butler (Clark Gable) threw against it in the second half of the movie.

Although Mitchell wrote only one novel, she was a prolific letter writer. In a letter to her mother-in-law in 1936, she describes the day she frantically gathered the GWTW manuscript to deliver to the editor of Macmillan Books: "For years [the manuscript] has been knocking about the house in about twenty very dirty manila envelopes. Some were under the bed . . . some were in the pot and pan closet. I had sixty first chapters, each worse than the other. So, I sat down and took off my garters and tore off a new first chapter. . . . It wasn't until I got to the lobby of [the editor's] hotel that I realized what I looked like, hatless, hair flying . . . my hastily rolled up stockings coming down around my ankles."

The museum is open Mon through Sat from 10 a.m. to 5:30 p.m.; Sun noon until 5:30 p.m. Admission for the house and museum is $13 for adults; $10 for seniors and students; and $5 for children ages 6 to 17. Mitchell was struck and killed by a taxi on her beloved Peachtree Street, 4 blocks from the house, in 1949. She's buried under a simple gravestone, with her married name Marsh, in downtown Atlanta's historic Oakland Cemetery.

One of the most interesting ways to delve into the city's history is on a tour led by the **Atlanta Preservation Center** (404-688-3353; atlantapreservation center.com). The center's 14 walking tours from March through November focus on the city's architectural and cultural heritage. The **Fox Theatre** tour (held throughout the year) takes you backstage at one of America's last surviving 1920s "picture palaces." Adorned with minarets, Moorish arches, Egyptian hieroglyphics, and a blue-sky ceiling that twinkles with electric stars, the "Fabulous Fox" (660 Peachtree St. at Ponce de Leon Ave.; 404-881-2100; foxtheatre.org) hosts a full schedule of touring musicals, concerts of all sorts, and a summertime classic movie festival.

MARTA, the Metropolitan Atlanta Rapid Transit Authority, is an up-to-date way to get around the city. The clean, 2-line rapid rail system intersects at Five Points Station downtown and is a swift way of getting to the Woodruff Arts Center/High Museum of Art, Hartsfield-Jackson International Airport, and other attractions.

The MARTA bus system is a more comprehensive but much slower way of getting about. Fare for either is $2.50 one way, including transfers. If you choose to buy the reloadable Breeze Card, that's another $1. For information call (404) 848-4711. Passes are available for 1-, 2-, 3-, 4-day or monthly passes.

If you are downtown, you may want to take advantage of MARTA's streetcar system. The 2.5-mile loop connects Centennial Park to the Martin Luther King, Jr. National Historic Site as well as most major tourist attractions in the downtown area. The cars run every 10 to 15 minutes and cost just $1 to ride. An all-day pass is available for $3.

For an ear on what's happening, check the *Atlanta Journal-Constitution*'s "Things-to-do" site (ajc.com/things-to-do). The alternative weeklies *Creative Loafing* (creativeloafing.com/things-to-do) and *InTown Atlanta* (atlantaintown paper.com) also keep updated events calendars.

Ansley Park, a lovely neighborhood dating to the 1920s, is a quiet place to walk, drive, or ride a bike. On Peachtree Street at the Woodruff Arts Center/ Colony Square area, turn east onto 15th Street and north onto Peachtree Circle and follow the meandering byways past sumptuous lawns and gardens skirting massive homes in a spectrum of styles. Stop for a picnic, a walk, or a giddy ride on a swing at the somewhat hidden **Winn Park,** at Peachtree Circle and Lafayette Drive. Follow a street called The Prado to Piedmont Avenue.

Cross this busy street and you're at the **Atlanta Botanical Garden** (404-876-5859; atlantabg.org). Take your time strolling through 30 acres of formal gardens, rose gardens, a Japanese garden, and a 15-acre hardwood forest with a marked walking trail, or better yet, walk high above it all with the canopy walk. The concrete walkway climbs up to 40 feet, allowing you a bird's eye view of the hardwood trees. Many state, regional, and national flower shows are held in the Day Building at the entrance. The Botanical Garden's center-piece is the Dorothy Chapman Fuqua Conservatory, with 16,000 square feet of tropical, desert, Mediterranean, and endangered plants. The Fuqua Orchid Center displays tropical orchids from around the world in their natural habitat. There's also a gift shop, snack bar, and nice restaurant. Open Tues through Sun 10 a.m. to 6 p.m. Admission is $21.95 for adults, $18.95 for ages 3 to 12; under age 3 free. Check the calendar for special events like Summer "Sip and Stroll" wine events and the spectacular "Garden Nights, Holiday Lights" from mid-Nov through mid-Jan.

After the Botanical Garden, wander into adjoining *Piedmont Park.* Dating back to 1887, the 189-acre park has tennis courts, a swimming pool, softball fields, playgrounds, and paved, auto-free roadways for jogging, hiking, biking, and rollerblading. In summer, the park's lawns and hillsides fill up with tanning bodies. You can rent (or buy) skateboards, in-line skates, roller skates, and bikes at *Skate Escape* (404-892-1292), across from the park at 1086 Piedmont Ave.

The *Virginia-Highland neighborhood,* about 1.5 miles east of Piedmont Park, is one of the city's favorite dining, shopping, and entertainment areas. It's divided into 3 parts: From Ponce de Leon Avenue, a lively strip of restaurants, bars, coffee shops, and offbeat shops extends about 3 blocks north on North Highland Avenue; after a 3-block residential break, it comes back to life around the Virginia Avenue–North Highland Avenue corner; after another residential break, you'll find more fun stuff at North Highland and Amsterdam Avenues and at another strip at North Highland and Morningside Drive.

Follow Highland north past the Morningside-Lenox Park neighborhood and it will fork off to Lenox Road as a backway into the Buckhead area of Atlanta. If you want to escape the city into nature, make a detour and stop at the *Daniel Johnson Nature Preserve* and *Herbert Taylor Park.* The pre-serve is located within the 26-acre park. There are beautiful trails through old growth forests along Rock Creek and the south fork of Peachtree Creek (1301 Beech Valley Road NE, Atlanta; 404-546-6788; mlpa.org).

The *Buckhead neighborhood,* off Peachtree Street/Road about 6 miles due north of downtown, has long been Atlanta's most splendid residential enclave. West of Peachtree Road, follow the green-and-white scenic drive markers past Spanish and Italian villas, French chateaux, Old English Tudor homes, and white-columned Greek Revival, Georgian, and even Japanese-style

How Buckhead Got Its Name

Buckhead, Atlanta's most affluent, most fashionable neighborhood, owes its unique name to an early settler. In 1838, Henry Irby paid a few dollars for a small piece of wilderness near the modern-day intersection of Peachtree, Roswell, and West Paces Ferry Roads, calling it Irbyville. He put up a tavern and a general store that became a meeting place for farmers, hunters, and tradesmen. One day while hunting in the dense woods, he shot a buck, posted the deer's impressive head on his door, and christened the establishment The Buck's Head Tavern. In time, the tavern gave its name to the entire neighborhood. Irbyville no longer exists, but Irby Avenue remembers the founding father.

showplaces that preside over immense lawns and great stands of trees and flowering shrubbery. Some of the most beautiful homes are on West Paces Ferry, Andrews, Habersham, Blackland, Valley, and Tuxedo Roads.

The neighborhood also has some of the city's finest restaurants. The upscale **Buckhead Village District** near the intersections of Peachtree, Roswell, and Paces Ferry Roads offers up designer shops like Hermès or Dior or trendy restaurants comparable to Rodeo Drive in Beverly Hills. Lenox Square and Phipps Plaza, tony malls at the Peachtree Road/Lenox Road intersection, offer the treasures of Saks, Neiman Marcus, and other upscale retail chains.

You'll have a better understanding of what makes Atlanta the kind of city it is after a day at the **Atlanta History Center** (404-814-4000; atlantahistory center.com). The tree-shaded, 30-acre sanctuary at 3101 Andrews Dr. includes 3 fascinating attractions: the insightful and very well done Museum of Atlanta History; the circa 1836 "plantation plain" Tullie Smith Farmstead; and the Swan House, an opulent Italian-Palladian villa, built in 1926 and appointed with European and Asian furnishings and set among formal gardens and terraced fountains. It's also home to **Cyclorama,** a massive painting depicting a crucial point in the July 22, 1864, Battle of Atlanta. Forty-two feet high and 358 feet long, it is one of two remaining paintings created in the 1880s to depict famous Civil War battles. (The Battle of Gettysburg *Cyclorama* is at the National Battlefield Park.) Open daily. Admission is $23.41 for adults; $19.60 for seniors 65 and older and students ages 13 and over with ID; $9.80 for youths 4 to 12; children under 4 are free.

The center has 6 signature exhibits, the largest of which is the **Centennial Olympic Games Museum.** The 27,500-square-foot, 3-story museum traces Atlanta's dark-horse bid for the 1996 games, the building of venues, and a timetable of events at the 16-day games. Exhibits include medals dating to 1896, a collection of Olympic torches, and gifts to the city from the 197 participating teams. An interactive Sports Lab lets kids and adults test their skills against Olympic athletes.

If you still pine for the flower-child days of the 1960s or feel like dyeing your hair electric blue or orange and skateboarding on the sidewalk, *Little Five Points* is your kind of place. You can be totally mainstream and still enjoy an outing at this Southern-style East Village/Soho area. Around the intersection of Moreland and Euclid Avenues, across Ponce de Leon Avenue from Virginia-Highland and about 3 miles east of downtown, you'll find a cluster of good, inexpensive restaurants—Indian, Caribbean, Mexican, Italian, Cajun—coffee bars, bars with and without music, brew pubs, tattoo parlors, and funky shops selling vintage clothing and books on astrology, herbal medicine, and other esoteric subjects. Just like the good old days, street musicians perform for your pleasure and spare change.

East Atlanta Village, off I-20 and Moreland Avenue about 10 minutes south of Little Five Points, is one of the more hidden old neighborhoods to get the Lazarus treatment. Young entrepreneurs have turned vacant storefronts around the Flat Shoals Avenue–Glenwood Avenue intersection into kitschy shops with unique and offbeat gifts, art, antiques, and imports. The resurgent old neighborhood's newfound diversity is reflected in inexpensive to moderately priced eateries that serve French, vegan, Italian, Australian, Caribbean, and contemporary American fare. Hot local bands draw the young and sleepless to *The Earl* (488 Flat Shoals Ave.; 404-522-3950; badearl.com). *Elder Tree Public House* is a traditional Irish pub with gastropub fare and it helps if you love soccer because there's usually a game on (460 Flatshoals Rd.; 404-600-5254; eldertreeatl.com). *Mary's* (1287 Glenwood Ave.; 404-624-4411; marysatlanta.com) is a popular gay bar. For a quick pick-me-up, find a sofa at *Joe's East Atlanta Coffee House* (510 Flat Shoals Ave.; 404-521-1122). The anti-corporate java and dessert shop is the unofficial "living room" for urban pioneers, who meet for jolts of espresso while they read, study, and revel in the urban slacker lifestyle.

Zoo Atlanta, in Grant Park (800 Cherokee Ave.; 404-624-5600; zooatlanta .org), a few blocks from the Village and 2 miles from downtown, is a fun place to spend a day. A top attraction is the growing giant panda family. On loan from China, Lun-Lun and Yang-Yang are proud parents to twins Ya Lun and Xi Lun, born September 4, 2016. These kids are their second set of twins and sixth and seventh offspring. Twins Me Huan and Mei Li (born July 15, 2012) and their three older sons Xi-Lan (born August 30, 2008), Po (born November 3, 2010), and Mei-Lan (born September 6, 2006), have all returned to China. The pandas spend a lot of time sleeping and munching bamboo, but when they move around and climb trees in their lavish habitat, you'll wish you could rush in and give them a big bear hug. The zoo's other big attraction is the Ford African Rain Forest, a natural habitat for families of silverback mountain gorillas. In early 2000, Willie B., the zoo's beloved 41-year-old silverback—the king of the zoo since his childhood—died of old age. A life-size statue of the world-famous silverback is in the zoo's sculpture garden. Other zoo habitats house more than 1,000 tropical birds, big cats, bears, giraffes, reptiles, and other exotic creatures from around the world. Open daily. Admission is $27.99 for adults, $19.99 for children 3 to 11.

Your suspicions that the government "has money to burn" will be confirmed when you visit the *Federal Reserve Bank of Atlanta's Monetary Museum*. During your prearranged guided tour, you'll see millions of dollars' worth of damaged paper bills being shredded. You'll receive a complimentary bag of Uncle Sam's "confetti" and see "live" currency counted and sorted and sent out to Southeastern banks. The tour also takes you through the Visitors Center, where interactive and multimedia exhibits give in-depth lessons in the US economy. The Federal Reserve Bank is at 1000 Peachtree St., across from the Margaret Mitchell House, in Midtown Atlanta. To arrange a free tour, phone (404) 498-8500 or visit frbatlanta.org/about/tours/museum.

The *Robert C. Williams American Museum of Papermaking,* on the Georgia Tech campus (500 10th St.; 404-894-7840; paper.gatech.edu), takes you on a self-guided tour through thousands of years of paper and paper technology. "Pre-paper" exhibits include tree leaves from India, Egyptian papyrus, Indonesian bark, and other substances that ancient peoples used before the invention of the real thing, in China around AD 105. Contemporary exhibits feature North America's first paper mill in 1690 and mills that produce paper in the 21st century. Papermaking workshops are held periodically. Open Mon through Fri 9 a.m. to 5 p.m. Free admission.

William Breman Jewish Heritage Museum (1440 Spring St., Midtown Atlanta; 678-222-3700; thebreman.org), explores the history of Judaism and Atlanta's own rich Jewish history. In addition to 2 main galleries, the museum offers a genealogy center, extensive archives, a resources library, and changing exhibits such as "Shalom, Y'all," a history of Judaism in the South. Open Mon through Thurs 10 a.m. to 5 p.m.; Fri 10 a.m. to 4 p.m.; and Sun 10 a.m. to 5 p.m. Admission for adults is $12; seniors 62 and over $8; students $6; children ages 3 to 6 $4. Age 3 and under free.

Children as well as adults will enjoy the *Center for Puppetry Arts* (404-873-3391; puppet.org), on the northern edge of downtown at 1404 Spring St. The converted redbrick school building houses a fascinating puppetry museum and puts on a year-round program of puppet theatricals, some aimed at youngsters, others tailored for adults. Check their schedule online to see what's on.

Oakland Cemetery (248 Oakland Ave. at Memorial Drive; 404-688-2107; oaklandcemetery.com), offers a look toward Atlanta's past, right behind the ultramodern King Memorial MARTA Station. Established in 1850, Oakland's redbrick walls enclose a wealth of architectural and cultural heritage. Victorian aristocrats are entombed in temple-like mausoleums, embellished with stained glass, gargoyles, and marble busts. You can walk through the original 8 acres, Confederate and Jewish sections; see the graves of the city's firstborn child and other celebrities, such as *Gone with the Wind* author Margaret Mitchell, golf champion Bobby Jones, governors, mayors, and beloved pets; and spread a picnic lunch under the magnolia trees. Open daily. Free tours are conducted on weekends—many with themes—and self-guided tours are encouraged. The cemetery supporters hold festivals and events to give insight as to the lives of their "residents" so check their website for activities.

A MARTA train to West End Station and a bus connection or 3-block walk will bring you to the **Wren's Nest,** the Victorian home of Joel Chandler Harris, creator of Br'er Rabbit, Br'er Fox, the Tar Baby, and other delightful critters who roam through his 1880s book, *Uncle Remus: His Songs & His Sayings.* Rooms are filled with furnishings and mementos of Harris and his family, editions of his book in many languages, and re-creations of his beloved characters. The house got its name when a mother wren decided that Harris's wooden mailbox would be perfect for her brood. The mailbox now has an honored place among the Wren's Nest's treasures. Especially if you have children, try to visit when storytelling sessions are scheduled, which is every Sat at 1 p.m. Wren's Nest (1050 Ralph David Abernathy Blvd.; 404-753-7735; wrensnest.org) is open Tues through Sat 10 a.m. to 2:30 p.m. Admission is $10 for adults, $8 for seniors, students, and children.

West of downtown, **Herndon Home** (587 University Pl.; herndonhome .org) is a landmark of black achievement. The dignified Beaux Arts–style mansion was built in 1915 by Alonzo Herndon, a former slave. Herndon founded Atlanta Life Insurance Company, the nation's largest black-owned insurance firm and became one of the first black millionaires in the US. He called the mansion "Diamond Hill" and it's easy to see why. The 15 rooms showcase his remarkable life. Most of the antique furnishings and family photos are original. The Herndon Home is open Tues through Thurs 10 a.m. to 4 p.m., other days by appointment. Admission is $10 for adults, $7 for children and military. For more information call (404) 581-9813.

Georgia's 19th-century poet Sidney Lanier sang the praises of the Chattahoochee River in his idyllic "Song of the Chattahoochee." The river rises in the

North Georgia mountains and flows through metropolitan Atlanta on its way to the Gulf of Mexico.

The *Chattahoochee River National Recreation Area,* a 48-mile stretch of river and gentle rapids flowing between wooded palisades, is the focus for recreational pursuits of all sorts. From spring through fall, Atlantans love to set their rafts, canoes, and kayaks loose in the river for a lazy day of relaxation. If you don't have your own, they are available for rental. There are two spots, both operated by the Nantahala Outdoor Center (noc.com). One is at *Power's Island* (5440 Interstate N Pkwy., Sandy Springs; 404-696-7517) and the other is technically in Marietta (301 Johnson Ferry Rd. SE; 404-678-5902) but is at the north end of the recreation area across the river from Power's Island. If rafting isn't your pleasure, you can also spread a picnic, hike, bike, jog, bird-watch, and exercise on the 22-station fitness trail. The park's main entrance is at US 41 and the Chattahoochee River bridge. Contact the Park Superintendent at 1978 Island Ford Pkwy. (678-538-1200; nps.gov/chat). There is a $5 entrance fee.

The river's fauna and flora are celebrated at the *Chattahoochee Nature Center* (9135 Willeo Rd., Roswell; 770-992-2055; chattnaturecenter.com). The private, nonprofit natural-science center's exhibits of plants and wildlife, special programs, and workshops are in a tranquil 50-acre setting by the riverbank, about 20 miles north of downtown Atlanta. Guided walks on Sat and Sun at noon and 2 p.m. weave through 20 acres of nature trails and along a 1,400-foot boardwalk over the river. You can also pick up a brochure and take a self-guided tour. Make a full day of it with a picnic lunch. Check the schedule because there is almost always something special planned for families and kids.

The center is open Mon through Sat from 9 a.m. to 5 p.m.; Sun from noon to 5 p.m. Adults $10, seniors $7, and ages 3 to 12 $6.

On December 22, 1853, Mittie Bulloch, a **Roswell** debutante, married New Yorker Theodore Roosevelt in the dining room of **Bulloch Hall** (180 Bulloch Dr., Roswell; 770-992-1731; bullochhall.org), her family's Greek Revival showplace. The happy couple, of course, had no inkling of the far-reaching consequences of their union. After the nuptials, they moved to New York and in 1858, had a son, Theodore, who became our 26th president when William McKinley was assassinated in 1901. Their other son, Elliot, had a daughter, Eleanor, who married her cousin Franklin.

In 1905, President "TR" made a sentimental journey to his mother's ancestral home. If he came back today, he'd find Bulloch Hall looking pretty much as it was when his mother was a blushing bride. Mittie's father, Maj. James Stephens Bulloch, grandson of Georgia's Revolutionary War Gov. Archibald Bulloch, built the house in 1839, the same year Roswell King, a Connecticut Yankee, founded the town and built textile mills on the Chattahoochee River.

One of the South's rare examples of pure temple-form architecture, with a fully pedimented portico. In 1978, the city of Roswell purchased the house and 16 acres and opened it to the public. A few of the Bulloch family's original furnishings are complemented by period pieces. Modern brides say their vows in the same dining room where Mittie said hers. A reenactment of Mittie and Theodore's wedding is a highlight of "Christmas in Roswell," which also includes Victorian holiday decorations, high teas, parades, seasonal storytelling, and the lighting of the town square.

Bulloch Hall is one of more than 100 Roswell structures on the National Register of Historic Places and part of what the city calls its "Southern Trilogy" along with **Archibald Smith Plantation** and **Barrington Hall.** Archibald Smith is an 1845 cotton farm with 12 original buildings (935 Alpharetta St., Roswell; 770-641-3978). The farm is probably one of the best examples of historical and cultural interpretation of 19th century farm life in the region. Barrington Hall (535 Barrington Dr.; 770-640-3855) was built by one of the founders of the town of Roswell, Barrington King (son of Roswell King), in the 1830s. Decorated with many of the home's original furnishing, you get a real insight into the time period. The 7-acre grounds include outbuildings and a public garden. All are open Tues through Sat 10 a.m. to 4 p.m.; Sun 1 to 4 p.m. Guided tours are $5 per house for adults and $4 for children.

Teaching Museum North, in a former elementary school (791 Mimosa Blvd., Roswell; 770-552-6339), is a hands-on, participatory extension of the classroom designed to get kids involved in their curriculum. It's also a good place to learn about the history of Roswell, the state of Georgia, and the United

Where's the Olympic Stadium?

If you'd like to visit Atlanta's *Olympic Stadium*, you'll have to take a swing by Center Parc Credit Union Stadium on Hank Aaron Drive. The stadium where the 1996 Summer Games opening and closing ceremonies and track and field events were held was ingeniously constructed so that about half of the 85,000 seats could easily be taken out after the games and the stadium converted to serve a single sport. First, it was converted to be home to the Atlanta Braves baseball team and called Turner Field after former Braves owner Ted Turner. The Braves vacated in 2016 to head north to Truist Park in Cobb County, opening the way for Georgia State's Panther football team. The giant brick pillars on the outside of the courtyard of the main entrance were part of the Olympic stadium and will give you a sense of its original size.

States. The Roswell Room's exhibits depict the town's antebellum homes and other buildings spared by the Civil War. A mural traces the region's history from Native Americans to the present. Georgia's many authors, including Pat Conroy, Flannery O'Connor, Sidney Lanier, Alice Walker, Margaret Mitchell, James Dickey, Eugenia Price, and Erskine Caldwell, are honored in the Writers Corner. There are even greenhouses where kids can learn to plant. Open Mon through Fri 8:30 a.m. to 3:30 p.m. Free to public but donations are appreciated. Study guides are available through their website: fultonschools.org/teachingmuseum.

Roswell King laid out the Town Square in New England fashion, with a park in the center and a bandstand where "TR" spoke to townsfolk in 1905, surrounded by brick shop buildings. It's still a central gathering point for the locals and a site for festivals and weekend events during the spring and summer.

A town as old as Roswell naturally (or supernaturally) has plenty of rumored ghosts. *Roswell Ghost Tour* (770-649-9922; roswellghosttour.com) every Friday evening takes you on a stroll through the Historic District, where you'll hear legendary tales, ghost stories, scandals, and very likely an outright fabrication or two. The biggest mystery is the fate of 400 women and children textile workers, charged with treason by the Union army in 1864 and taken north, most of them never heard from again. The Lost Workers of Roswell Monument, in Old Mill Park on Sloan Street, is their memorial. Adults $15, children under 12 are $10.

Antiques shops and galleries are foremost on many visitors' minds. Canton and Alpharetta Streets are chock full of cozy shops to wander and explore. At 1160 Canton St., you'll find the celebrated *Raiford Gallery* (770-645-2050; raifordgallery.com). You could stay busy for hours exploring the one-of-a-kind works from more than 400 artists, including 50 jewelers, in the gallery's beautiful open wooden structure.

If you want to pay respects to the fallen of Vietnam, the **Roswell Faces of War Memorial** can be found on the corner of Hill and Atlanta Streets on the grounds of City Hall. The solemn bronze sculpture features a soldier reaching out to clasp the hand of a little girl while behind him are 50 faces showing a range of emotions. On most days, a cascade of water falls from the top where you can read the words "You Are Not Forgotten."

To arm yourselves with information on what to see and do, stop first at the **Roswell Visitors Center** on the square (617 Atlanta St., Roswell; 800-776-7935, 770-640-3253; visitroswellga.com) for a video overview, historical exhibits, and walking/driving maps. Guided walking tours with a docent from the Historical Society are available by appointment, but audio tours of the Civil War Walk and the Roswell Mill Village Walk are available for free download through their website.

With a population of 714,350, **DeKalb County** is the Metro area and Georgia's third most populous county and one of Georgia's most ethnically diverse. You'll find many off-the-beaten-path attractions among the county's busy streets and freeways, shopping malls, and subdivisions.

There's an Andrew Young International Boulevard in downtown Atlanta, but the metro area's real "international" boulevard is **Buford Highway** (GA 23). A 10-mile stretch of multilane urban roadway from Lenox Road in the city of Atlanta north through the DeKalb towns of Chamblee and Doraville to Jimmy Carter Boulevard in Gwinnett County is lined with more than 700 businesses and services run by Asian and Hispanic immigrants. Since the early 1980s, old strip shopping centers and newly built malls have filled up with supermarkets where shoppers come from around the Southeast for Korean, Thai, Chinese, Vietnamese, Caribbean, Mexican, Central American, and South American produce, seafood, rice, spices, and other staples.

Dozens of restaurants offer a selection of authentic cuisines you might expect to find only in Seoul, Bangkok, and Lima (or in Los Angeles, San Francisco, and New York). A great place to be transported to a different country is **Plaza Fiesta,** at the busy Buford Highway–Clairmont Road intersection (4166 Buford Hwy.; 404-982-9138). Here you can buy hecho en Mexico (made in Mexico) shoes, sandals, Western wear, apparel of all kinds, religious items, DVDs, candy, breads, pastries, and cakes; get your hair styled; see a doctor; have your taxes prepared; and explore dozens of stores and kiosks. Walk-up eateries serve inexpensive Mexican and Latino fast food.

While you're in northeast DeKalb, you can explore an assortment of antiques shops and flea markets around the Peachtree Road–Broad Street

Junction in "old" downtown Chamblee (antiquerow.com). You're bound to find something you can't resist and didn't realize you needed at the ***Antique Factory*** (5506 Peachtree Rd.; 770-455-7570), ***Broad Street Antique Mall*** (3550 Broad St.; 770-458-6316), and ***Chamblee Antiques and Collectables*** (3509 Broad St.; 770-986-7460).

Only 3 miles due east of downtown Atlanta is the quaint town of ***Decatur,*** the DeKalb County seat. ***Court Square,*** across from the historic county courthouse, is a bustling hub of upbeat restaurants, taverns, and distinctive shops.

In a cul-de-sac off East Ponce de Leon Avenue there is a choice of popular American and ethnic eateries and bars, including the sumptuous ***Iberian Pig*** (121 Sycamore St.; 404-371-8800; iberianpigatl.com). Known for its Spanish-styled tapas, it's a place people from across metro seek out. Nearby is the highly acclaimed ***Brick Store Pub*** (404-687-0990; brickstorepub.com). The Brick Store is considered to have one of the top beer collections in the country, featuring an entire cellar devoted to Belgian brews. With the quaint setting and diverse selection of places, you'll probably have to wait for a table on weekends. In warm weather, you can sit at outdoor tables that line the sidewalks. If you don't need as wide a beer selection, you can also walk around the corner to its sister restaurant ***Leon's Full Service*** (131 E. Ponce de Leon, Decatur; 404-687-0500; leonsfullservice.com). There are a lot of great restaurants right outside the Decatur MARTA rail station, with a spacious open plaza with benches and a fountain, about a 10-minute ride from downtown Atlanta. On summer Saturday nights, Decaturites spread blankets and picnic suppers on the courthouse lawn and enjoy live music at the bandstand.

You wouldn't expect a world-class antiquities museum to be somewhat hidden on a university campus but Emory University's ***Michael C. Carlos Emory University Museum of Art and Archaeology*** (571 South Kilgo St.; 404-727-0516; carlos.emory.edu) holds a trove of artifacts from around the world. Treasures in this beautifully planned building on the Emory Quadrangle include Greek and Roman coins, statuary, and amphorae; an Egyptian mummy with a gilded face; and European, pre-Columbian, and Asian art objects. Floors are inlaid with diagrams of ancient temples and palaces. Special exhibitions are held regularly. An $8 donation is requested and an extremely helpful audio guide can be rented for $2. Open Tues through Fri 10 a.m. to 4 p.m.; Sat 10 a.m. to 5 p.m. The museum is on the Emory Quadrangle, near the university's main entrance at North Decatur and Oxford Roads. On-campus paid parking is available.

Across from the campus on North Decatur and Oxford Roads in an area known as ***Emory Village***, you'll find a row of popular student-oriented eateries, including Rise-n-Dine, Doc Chey's Dragon Bowl, Dave's Cosmic Subs, Chipotle Mexican Grill, Romeo's New York Pizza, and Falafel King.

What can you do on a rainy day in Atlanta? Rain or shine, you can spend all of it at the ***Fernbank Museum of Natural History*** and the companion ***Fernbank Science Center.*** Both are operated by the DeKalb County Board of Education. The natural history museum's attractions include the hands-on "A Walk Through Time in Georgia," "Reflections of Culture," and "The World of Shells," children's discovery rooms, towering dinosaur skeletons, and an IMAX theater. Located at 767 Clifton Rd. between downtown Atlanta and Decatur (404-929-6400; fernbankmuseum.org), the museum is open Mon through Sat 10 a.m. to 5 p.m. and Sun noon to 5 p.m. Adults, $20; students and senior citizens, $19; ages 3 to 12, $18. IMAX theater: adults, $13; students and seniors, $12; ages 3 to 12, $11. Combination museum-IMAX are just $5 more. Check their schedule for "adult fun nights" which feature events such as Latin Dance Night or Adult Prom.

Fernbank Science Center (156 Heaton Park Dr.; 678-874-7102; fernbank .edu) in a 65-acre hardwood and pine forest threaded with walking trails, has a 500-seat planetarium offering seasonal looks at the heavens. You can also look at far-flung galaxies through the Southeast's largest telescope. Other exhibits focus on Georgia's varied plant and animal life, as well as special exhibits like an Apollo Space Capsule on loan from the Smithsonian. Open Mon through Wed, noon to 5 p.m.; Thurs to Fri, noon to 9 p.m.; Sat 10 a.m. to 5 p.m. The observatory is open Thurs and Fri from 9 p.m. to 10:30 p.m. weather permitting. Admission is free but planetarium shows are $7 for adults and $5 for students. Gates to the forest are locked at 5 p.m.

A granite monolith 825 feet high and 6 miles around, with numerous attractions and 6 million visitors yearly, is hardly off the beaten path. However, many ***Stone Mountain Park*** visitors include a visit to ***Stone Mountain Village.*** Outside the park's gates, the village's 19th-century Main Street is flanked by covered sidewalks and 3 blocks of stores stocked with vintage books, arts and crafts, Civil War artifacts, antiques, geodes, apparel, jewelry, and oddities. In fact, the downtown area is on the National Register of Historic Places.

Buster, Hero Dog

Buster, a heroic police dog, is remembered with a granite tribute in front of the Jonesboro police headquarters on North McDonough Street. The inscription reads: NOT JUST A DOG, BUT A POLICE OFFICER, A PARTNER, A FRIEND, ONE WHO MADE A DIFFERENCE. Buster's fellow officers put up the monument bearing Buster's image after bad guys brought down the fearless, 5-year-old crime fighter in 1990.

You can get a haircut in an old-fashioned barbershop and buy an ice cream, a sandwich, or a full meal at several cafes and restaurants. The town's visitor center is located in an old railroad caboose (891 Main St.; 770-879-4971; stnemountaincity.org).

Housed in the old trolley station, **ART Station** (5384 Manor Dr., just off Stone Mountain's Main St.; 770-469-1105; artstation.org) exhibits paintings, sculpture, and other works by local and regional artists. Feeling artistic? You can also sign up for classes.

Yellow River Wildlife Sanctuary (4525 Hwy. 78, Lilburn; 770-972-6643; yellowrivergameranch.com) is a peaceful place in the woods in the midst of south Gwinnett County's suburban explosion. Just off very busy US 78, 3 miles east of Stone Mountain Park, the 24-acre privately owned nature preserve is home for dozens of free-roaming brown deer, huggable bunnies, goats, sheep, coyotes, ducks and geese, pigs and porcupines, foxes, wolves, donkeys, a skunk named William T. Sherman, and a spring-forecasting groundhog named Gen. Beauregard Lee. It's also home to what's purportedly the largest herd of American buffalo east of the Mississippi.

First established as a home for injured and orphaned wildlife, Yellow River is now a great place to learn about native animal species. You can really get to know the animals up close and personal. You may reserve Yellow River's **Birthday House** for your youngster's special day or for a family reunion or other group activity. Yellow River Wildlife Game Ranch is open daily 10 a.m. to 5 p.m. Admission is $18 for adults; $12 for children 3 to 11; free for children 2 and under.

You may do a double take if you are driving down Rockbridge Road in Lilburn. The traditional Hindu **BAPS Shri Swaminarayan Mandir** rises like a wedding cake above the landscape. Constructed of hand-carved Italian marble, Turkish limestone, and Indian pink sandstone, the design is in accordance to ancient scriptures. Set on 30 acres, it is the largest Mandir outside of India. Open daily at 460 Rockbridge Road.

Clayton County, south of downtown Atlanta, was the fictional setting for Tara, Twelve Oaks, and other *Gone with the Wind* landmarks. Appropriately, the **Road to Tara Museum,** in Jonesboro's Depot Welcome Center (104 N. Main St., Jonesboro; 770-478-4800, 800-662-7829; claytoncountyfilmtourism .com), houses one of the largest collections of GWTW memorabilia in the world. Exhibits include re-creations of some of the movie's most famous costumes, first editions of the book in many languages, posters, continuous showings of the film, and souvenir items. If you look closely at a mural, you'll see the familiar face of Elvis Presley, carrying the Confederate battle flag. The mural's artist, Del Nichols, includes Elvis in everything he does. The museum

Where Bobby Learned to Play

Bobby Jones is considered by many to be the greatest golfer who ever picked up a stick. Young Bob Jones was just 5 years old when the Atlanta Athletic Club at East Lake opened its golf course on 2575 Alston Drive on July 4, 1906. Jones's family lived across the street and he would come over to watch the golfers and mimic the golf pro Stewart Maiden who had just arrived from Carnoustie, Scotland. Maiden would shape not only Jones, but other phenoms such as Alexa Stirling and Charlie Yates. East Lake was considered one of the best courses in the US in the early 1900s but saw a decline in the 1960s and '70s. Atlanta businessman Tom Cousins purchased East Lake in 1993 and not only restored the club to its original splendor, but helped revitalize the entire neighborhood by creating partnerships with the community. Now home to the PGA's Tour Championship, *East Lake Golf Club's* motto is "Golf with a Purpose." A small park is dedicated to Maiden across from the East View Cemetery on 4th Street, just two blocks from the East Lake entrance; eastlakegolfclub.com.

is open Mon through Fri 8:30 a.m. to 5:30 p.m.; Sat 10 a.m. to 4 p.m. Adults, $7; seniors and students, $6.

As long as you are feeling the tug of *Gone with the Wind*, you may want to also take in **Stately Oaks Plantation Historic Site**, also available through the visitor's center. Built in 1839, it is believed this Greek Revival home was the inspiration for Scarlett O'Hara's home, Tara.

If that's not enough Scarlett and Rhett for you, you can hop a bus at the center for either the **Southern Belles & Whistles Tour** or **Peter Bonner's Gone with the Wind Tour.** You'll be treated to a full array of GWTW connections to Jonesboro. Tour reservations can be made at (800) 662-7829. Adults are $24.95, $21.95 for seniors, and $13.95 for children 12 and under.

Monks, a Mountain & Gone with the Wind

Like other Metro Atlanta counties, **Gwinnett** (population about 860,000) has grown so rapidly the past 35 years, it seems to be one vast, unbroken landscape of mammoth shopping malls, subdivisions, and apartment complexes. It's now Metro Atlanta and Georgia's second most populous county. But if you peek behind the "new" Gwinnett, you'll find that many of its old towns and cities have become walkable havens with unique shops, restaurants, and art galleries.

Norcross's Historic Old Town is a pleasant throwback to yesteryear a few minutes off traffic-crazy I-85 and Jimmy Carter Boulevard. Take North Norcross–Tucker Road off Jimmy Carter and follow the Historic Norcross signs to South Peachtree Street. Antiques and gift shops include *Taste of Britain* (73 S. Peachtree St.; 770-242-8585; tasteofbritain.com), with imported teas, biscuits, jams, china, and gifts. There is also an old-fashioned barbershop, a vintage hardware store, and other small businesses in the well-preserved 19th-century buildings grouped around the old wooden train depot. *The Crossing Steakhouse,* in the done-over depot, and *Dominick's Little Italy* across the street, are detailed in "Places to Eat in Metro Atlanta," at the end of this chapter.

Not to be outdone by other Gwinnett County cities, *Lawrenceville,* the county seat, has done a vibrant renovation of its Courthouse Square. The centerpiece is the majestic 1885 redbrick courthouse with the tall white turret and clock tower. No longer the seat of county government since a modern courthouse was built in the early 1990s, the historic building, with its manicured lawns, brick-paved sidewalks, benches, retro streetlights, and memorials to soldiers who died in the Civil War and Creek Indian War, has historical displays and meeting rooms.

The *Aurora Theatre* (1128 E. Pike St.; 770-476-7926; auroratheatre.com) is Lawrenceville's most popular attraction. Located in a renovated historic church, a professional repertory company performs in the 200-seat main auditorium year-round. The Aurora is also home to a performance academy and hosts dances when performances are not underway.

The food is as much fun as the Lawrenceville shops. Choices include *Blue Rooster Bake Shop and Eatery* (169 W. Pike St.; 770-995-0065; bluerooster bakeshop.com), with sandwiches, salads, soups, and delectable sweets; and the ever-popular *McCray's Tavern* (100 N. Perry St.; 770-407-6745; mccraystavern .com). McCray's has a huge beer selection and its menu ranges from pub fare to shrimp and grits or a garlic rib eye. If your craving good, old-fashioned Southern cooking like you wish your grandma could make, then try the *Corner Stop Café* (195 N. Perry St.; 770-962-4112; cornerstopcafe.com).

For a look at Gwinnett County "when," take a walk through the *Lawrenceville Female Seminary* (455 S. Perry St.; 770-904-3500). Built in the 1850s after the original burned, the 2-story brick Greek Revival building was a finishing school that tutored antebellum young ladies in reading, writing, and etiquette. Over the years the old school building taught boys and hosted civic clubs, the United Daughters of the Confederacy, and a radio station. In the 1970s, when Dairy Queen coveted the site, the county government purchased it, had it placed on the National Register of Historic Places, and made it the home of the Gwinnett County History Museum's collections of farm implements, textiles, historic photos, and exhibits on schools, religion, music, and other aspects of the county's life. Open Mon through Thurs, and Sat by appointment. No admission charge.

Directly next door is the stately *Isaac Adair House* (15 South Clayton St.). Built in 1827, the house is one of the oldest in the county and was moved to the 10-acre site in the mid-1980s when it was threatened by demolition to make way for a shopping center. For information on both locations, visit gwinnett county.com.

In the mood for authentic Mexican tacos and moles, Ecuadorean and Salvadorean empanadas, pad Thai, Korean barbecue, Cantonese dim sum, fiery Szechuan, Vietnamese pho, Indo-Pak curries and dosai, and the ingredients to make your own? One of Georgia's most ethnically diverse counties, Gwinnett has scores of restaurants, food markets, and other services catering to large communities from Asia, Mexico, Central and South America, and homegrown Anglos and others looking for some adventure for their palates.

For information contact the *Gwinnett Convention and Visitors Bureau,* (6500 Sugarloaf Pkwy., Duluth; 770-623-3600 or 888-494-6638; exploregwinnett .org).

North of Lawrenceville, tucked in the town of Buford, is the off-the-beaten-path gem the *Gwinnett Environmental and Heritage Center* (2020 Clean Water Dr., Buford; 770-904-3500). Indoor, outdoor, and hands-on exhibits will entertain both children and adults. If you do nothing but walk the outdoor paths, it's worth the visit. Think "dinosaurs in the woods!"

The *Sugar Hill Municipal Golf Course* (8 miles north of the Suwanee exit off I-85; 770-271-0519; sugarhillgolfclub.com), is a sweet layout for those who'd like to play like the pros but have an amateur's budget. Spread over 300 acres at the north Gwinnett County town of Sugar Hill, the well-maintained par-72, 18-hole course offers plenty of challenges as it swoops up and down hills and around 6 lakes and 45 traps.

McDaniel Farm Park (3251 Daniel Rd., Duluth; 770-814-4920) isn't just a park—it's a trip back through time. The park is a former cotton farm that was first part of an 1800s land lottery. Run by sharecroppers, it now serves as a living history lesson and includes an original barn, well house, chicken coop, blacksmith shed, and restored tenant farmer house.

The *Southeastern Railway Museum* in Duluth, 25 miles northeast of downtown Atlanta (3395 Buford Hwy., Duluth; 770-476-2013; train-museum .org), honors the golden age of passenger trains. Owned and operated by the Atlanta Chapter of the National Railway Historical Society, the 30-acre indoor and outdoor museum invites train buffs to sit in red cabooses, hauled around the yards by vintage diesel locomotives. Each Saturday and most Thursdays (except June and July on Wednesday), the cabooses are hooked to huffing, puffing steam locomotives. Before and after the ride, there's time to look at more than 90 pieces of rolling stock, exhibits, and displays. One of the

I'll Have a Co-Coler

For millions of people around the world, Atlanta is synonymous with **Coca-Cola**. The soft drink was created in a Peachtree Street pharmacy in 1886. Dr. John Stith Pemberton, originally from Columbus, Georgia, was seeking a nonalcoholic cure for the common headache. He blended coca leaves, African kola nuts, and other ingredients into an elixir he called Coca-Cola. It was first sold as a heavy syrup diluted with water. But one day the clerk substituted soda water for tap water, and voilà, Coke was on its way around the world.

Headquartered in Atlanta, the company closely guards its secret formula. If you visit the massive interactive **World of Coca-Cola** near Centennial Olympic Park and the Georgia Aquarium (121 Baker St.; 404-676-5151; worldofcoca-cola.com), you'll be treated to animated films and videos on Coke's history, as well as hundreds of exhibits and souvenir items, a bottling room, an art gallery, a gift store, and free samples of Coke and soft drinks the company tailors for specialized tastes around the world. It's open for self-guided tours daily 9 a.m. to 5 p.m.; 8 a.m. to 6 p.m. in June, July, and Aug. Admission is $17 for adults; $17 age 65 and over; $17 ages 3 to 12; children 2 and under free. Paid parking is in the attraction's deck on Ivan Allen Jr. Boulevard.

showpieces is "Superb," the 1911 Pullman car that carried President Warren G. Harding across the country in the early 1920s. When Harding died in San Francisco in 1923, "Superb" carried him back to Washington and then to burial in Ohio. Army chefs prepared meals for the troops in a military kitchen car parked nearby. You can walk through locomotives, passenger coaches, dining cars, a railway post office, and Pullman sleeper cars. Kids and grown-up "kids" who enjoy the sport of model railroading can see the miniature train in the exhibit hall. From downtown Atlanta, take I-85 North to exit 104/Pleasant Hill Road and follow the signs. There is no set schedule on park train rides, but the museum is open Thurs through Sat from 10 a.m. to 5 p.m. throughout the year, as well as Mon and Wed during summer months. Admission is $18 adults; $15 age 65 and over; $13 ages 2 to 12. Caboose rides and park train rides are an additional $4. The complex is available for birthdays, meetings, and other events.

Amid the burgeoning suburbs of Rockdale County, a short drive off the busy lanes of I-20, about 25 miles east of downtown Atlanta, the **Monastery of the Holy Ghost** is a place of inordinate peacefulness. Since the late 1940s, Benedictine Trappist monks have dwelt and prayed in this cloistered sanctuary at 2625 Hwy. 212 in Conyers (770-483-8705; trappist.net). The Spanish Gothic–style buildings, even the stained glass in the main church, are all products of their labors.

Men and women can attend Sunday morning Mass in the church, which is highlighted by the monks' chants and prayers. Men may make retreats at the modern guesthouse nearby. A small shop sells bread, cheese, jam, religious items, and produce and herbs grown in the monastery's fields. They also operate a stained-glass studio that originally produced pieces for the monastery itself. Now you can order windows, doors, etc. for your own home. You may also bring a picnic lunch to tables that sit by a lake beside the cloister.

The abbey does not observe a strict rule of silence, and most monks can converse with visitors.

Just east of Conyers on I-20 is Covington in Newton County. Film buffs can walk around **Covington Square** and recognize locations from numerous movies and television shows including *The Walking Dead*, *Vampire Diaries*, and *Selma*. Many beautiful white-columned homes are on the tree-shaded streets radiating from the square.

You'll also find a trove of antebellum treasures around nearby **Oxford College of Emory University,** which welcomed its first freshman class in 1839.

Twenty miles southeast of downtown Atlanta, via GA 155, **Panola Mountain State Conservation Park** is a peaceful 585-acre day-use park where you may have a walk in the woods, enjoy a picnic, and wonder at a 100-acre granite outcropping that's been part of the Henry County landscape for about a million years. The lichen-covered monadnock is part of a major belt of granite, most dramatically evidenced by Stone Mountain a few miles away.

Stop first at the park's Nature Center for information on trails leading through the woodlands and around the mountain. Meandering through hardwood and pine forests, the 1.25-mile Watershed Trail is a moderately strenuous course. Several stations along the way have benches and markers describing the park's fauna and flora. At the base of Panola Mountain, a 3-acre pond is alive with turtles, frogs, fish, and small reptiles.

We Like it Sweet

Georgians, like their fellow Southerners, are addicted to iced tea. We drink gallons of it summer, winter, fall, and spring. And the sweeter, the better. Real Southern iced tea has the sugar brewed in; adding it later doesn't have the same effect. When you order, you'll usually be asked, "Sweet or unsweetened?" If you want it sugarless and aren't asked for a preference, you're liable to get a glassful so syrupy it will make your teeth and gums ache. Half & half is also a good and accepted option.

The 0.75-mile **Rock Outcrop Trail** takes you through the woods to an overlook on one of the mountain's major outcroppings. The truly ambitious could tackle the 12-mile PATH foundation/Panola Mountain Trailhead which connects Panola Mountain with Arabia Mountain and Stonecrest Mall. On Saturday and Sunday afternoon, park naturalists conduct walks and give talks at the small amphitheater close to the Nature Center. Picnic tables are located near restrooms and soft drink machines. Pets on leashes may be walked in the picnic area but aren't allowed on the nature trails. The park is open daily from 7 a.m. to sundown. There is a $5 parking fee. Contact the superintendent in Stockbridge, (770) 389-7801, (800) 864-PARK; gastateparks.org/Panola.

If you didn't surmise it while battling the perpetual traffic on **Henry County's** streets and highways, the south suburban metro county is the third-fastest-growing county in Georgia and fourth-fastest in the entire United States. So it's a pleasant surprise to drive into the courthouse square in **McDonough,** the county seat, and wonder if you haven't drifted plum out of Henry into some rural place far from Metro Atlanta.

With a population of about 22,000, tidy, compact McDonough (pronounced "Mcdunnah") is a throwback to calmer, less frantic small-town times. Stop first at the McDonough Hospitality and Tourism Bureau in a regeared 1920s Standard Oil station on the square, pick up a map and helpful pointers, and start poking around the antiques malls, "attics," flea markets, gift, and specialty shops. The **Gerbardts's World** offers antiques and gifts (678-782-3915); **Moye's Pharmacy and Gifts** is the oldest pharmacy in Henry County and also sells unique gifts, foods, and collectibles (770-957-1851; moyespharmacy .com); **Planter's Walk Antique Mall** sells thousands of antiques and collectibles (678-432-5250; planterswalkantiquemall.com); and **Secret Garden** (678-432-6888), with its home accessories and unique gifts for the young and old, are good places to start.

Dining on the square includes **KirbyG's Diner and Pub,** a 1950s style diner near the square that serves up cooked-to-order burgers (45 Macon St.; 678-583-8777; kirbygs.com); **Gritz,** serving Southern-style breakfast and lunch (14 Macon St.; 770-914-0448; gritz-family-restaurant.business.site); **PJ's Cafe,** American cuisine and a popular bar (30 Macon St.; 770-898-5373); and **Queen Bee Coffee Company,** coffee and pastries (58 Griffin St.; 678-883-2233; queen beecoffee.com).

"The Geranium City" lives up to its nickname during late January's **Geranium Festival.** Blooming with thousands of the colorful plants, the park in the square features music, entertainment, food, and more than 300 craftspeople selling their wares. For information, contact **McDonough Hospitality and Tourism Bureau** (5 Griffin St., McDonough; 770-898-3196; visitmcdonoughga.com).

Bargain lovers should put the Spalding County seat of **Griffin** high on their shopping lists. The textile town of 20,000, on US 19/US 41, 40 miles south of Atlanta, has some especially tempting values in antiques and socks.

Spalding Hosiery Shoppe, aka *"The Sock Shoppe"* (770-227-4362; sock shoppe.com) is a local institution. Founded in 1939 in a building across from the massive redbrick Spalding Mills, the store used to sell goods made at the mills. You can still buy colorful argyles, athletic socks, dress socks, and heavy-duty work socks, as well as pantyhose, sweatshirts, and other items made by major manufacturers. The company has expanded to three other locations, but there's nothing like the original at 432 E. Broad St. It's open Mon through Sat from 8:30 a.m. to 5:30 p.m.

There's a ton of good antiques hunting to be done. **The Auction Block Antique Mall** (314 E. Solomon St.; 678-315-3402) and the next door **Cotton Mill** (312 E. Solomon St.; 770-412-8888) display vast amounts of treasures in old mills featuring dozens of dealers, including a blacksmith/welding art center in downtown Griffin. Take your pick of china, old coins, Civil War relics, vintage toys, country primitive and Victorian furniture, decorative accessories, jewelry, and folk art. **Aging Gracefully Antiques** (103 N. Hill St.; 770-233-9000), has eclectic selections of pottery, furniture, quilts, and oil, gas, and kerosene lamps.

Architecture buffs can stroll downtown Griffin and see a range of styles surviving from the late 1800s to the 1930s. Most of the downtown commercial buildings, on Broad, Solomon, and Taylor Streets, are two stories high, constructed of brick, with wood or cast-iron storefronts and plate glass display windows. Many of the old buildings have been adapted for contemporary use.

Lewis Grizzard & Antebellum Newnan

Coweta and Fayette Counties, on Metro Atlanta's southwest periphery, are perfect for a one-day getaway from the big city, and they have more than enough to keep you happily occupied for much longer than that.

Take I-85 exit 47, 40 miles south of Atlanta, and follow Bullsboro Drive/ GA 34 into downtown **Newnan**. First stop is the **Coweta County Visitor Center,** 200 Courthouse Sq. in the heart of Newnan. Call (770) 254-2627 or visit explorecoweta.com. They'll fill you in on every place to see, do, eat, and sleep in and around the city of 22,000. Open Mon through Sat, 9 a.m. to 5 p.m. Be sure to pick up an **Historic Driving Tour of Homes** guide, which describes five different National Historic Registry Districts in downtown Newnan, including antebellum and Victorian mansions as well as 23 pre–Civil War landmarks. Many of the homes welcome visitors during the annual **Tour of Homes and Arts and Crafts Show** the third week of April. Before your driving tour, park

Judge Landis

In the wake of the Chicago "Black Sox" betting scandal during the 1919 World Series, *Judge Kenesaw Mountain Landis* was named Major League Baseball's first commissioner. He is credited with restoring the game's integrity and saving it from self-destruction. Although he was born and raised in Indiana, he was named for Marietta's Kennesaw Mountain, where his father was wounded during the Civil War. His father spelled the name with only one *n* instead of two.

around the majestic old courthouse in the center of the square and browse the many antiques, gift, and bookshops that lure locals away from the ubiquitous malls on the outskirts. Griffin has been certified as a "Camera Ready Community" by the Georgia Film Commission so don't be surprised if you bump into a famous actor or a production crew shooting a commercial, television show, or film.

Male Academy Museum (30 Temple Ave., Newnan; 770-251-0207; newnancowetahistoricalsociety.org/museums.html) and the accompanying *McRitchie-Hollis Museum* are musts for Civil War enthusiasts. The historic school building displays a major collection of uniforms, weapons, artifacts, and soldiers' personal effects. You'll also find clothing, furniture, and photographs from the mid-19th to the early 20th centuries and an 1890s classroom. Open Tues through Sat 10 a.m. to 12 p.m. and 1 p.m. to 3 p.m. Admission is $5, children $2.

For a little town—population less than 500—tiny *Moreland* has a huge literary legacy. The late syndicated humor columnist Lewis Grizzard wrote fondly about growing up in Moreland. In appreciation, townsfolk opened *The Lewis Grizzard Museum.* The collection ultimately outgrew its original home in an old gas station and was relocated to the historic Moreland Mill to be part of the *Hometown Heritage Museum* (7 Main St.; 678-492-3161; moreland adventure.com), which also houses artifacts of Moreland's history. The museum is open Thurs through Sat 10 a.m. to 3 p.m. The Grizzard collection takes up a large portion of the exhibit area and displays his many books, photos, battered manual typewriters, his favorite Gucci loafers, high school letter jacket, and other memorabilia. A shameless male chauvinist, he even found humor in his three failed marriages. A bumper sticker urges, "Honk if you've been married to Lewis Grizzard." He died of heart disease in 1994 at the age of 47. A section of I-85 in Coweta County is called Lewis Grizzard Highway.

Although he was vilified by Southerners for his scathing takes on rural morals and manners, Coweta Countians have restored *"The Little Manse,"* birthplace of novelist **Erskine Caldwell**. The author of *God's Little Acre* and *Tobacco Road* was born in The Manse in 1903 when his father was a Presbyterian pastor here. The family left when Caldwell was 5 years old, and he never lived here as an adult. But the simple frame house is very much as he knew it. Biographical exhibits, personal items, copies of his books in several languages, and a video trace the career of the author, who died in 1987. The house is on Moreland's Town Park, on East Camp Street off US 29, Moreland; open Fri 9 a.m. to 1 p.m. and Sat 10 a.m. to 3 p.m. Admission is $5 for adults, $1 for children 6 to 12. Call (678) 492-3161 for more information. You can go directly to Moreland from I-85 exit 41 and driving south on US 29.

Dunaway Gardens (3218 Roscoe Rd./GA 70, Newnan; 678-423-4050; dunawaygardens.com), was created in the 1920s and 1930s by popular Chatauqua Circuit actress **Hettie Jane Dunaway**, as a theatrical training center and floral rock gardens. In its prime, the gardens hosted ballet and modern dance troupes, a drama school, indoor and outdoor theater, and celebrities such as Walt and Roy Disney. Sarah Ophelia Colley, later famous as the Grand Ole Opry's Minnie Pearl, headed the drama school. After Dunaway's death in the early 1960s, the 25-acre gardens were abandoned to weeds, vines, kudzu, and poison ivy. Now, thanks to work by Jennifer and Roger Bigham of Newnan, visitors are once again welcome to explore 5 descending staircases, with rock walls, a natural rock amphitheater, slate patios, waterfalls, goldfish ponds, hanging gardens lush with native plants and flowers, and a 1-acre granite outcropping called "Little Stone Mountain." The gardens are open from Mar through Nov Thurs through Sat 10 a.m. to 5 p.m. and Sun 1 to 5 p.m. Adults $10, children $8. Group tours are available by appointment. It's a popular, picturesque setting for weddings.

Senoia is a deceptively drowsy little Coweta County town on GA 85, 40 miles south of Atlanta. The delightful trip through Norman Rockwell–land is also movie/TV central. With over 113 sites on the National Historic Register, it is a perfect movie location so don't be surprised if you run into some sort of production underway during your visit. In fact, the popular television show *The Walking Dead* calls this town "Woodbury." There are tours of the town to show off sites from the show and the **Woodbury Shoppe** (48 Main St.; 770-727-9394; woodburyshoppe.com) is full of fun souvenirs and collectables. The undead aside, the entire town is so dedicated to maintaining its looks, any new building has to be constructed to fit in with the historic motif. Stop by the Visitor Information Center at Main Street (770-599-3679; enjoysenoia.net) for a guide to many of the historic homes.

The **Culpepper House** in Senoia dates to 1871, when it was built by Dr. John Addy, a returning Civil War veteran. Innkeepers Suzanne and Sam

Helfman have 3 guest rooms with private baths and furnished with Victorian antiques. Public areas shine with gingerbread trim, stained glass, and pocket doors. A full Southern breakfast is included in the inexpensive to moderate rate for a double with private or shared bath. Contact them at 35 Broad St., Senoia, or call (770) 599-8182, culpepperhouse.com.

Four miles north of Senoia, at the junction of GA 85 and GA 74, stands **Starr's Mill,** one of Georgia's most photographed landmarks. One look at the 200-year-old red frame mill, by a pond and waterfall, and you'll be rushing for your camera, too. When you go, be sure to bring along a blanket and picnic.

If you are feeling more adventurous you may want to check out **Historic Banning Mills** (770-834-9149; historicbanningmills.com) near the little town of Whitesburg off US 27. Now a popular corporate retreat location, ruins of centuries-old mills dot Snake Creek, which meanders through the 1,200-acre forest preserve. In addition to its conference center, Banning Mills is home to the longest and largest zipline canopy tour in the world. It features 6 levels including the intimidating Screaming Eagle. You can choose a day of it, or spend a few days completing all the courses available.

Sherman Meets the Suburbs

Since 1968 the picturesque rapids of Sweetwater Creek and the adjacent hardwood and piney woodlands have been the heart of **Sweetwater Creek Conservation Park,** a peaceful day-use state park. A short drive off I-20, 15 miles west of downtown Atlanta, the park serves the populace of rapidly growing Douglas County and many others who find it a delightful retreat from the hurly-burly of big-city life.

The ghostly ruins of the **New Manchester Manufacturing Company,** a Civil War–era enterprise torched by General William T. Sherman's troops, stands by the churning rapids, which provided the company with power to produce uniforms for the Confederate army. During the summer, kick off your shoes and join others wading in the swift, cool waters. Be careful of the slick patches of moss covering the rocks.

Five miles of nature trails lead you through the woods beside the creek. A 250-acre reservoir is stocked with bass, catfish, and bream, which you can fry in a pan and serve on one of the park's picnic tables. Fishing supplies are available at the park's bait shop, and during warmer months boat rentals are also available. The park is open daily from 8 a.m. to sundown. There is a $2 parking fee. Contact the superintendent at (770) 732-5871, (800) 864-PARK, or gastateparks.org/SweetwaterCreek.

With more than 765,000 residents, affluent **Cobb** is one of the nation's fastest-growing counties and the northwest flagship of the Atlanta metropolitan area. Off the well-beaten paths of freeways and around the corner from highrise hotels, glitzy shopping galleries, and trendy eateries, you'll find fascinating historic sites, charming town squares, and outdoor recreation.

Acworth, in northern Cobb County, is another of Metro Atlanta's transformed once-sleepy little towns by the train tracks into a buzzing hub of contemporary dining and shopping.

Along 2 blocks of Main Street, just off busy I-75, exit 277, diners choose from an eclectic array of cuisines. **Brix on Main** (770-693-0077; brixonmain .com) brags that it's like a fru-fru place and a non fru-fru place had a baby; a long-time staple is **Henry's Louisiana Grill** (770-966-1515; chefhenrys.com); and **Fusco's Via Roma** (770-974-1110; fuscosviaroma.com). Just one street behind is the lively hangout **Center Street Tavern** (4381 Center St.; 770-917-0004; centerstreettavern.com). **Teacup Cottage** (678-574-6011; teacupcottage .com) pours international teas with soups, salads, sandwiches, and desserts in a delightful gift shop. Antiques, book, jewelry, clothing, housewares, garden accessory, and wine shops and an ice-cream store are spaced among the restaurants. For information: Acworth Area Visitors Bureau, 4762 Logan Rd., Acworth; (770) 917-1234; acworthtourism.org.

After the fall of Chattanooga in late 1863, the Confederates grudgingly fell back to Kennesaw Mountain, 25 miles north of Atlanta and the site of **Kennesaw Mountain National Battlefield Park.** For 2 weeks in June 1864, 60,000 soldiers dug into the wooded flanks of the 1,808-foot mountain. When a series of assaults failed to dislodge the Southerners, Union commander General William T. Sherman executed a flanking strategy, which forced the Confederates to leave the mountain and retreat to Atlanta.

Stop first at the National Park Service Visitors Center and view the slide presentation and exhibits. Outside are some of the cannons that took part in the battle. From Mon through Fri you may drive your car up a paved road to a parking area 200 yards below the summit. From there take an easy walk through the woods studded with cannons, earthworks, and markers telling the story of the battle. The mountain road is open only to a free shuttle bus that makes the trip every half hour on Sat and Sun. In fair weather many visitors hike at least one way on an easy 1-mile trail. If you've the stamina, you can extend your hike from the Kennesaw summit 4 miles to **Cheatham Hill** and 7 miles to **Kolb's Farm,** other principal battlegrounds in the Kennesaw theater. The two areas are also accessible by car.

Picnic tables, grills, and restrooms are in a grove of trees near the visitor center parking area. The park, about 4.5 miles west of I-75 exit 269 (Barrett

Parkway) in Kennesaw, is open Mon through Fri from 8:30 a.m. to 5 p.m.; Sat and Sun to 6 p.m. A KEMO day pass is $5 and allows for shuttle riding as well as parking. Contact the superintendent at 900 Kennesaw Mountain Dr., Kennesaw; (770) 427-4686; nps.gov/kemo.

Civil War and old-time train buffs can have a great day exploring the **Southern Museum of Civil War and Locomotive History** in Kennesaw. The celebrated steam locomotive "General" is the centerpiece of the 40,000-square-foot, Smithsonian-affiliated museum. In April 1862, Union raiders hijacked the engine and several cars at the Kennesaw depot and drove it north toward Chattanooga. The train's crew, breakfasting at a trackside hotel during the heist, pursued the hijackers by foot, platform car, and locomotive for 87 miles. When the "General" ran out of fuel, near Ringgold, Georgia, 22 raiders were captured and 8 were hanged as spies. The secretary of war later presented 14 of the raiders with the Congressional Medal of Honor. In 1956, Walt Disney Pictures dramatized the episode in *The Great Locomotive Chase*, starring Fess Parker. With 8 wheels, a barrel-shaped smokestack, and a bright red cowcatcher, the "General" sits on original track in its own spacious exhibit hall. The museum's other displays include a history of Southern railroading, Civil War weapons, uniforms, and soldiers' personal items. A large wing re-creates the Glover Machine Works, a foundry in nearby Marietta where 300 locomotives were built during the early 1900s. Special exhibits from the Smithsonian are held all year. The museum is at 2829 Cherokee St., Kennesaw, off I-75 exit 273, about 25 miles north of downtown Atlanta. Open Mon through Sat 9:30 a.m. to 5 p.m.; Sun 11 a.m. to 6 p.m. Adults, $10; military, seniors, and children 3 to 17, $5; under age 2, free. Phone (770) 427-2117 or visit southernmuseum.org.

Londoners rendezvous by Big Ben, New Yorkers under the Grand Central Station clock. Since the early 1960s, motorists navigating the highways of Marietta and Cobb County have set their sights by **The Big Chicken,** a 56-foot red-and-white sheet-metal rooster that preens on the façade of a KFC outlet on busy US 41/Cobb Parkway (12 Cobb Pkwy. N). The Big Chicken was "hatched" in 1963 by S. R. "Tubby" Davis, who wanted a really big sign to ballyhoo his fast-food restaurant. In the 1970s, KFC bought out Tubby and reluctantly retained the Chicken, which had become a landmark and popular icon. When it was severely damaged by a 1993 tornado, KFC bowed to public demands and spent "buckets" on a makeover.

The Chicken's flapping beak and rolling eyes point travelers a mile west to Marietta's lovely old courthouse square. Something of an anomaly in a city of nearly 61,000, seat of 760,000-strong Cobb County, the square's centerpiece, **Glover Park,** is a peaceful Victorian throwback, with big trees, flowering plants, a gazebo, a bandstand, benches, and kids' play areas.

TOP ANNUAL EVENTS

MARCH

Conyers Cherry Blossom Festival
Georgia International Horse Park
(770) 918-2169
conyersga.com/events-and-attractions

APRIL

Atlanta Dogwood Festival
Piedmont Park, Atlanta
(404) 817-6642
dogwood.org

Georgia Renaissance Festival
Fairburn
(770) 964-8575
garenfest.com

Inman Park Spring Festival and Tour of Homes
Euclid and Edgewood Avenues, Atlanta
inmanparkfestival.org

JUNE

Virginia-Highland Summerfest
Atlanta
Vahisummerfest.org

JULY

Peachtree Road Race 10K
Atlanta
(404) 231-9064
peachtreeroadrace.org

OCTOBER

Atlanta Gay Pride Parade and Festival
Atlanta
(678) 368-6435
atlantapride.org

NOVEMBER

Christmas at Bulloch Hall
Roswell
(678) 639-7500
bullochhall.org

DECEMBER

Christmas at Callanwolde
Callanwolde Fine Arts Center
(404) 872-5338
callanwolde.org/christmas-at-callanwolde

Low-rise late 19th- and early 20th-century buildings on three sides of the square house a slew of antiques shops and others with clothing, jewelry, gifts, stationery, toys, garden accessories, folk art, and a pet bakery. Restaurants cover the map, with Turkish, Slovakian, Italian, Mexican, Australian, Irish, and American cuisines. Pubs and music clubs feature live music. ***Marietta's New Theatre in the Square*** (11 Whitlock Ave.; 770-426-4800; theatreinthesquare .net) is one of Metro Atlanta's finest professional companies. MNTITS is a resurrection of the long-standing theater which closed its doors in 2012. Raul Thomas and his family are dedicated to presenting a range of multi-cultural experiences. They also make sure patrons are as involved as the vibrant members of the theater company. Since reopening, it has racked up an array of prestigious awards including Broadway World's Regional Theatre of the Year award, Best Director of N. Emil Thomas's *In the Heights* work—which also won Best Musical.

Before ducking into any of the above, stop in the Marietta Welcome Center, in the 1898 Western & Atlantic railroad depot (4 Depot St., Marietta; 800-835-0445 and 770-429-1115; mariettasquare.com), for maps and information on museums and walking and driving tours of the city's five National Register historic districts.

The **Marietta Museum of History** is located in a historic landmark (1 Depot St., Marietta; 770-794-5710; mariettahistory.org). The museum is open Mon through Sat 10 a.m. to 4 p.m. Admission is $7 for adults; seniors ages 55 and up and students, $5. In its original life as the Kennesaw Hotel, the 1845 building housed James Andrews and his Union raiders the night before they train-jacked the locomotive "General" from the depot in nearby Kennesaw, an event immortalized in the Disney film *The Great Locomotive Chase.*

Marietta's **Gone with the Wind *Museum*** exhibit runs neck and neck with the previously mentioned Jonesboro museum. Now located in Brumby Hall (472 Powder Springs Rd.; 770-794-5576; gwtwmarietta.com), this antebellum home is a perfect spot to learn all about Atlanta author Margaret Mitchell's all-time best-selling novel and the 1939 film. Several hundred pieces collected by Dr. Christopher Sullivan of Akron, Ohio, include costumes, conceptual artwork, rare press and publicity books, film posters, editions of the novel in many languages, programs from the 1939 Atlanta movie premiere, contracts, promotional items, and much more. One of the most valuable artifacts is the bengaline silk gown that Vivien Leigh, as Scarlett O'Hara, wore on her New Orleans honeymoon with Rhett Butler/Clark Gable. Other exhibits highlight Mitchell's life and a tribute to Hattie McDaniel, the first African American to receive an Oscar, for her role as "Mammy." Brumby was built in 1851 and is a popular wedding venue because of its courtyard and gardens.

The museum is open Mon through Fri 10 a.m. to 5 p.m. Adults, $7; seniors 60 and over, and children 8 and older, $6; and $5 per person for groups of 15 or more.

Cinch up your hiking shoes, pump up your bike tires, and head for a blissful day on the **Silver Comet Trail.** The tree-shaded, 61-mile paved path takes you from suburban Smyrna into northwest Georgia's peaceful rural countryside. As you head for the Alabama border, you'll cross a towering 500-foot-long railroad trestle, over streams, around rock formations, through tunnels, pine forests, modest hills, and farmlands. Mavell Road in Smyrna, the trail access closest to Atlanta, is the busiest, but once you're free of the suburbs, it's just you and your fellow travelers, with no hassles from trucks and cars. The Silver Comet extends across the Alabama border, where it connects with the Chief Ladiga Trail, providing a 101-mile trail from Atlanta to Anniston, Alabama. It's part of a metro-wide greenways system being developed by the nonprofit PATH

Foundation. In the city of Atlanta, PATH partnered with the Atlanta Development Authority to create a 22-mile "beltline" of trails and parks around the city and an additional 11 miles of spur trails utilizing former railway corridors. The BeltLine has been developed in stages, but the Eastern Corridor near the Carter Presidential Center has proven very popular, and is credited with launching countless business and residential projects along its path. For information on the BeltLine, go to beltline.org, for Silver Comet go to silvercometga.org, and for other pathways, phone (404) 875-7284; pathfoundation.org.

Pickett's Mill Battlefield Historic Site, 5 miles northeast of Dallas, should be high on Civil War buffs' "must-do" list. The battlefield is much as it was when blue and gray troops fought here during the Battle of Atlanta campaign. Living-history programs demonstrate cooking, weapons firing, and military drills of the Civil War era. Artifacts and exhibits are in the interpretive center/visitor center. The battlefield is at 4432 Mt. Tabor Rd., Dallas (770-443-7850, 800-864-PARK; gastateparks.org). Admission is $5 for adults, $3 for students. Open Thurs through Sat.

Places to Stay in Metro Atlanta

ATLANTA

The Ellis Hotel
176 Peachtree St.
(404) 532-5155
ellishotel.com
Expensive
Now one of Atlanta's most popular boutique hotels; 127 guest rooms and suites have all the modern comforts and conveniences

The Glenn Hotel
110 Marietta St.
(404) 521-2250
(866)-40GLENN
glennhotel.com
Expensive
Downtown Atlanta's first boutique hotel is a hip makeover of a 1920s office building; 93 guest rooms and 16 suites

Hotel Clermont
789 Ponce de Leon Ave.
(470) 485-0485
hotelclermont.com
Moderate
One of Atlanta's newest/oldest hip hotels, completely refurbished, offering a mixture of rooms, suites and even "bunkrooms" with bunk beds

Hotel Indigo
683 Peachtree St.
(404) 874-9200
igh.com/hotelindigo
Moderate to expensive
In the heart of Midtown's thriving dining, entertainment, and cultural area; 140 guest rooms and suites with contemporary furnishings and amenities; pets welcome; parking on premises

The Social Goat
548 Robinson Ave.
(404) 626-4830
thesocialgoat.com
Moderate
Located across from Grant Park and Zoo Atlanta;

7 rooms that include a private carriage house, a master suite, a third-floor suite, and a small house located across the street; miniature barnyard with a menagerie of goats; includes full breakfast

Stonehurst Place
923 Piedmont Ave.
(404) 881-0272
stonehurstplace.com
Moderate to expensive
Beautifully restored 19th-century mansion with 8 rooms and suites, including a honeymoon suite; includes full breakfast

Sugar Magnolia
804 Edgewood Ave.
(404) 222-0226
sugarmagnoliabb.com
Moderate to expensive
The spectacular Queen Anne–style "painted lady" mansion in Inman Park; 4 guest rooms, including 2 suites with antiques and modern amenities; includes full breakfast

Urban Oasis
130A Krog St.
(770)714-8619
urbanoasisbandb.com
Moderate to expensive
Three guestrooms in a quirky, former warehouse industrial space; owners require a 2-night minimum stay; includes full breakfast

NEWNAN

Casa Bella Bed and Breakfast
61 Temple Ave.
(770) 755-6750
Casabellabb.com
Inexpensive
Two large guest rooms in the main historic house, and 2 guest cottages; saline pool open in the summer; includes 2 course breakfast

POWDER SPRINGS

Georgia Palms and Gardens
3228 Powder Springs Rd.
(678) 402-6861
georgiapalmsandgardens.com
Moderate
Family-owned and -operated, this is a popular wedding venue; 5 guest rooms; includes big Southern breakfast

MARIETTA

The Stanley House
236 Church St. Northeast
(770) 426-1881
Moderate
Victorian mansion features Savannah-style courtyard, wraparound porch, and elegant ballroom; 5 guest rooms available; includes full breakfast

HELPFUL WEBSITES

Georgia Tourist Division
georgia.org and gastateparks.org
(Both sites have information on all the state's regions.)

Atlanta Convention & Visitors Bureau
discoveratlanta.com

Atlanta Braves Baseball
atlantabraves.com

High Museum of Art
high.org

DeKalb County Convention & Visitors Bureau
discoveredekalb.com

Marietta Welcome Center
visitmariettaga.com

Historic Roswell Convention & Visitors Bureau
visitroswellga.com

Georgia State Parks
gastateparks.org

Whitlock Inn Bed & Breakfast
57 Whitlock Ave.
(770) 428-1495
whitlockinn.com
Moderate
Five guest rooms with private baths in Victorian mansion; includes continental breakfast

STONE MOUNTAIN

Stone Mountain Manor
1037 Main St.
(770) 879-6800
stonemountainmanor.com
Inexpensive to moderate
Reproduction of an old plantation home; comfortable, modern rooms within walking distance of village shops and restaurants; includes full breakfast

Places to Eat in Metro Atlanta

ATLANTA

The Consulate
10 10th St. NW
(404) 254-5760
theconsulateatlanta.com
Moderate to expensive
International small plates and dim sum–style lunch, rotating menu

Desta Ethiopian
3086 Briarcliff Rd. NE
(404) 929-0011
destaethiopiankitchen.com
Inexpensive to moderate
Ethiopian

Doc Chey's Noodle House
1424 N. Highland Ave.
(404) 888-0777
doccheys.com
Inexpensive
Vietnamese soup and Pan-Asian noodle dishes

Eats
600 Ponce de Leon Ave.
(404) 888-9149
eatsonponce.net
Inexpensive
Pasta, jerk chicken, and fresh veggies at rock-bottom prices

Fontane's Oyster Bar
1026 N. Highland Ave.
(404) 872-0869
facebook.com/fontainesoysterhouse
Inexpensive
Gumbo and other Southern fare, rustic dining area and outdoor patio

George's Restaurant
1041-A N. Highland Ave.
(404) 892-3648
Inexpensive
Tavern food and best hamburgers in town

Havana Restaurant
3979 Buford Hwy., #108
(404) 633-7549
havanaatlanta.com
Inexpensive
Cuban fare, milkshakes

Limerick Junction
824 N. Highland Ave.
(404) 874-7147
limerickjunction.com
Inexpensive
Pub food; nightly entertainment including musicians from Dublin and Belfast (and Limerick)

Man Chun Hong
5953 Buford Hwy.
(770) 454-5640
Manchunhong.com
Inexpensive to moderate
Chinese

Manuel's Tavern
602 N. Highland Ave.
(404) 525-3447
manuelstavern.com
Inexpensive
American classics and pub favorites

Mary Mac's Tea Room
224 Ponce de Leon Ave.
(404) 876-1800
Marymacs.com
Inexpensive
Southern

Max Lager's American Grill and Brewpub
320 Peachtree St.
(404) 525-4400
maxlagers.com
Inexpensive to moderate
Pub fare and variety of house-brewed beers

Surin of Thailand
810 N. Highland Ave.
(404) 892-7789
surinofthailand.com
Inexpensive to moderate
Thai

Ted's Montana Grill
133 Luckie St.
(404) 521-9766
tedsmontantagrill.com
Moderate to expensive
Steaks and burgers, comfort food sides

Trader Vic's
Atlanta Hilton Hotel
255 Courtland St.
(404) 659-2000
tradervics.com
Moderate to expensive
Polynesian menu and
theme with faux palm trees
and a tiki bar

Trattoria Il Localino
467 N. Highland Ave.
(404) 222-0650
localino.info
Moderate to expensive
Italian

The Vortex Bar & Grill
438 Moreland Ave.
(404) 688-1828
878 Peachtree St.
(404) 875-1667
thevortexbaratl.com
Inexpensive
Burgers

The Varsity
61 North Ave., near
Georgia Tech
(404) 881-1706
thevarsity.com
Inexpensive
Diner fare, an Atlanta
landmark and self-
proclaimed "World's
Largest Drive-In"

**White Oaks Kitchen and
Cocktails**
270 Peachtree St. NW 100
(404) 524-7200
whiteoakkitchen.com
Moderate to expensive
Southern food with a twist

DECATUR

Brick Store Pub
125 E. Court Sq.
(404) 687-0990
brickstorepub.com
Inexpensive
Pub fare; Belgian bar
features high-octane beers
and ales

Cafe Alsace
121 E. Ponce de Leon Ave.
(404) 373-5622
cafealsace.net
Moderate
French Alsatian bistro

Iberian Pig
121 Sycamore St.
(404) 371-8800
theiberianpigatl.com
Moderate to expensive
Modern Spanish cuisine
and tapas

Taqueria del Sol
359 W. Ponce de Leon
Ave.
(404) 377-7668
taqueriadelsol.com
Inexpensive
Spanish, seafood, and
Southern sides with a twist

Wahoo! A Decatur Grill
1042 W. College Ave.
(404) 373-3331
wahoogrilldecatur.com
Moderate to expensive
Seafood, Southern

NEWNAN

The Oink Joint
9 E. Washington St.
(770) 755-7999
theoinkjoint.com
Moderate to expensive
BBQ and craft beers

The Redneck Gourmet
11 N. Court Sq.
(770) 251-0092
redneckgourmet.com
Inexpensive
Southern

NORCROSS

The Crossing
40 S. Peachtree St.
(678) 280-9081
Thecrossingofnorcross.com
Moderate to expensive
Steakhouse, signature
drinks

Dominick's Little Italy
95 S. Peachtree St.
(770) 449-1611
dominicksitalian.com
Moderate
Italian

Iron Horse Tavern
29 Jones St. NW
(678) 291-9220
Iron-horse-tavern.com
Moderate
American and British pub
fare

ROSWELL

Greenwood's
1087 Green St.
(770) 992-5383
greenwoodsongreenstreet
.com
Inexpensive
American

**The Swallow
at the Hollow**
1072 Green St.
(678) 352-1975
swallowatthehollow.com
Inexpensive
BBQ and Southern
favorites, lively music

Table & Main
1028 Canton St.
(678) 869-5178
Moderate to expensive
Southern food and
signature cocktails

The Whiskey Project
45 Oak St.
(678) 373-1981
twpatl.com
Moderate to expensive
1,200 kinds of whiskey,

50 craft cocktails, 45 wines
by the glass, and 16 draft
beers

Southwest Georgia

Chattahoochee Trace

LaGrange, a pretty town of 30,000 near the Georgia–Alabama border, was named in honor of the Marquis de Lafayette's French estate, which accounts for the bronze likeness of the marquis in the center of downtown Lafayette Square. Away from the square, regal white-columned mansions preside over well-tended lawns, gardens, and tree-shaded streets.

Bellevue Lagrange Women's Club (204 Ben Hill St., LaGrange; 706-884-1832; visitlagrange.com) was the stately Greek Revival home of US senator and acclaimed orator Benjamin Harvey Hill. Built in the early 1850s, the home is an architectural treasure inside and out, filled with magnificent furnishings and artwork. It's the LaGrange area's favorite wedding venue. Open Tues through Sat from 10 a.m. to 5 p.m. Admission is $5 adults; seniors, military, and children, $4.

Lamar Dodd Art Center (706-542-1511; lagrange.edu), on the neighboring LaGrange College campus, 302 Forrest Ave., LaGrange, is a strikingly modern museum displaying changing regional and national exhibitions and a permanent collection of Native American art. Named for late LaGrange

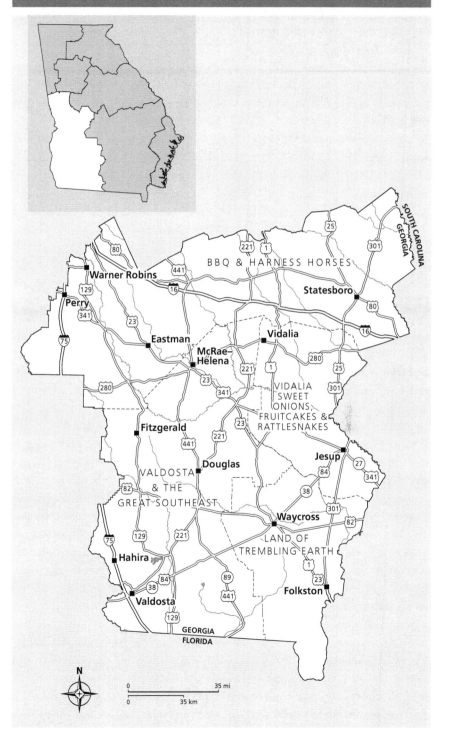

BBQ & HARNESS HORSES

Warner Robins

Statesboro

Perry

Eastman

Vidalia

McRae-
Hélena

VIDALIA
SWEET
ONIONS,
FRUITCAKES &
RATTLESNAKES

Fitzgerald

Jesup

Douglas

VALDOSTA
& THE
GREAT SOUTHEAST

Waycross

Hahira

LAND OF
TREMBLING EARTH

Valdosta

Folkston

GEORGIA
FLORIDA

SOUTH CAROLINA
GEORGIA

N

0   35 mi
0   35 km

artist Lamar Dodd, whose work is featured, the museum is open Mon through Fri from 8:30 a.m. to 4 p.m. Free admission.

The **LaGrange Art Museum** (112 LaFayette Pkwy., LaGrange; 706-882-3267; lagrangeartmuseum.org), near Lafayette Square, displays paintings, sculpture, and decorative arts in a restored 1890s jail building. It's open Tues through Fri from 9 a.m. to 5 p.m., Sat 11 a.m. to 5 p.m. Free admission, although nonresidents have a suggested $10 donation.

You'd never expect to find a bit of Israel in Georgia, but the **Biblical History Center** (130 Gordon Commercial Dr.; 706-885-0363; biblicalhistorycenter .com) is just that. Founded by archaeologist Dr. James Flemming, the center includes replicas of ancient life settings dating back to Biblical times. There are replicas for city gates, a village, ancient tombs, archeological gardens, and a Biblical Life Artifacts Gallery that houses 250 Biblical period artifacts from Israel. You can even sample food from the time period. Guided and self-guided tours are available. Guided are $21.50 for adults, $16.12 for children. Self-guided for adults are $17.25, $12.15 for children. Biblical meals can be reserved for $40 for adults, $25 for children. Open Tues through Sat 10 a.m. to 5 p.m.

In 1841, Sarah Ferrell created a formal boxwood garden in west Georgia wilderness that only a few years earlier had been part of Creek and Cherokee lands. Nearly 170 years later, Sarah Ferrell's garden is the centerpiece of **Hills & Dales Estate.** The home of two generations of the Callaway family, the estate, opened to the public in 2004, is one of west Georgia's most beautiful attractions.

Sarah Ferrell's garden was actually begun in 1832 by her mother, Nancy Ferrell. When she inherited it nine years later, Sarah expanded it into one of the Southeast's most acclaimed gardens. Deeply religious, she planted an area called "The Sanctuary," with religious symbols sculpted in boxwoods. A harp, a circular boxwood bed planted with yellow flowers, symbolized an offering plate full of coins. A nearby boxwood topiary is shaped like a church organ.

The "God" topiary, planted at the formal entrance to the garden, was a reference to the Genesis passage, "In the beginning, God created the heavens and earth." On the upper terrace near the house, she planted "God Is Love," and for her husband, Blount Ferrell, a judge and Mason, she created the Masonic emblem and Fiat justitia ("Let Justice Be Done").

Sarah continued working her garden until her death in 1903. In 1908, the property was purchased by Fuller E. Callaway and his wife, Ida Cason Callaway, who renamed the estate Hills & Dales. A wealthy west Georgia textile manufacturer, Callaway commissioned renowned Atlanta architect Neel Reid to design an opulent Georgian-Italianate villa. Completed in 1916, the 30-room house was furnished with American and European antiques and family keepsakes. The Callaways restored Sarah Ferrell's gardens and installed classical statuary, sunken gardens, terraces, and fountains to complement the Italian character of their house. They added greenhouses and herb gardens, and thousands of trees, flowers, and shrubs.

When Fuller Callaway died in 1928, followed by Ida in 1936, the estate was inherited by Fuller Callaway Jr. and his wife, Alice Hand Callaway. They enhanced the beauty of the house and gardens until their deaths in 1992 and 1998, respectively, after which the estate was granted to the Fuller E. Callaway Foundation and opened to the public. Cason Callaway, who created nearby Callaway Gardens, was Fuller Jr.'s older brother.

Tours of the estate begin at the Hills & Dales Visitor Center. Designed in classical style and inspired by Neel Reid's Italianate villa, the center includes an exhibit gallery, an orientation film, and a gift shop.

SOUTHWEST GEORGIA'S TOP HITS

Albany's Flint RiverQuarium	Kolomoki Mounds State Historic Park
American Camellia Society	LaGrange Art Museum
Andersonville National Cemetery and Historic Site	Lake Seminole
	Lapham-Patterson House
Bellevue Mansion	Little White House
Callaway Gardens	National Infantry Museum
Chattahoochee Riverwalk	Parks at Chehaw
Climax Swine Time	Pasaquan Folk Art Compound
Day Butterfly Center	Pebble Hill Plantation
Downtown Tifton	Port Columbus National Civil War Naval Museum
Florence Marina State Park	
Franklin D. Roosevelt State Park	Providence Canyon State Park
George T. Bagby State Park	Rattlesnake Roundup
Georgia Agrirama	"Swamp Gravy"
Georgia Rural Telephone Museum	Thomasville Rose Garden
Georgia Veterans Memorial State Park	West Point Lake
Hills & Dales Estate	Westville
Jimmy Carter National Historic Park	Windsor Hotel

A motorized tram takes visitors to the villa on a hill overlooking the gardens. Guests enter the home under four Doric columns, which support a covered two-story porte cochere and red tile roof.

Guided tours begin in the library, the Callaways' favorite room. Reminiscent of an English drawing room, the room is paneled in Circassian walnut, with American and English furnishings and family portraits. Although additions to the library and adjoining living room and dining room were made over the years, the house has retained the comfortable ambience of a fine country estate, in accordance with Fuller Callaway Sr.'s wishes for "a home in the real sense, to express, inside and outside, grace, naturalness and cheery friendliness."

Hills & Dales Estate is on the edge of the LaGrange College campus, a few blocks west of Lafayette Square, in downtown LaGrange. Open Mar to June, Tues to Sat from 10 a.m. to 6 p.m. and Sun 1 to 5 p.m.; July to Feb, Tues to Sat from 10 a.m. to 5 p.m. For House and Garden, adults and seniors, $15; age 7 to college students with ID, $7. Garden only tickets $10. For information contact Hills & Dales Estate, 1916 Hills and Dales Dr., LaGrange (706-882-3242; hillsanddalesestate.org).

West Point Lake, a mammoth 26,000-acre inland sea a few minutes from downtown LaGrange, offers plenty of opportunities for fishing, boating, swimming, waterskiing, and sunbathing. Contact the West Point Lake Resource Manager, 500 Resource Management Dr., West Point (706-645-2937; westpointlake .info). The lake's commercial outlets include Highland Marina Resort (1000 Seminole Rd., LaGrange; 706-882-3437; highlandmarina.com) where you can rent fishing boats and go after the lake's channel catfish and white and largemouth bass. Also at the marina, you can rent a houseboat or stay in a campground or furnished cottage. The lake is a US Army Corps of Engineers impoundment of the Chattahoochee River, which forms most of the Georgia–Alabama border.

In the mood for a hot dog? ***Charlie Joseph's*** has been serving them up, and Troup Countians have been gobbling them up, since 1920 when Charlie's opened as a fruit stand in downtown LaGrange. It's been at 128 Bull St. (706-884-5416; charliejosephs.com) since 1946. You can have your dog with just plain mustard and onions, or dressed up with slaw, chili, cheese, relish, and other fixins. Or try the hamburgers and breakfast-time egg-and-cheese sandwiches. Charlie's second location, 2238 West Point Rd. (706-884-0379; charliejosephs.net) serves breakfast, lunch, and early dinner. Both are open Mon through Sat.

Butterflies—over 1,000 of them, of more than 50 species, in all sizes and colors, from exotic places around the world—are free and on the wing at the ***Cecil B. Day Butterfly Center at Callaway Gardens*** in Pine Mountain. Opened to visitors in September 1988, America's first such natural attraction was inspired by similar preserves in Europe and Asia, with some distinctive Georgia touches. Named in honor of Cecil Day, late founder of the Days Inns of America motel corporation, it's a year-round, indoor-outdoor experience.

As you walk into an 8,000-square-foot, glass-enclosed "rain forest," you're suddenly caught in clouds of feathery giant swallowtails *(Papilio cresphontes)*, Paris peacock swallowtails *(P. paris)*, green-banded swallowtails *(P. palinurus)*, owl butterflies *(Caligo sp.)*, passion flower butterflies *(Heliconius sp.)*, and a rainbow of other iridescent beauties from Asia, the Andes, and the South Pacific. Over 1,000 butterflies and tropical birds perch side by side on exotic plants. A waterfall gently spatters. Bleeding-heart doves hide in the thick tropical foliage. Indoors, you'll find educational displays and a theater with a film all about the remarkable lives of butterflies.

Outside, the native butterfly garden is cunningly designed to lure home-grown butterflies to **Callaway Gardens** (17800 US 27, Pine Mountain; 800-852-3810; callawaygardens.com). If you'd like to have your own butterfly center, Callaway's horticulturists will show you how to plant a "tender trap" in your backyard.

While you're at Callaway Gardens, you can also take a driving tour of the 2,500 acres of gardens planted with 700 varieties of azaleas and more than 450 types of holly, mums, mountain laurel, rhododendron, dogwood, and wildflowers. These may be viewed in their natural habitat along 13 miles of roads and walking trails, and inside the **John A. Sibley Horticultural Center,** a stunning indoor-outdoor conservatory with pools, cascades, and scores of floral displays that change with the season.

Callaway's 14,300 rolling, wooded acres also embrace 13 lakes for swimming, fishing, boating, and waterskiing. Golfers may play 63 picturesque holes and sample from a recreational smorgasbord that includes tennis, skeet shooting, biking, and a summertime big-top circus. A half-dozen restaurants range from candlelight to casual.

Another unforgettable attraction is the **Virginia Hand Callaway Discovery Center.** Overlooking Mountain Creek Lake, at the end of a scenic 2.5-mile drive through woodlands and meadows, guests reach the Discovery Center from the gardens' main entrance at GA 18 and GA 354. (The former main entrance on US 27 is closed.) Named for founder Cason Callaway's late wife, the 35,000-square-foot center includes an information desk, a 100-seat orientation theater, interpretive exhibits, a gift shop, a lakeside restaurant, and interactive kiosks about the gardens' flora and fauna. A 3,000-square-foot museum displays late Italian artist Athos Menaboni's collection of bird paintings. From the Discovery Center, visitors can explore the gardens' many other attractions by foot, bike, tram, or water taxi.

The 40-acre **Callaway Brothers Azalea Bowl,** purportedly the world's largest azalea garden, contains more than 3,400 of the colorful shrubs in numerous domestic and exotic varieties. Set among streams, arched bridges, and wide, curving trails, the azaleas burst into banks of radiant, multicolored blooms in March and April. All-inclusive admission to most attractions is $25 for adults, $20 for seniors, $15 for children 6 to 12, 5 and under free. If you purchase online, you can get a discount.

Lodgings range from rooms at the **Mountain Creek Inn** to deluxe villas and cottages. The Marriott-operated **The Lodge and Spa's** 150 deluxe guest rooms have a wide range of decorative styles, contemporary comforts and conveniences, and balcony views of surrounding forests. The Lodge is associated with **Spa Prunifolia,** named for an azalea native to this area, which offers the full range of massages, wraps, facials, and other treatments. Callaway Gardens lies 12 scenic miles from Warm Springs and Franklin D. Roosevelt's **Little White House.**

At **Pine Mountain Wild Animal Safari** (1300 Oak Grove Rd., Pine Mountain; 706-663-8744, 800-367-2751; animalsafari.com), you can drive your own car or take the Safari Bus through a 500-acre preserve populated by zebras, giraffes, camels, axis deer, gnus, antelopes, water buffalo, and other wild, nonpredatory creatures. Also visit the petting zoo, monkey house, and serpentarium. Open daily from 10 a.m. to 5:30 p.m. Admission is $28.97 for adults; $25.97 for ages 60 and over and ages 3 to 12. Free for age 3 and under. If you'd rather not drive your vehicle through the park, you can rent a "Zebra Van," which holds 15 passengers, for $30. The 7-passenger "Zebra Mini-Van" is $25.

Blanton Creek Park (6111 Lickskillet Rd.; 706 643-7737), I-185 exit 11, is a nicely kept Georgia Power Company recreation area on 5,800-acre Lake Harding. The park features 51 RV ($30 a night) and tent camping sites ($25 a night), which have electrical and water hookups. The park also has boat ramps, picnic pavilions, and playgrounds.

If shopping's your favorite sport, indulge to your heart's content on **Pine Mountain's Main Street** (US 27). More than a dozen shops on both sides of the street have antiques and fine art, collectibles, handcrafted pottery, paintings, designer jewelry, books, toys, glass, and furniture. Before you begin, stop by the Pine Mountain Tourism and Welcome Center (101 E. Broad St.; 706-663-4000; pinemountain.org) in the center of town. They can also help point you to a number of moderately priced motels, bed-and-breakfasts, cottages, and chalets that are around Pine Mountain, Hamilton, and Warm Springs.

Columbus is Georgia's third largest city. To get your bearings in the city of 198,000, stop by the **Columbus Convention and Visitors Bureau**

(706-322-1613 and 800-999-1613; visitcolumbusga.org) at 900 Front Ave., Columbus, facing the Chattahoochee Riverwalk.

The *Chattahoochee Riverwalk,* a wide brick pathway with trees, benches, and attractive lighting, meanders 14 miles along the Chattahoochee and in the downtown historic district. It's adorned with lots of ornamental brick and ironwork, flowers and landscaping, and steps that lead right to the river's edge.

The *Historic Columbus Foundation* is located just a few blocks from the Riverwalk at 1440 Second Ave. and conducts a variety of tours. "Heritage Corner" features four homes at the corner of Broadway and 7th Street. They include an early-1800s pioneer log cabin; an 1828 Federal-style cottage; the Victorian cottage of Dr. John Stith Pemberton, a Columbus pharmacist who left here for Atlanta, where he invented Coca-Cola in 1886; a mid-19th-century farmhouse called the Woodruff Farm House; and the Victorian townhouse at 700 Broadway. The foundation also offers a tour explaining the city's "Soft Drink Heritage." Tours are by appointment only and begin at the headquarters for an all-inclusive $5. Phone (706) 323-7979 or visit historiccolumbus.com.

The self-guided *Columbus Black Heritage Tour* includes more than two dozen sites that played vital parts in the city's rich African-American culture. The tour begins with the last home of legendary blues singer Gertrude "Ma" Rainey (1886–1939) and includes churches, schools, theaters, businesses, and landmarks that showcase achievements of the city's black community.

If it's open—or holding one of its many regular stage productions—don't miss a chance to see the restored *Springer Opera House* (103 10th St.; 706-327-3688, 888-332-5200; springeroperahouse.org). Built in 1871, the Springer has hosted such illuminati as Oscar Wilde, Will Rogers, and Edwin Booth.

You can also take a walking/driving tour of numerous historic homes, churches, and public buildings with an illustrated brochure called "Original City Tours," available at the Historic Columbus Foundation.

The *Coca-Cola Space Science Center* (701 Front Ave., Columbus; 706-649-1470; ccssc.org) is one of Riverwalk's most exciting attractions. Developed in conjunction with Columbus State University, its components include the Mead Observatory, which captures high-detail images of far-flung celestial bodies (you can take a space flight and land on the moon); the Challenger Learning Center, an interactive, hands-on experience that helps sharpen science, math, team-building, and communications skills for schoolchildren and other groups; and the Omnisphere Theater, which projects laser shows, science and science fiction movies, concerts, and theatrical performances onto a giant domed ceiling. An accurate replica of the Apollo space capsule is one of the many permanent exhibits. Special events include "Night Out Under the Stars," an overnight campout at the Space Center that includes a Challenger Center

Mission, the Omnisphere Theater, construction and launch of a model rocket, a laser concert, and a science fiction movie. Open Mon through Thurs from 10 a.m. to 4 p.m.; Sat from 10:30 a.m. to 8 p.m. Closed Sun. Adults, $6; military and seniors, $5; ages 4 to 12, $4.

TOP ANNUAL EVENTS

JANUARY

Rattlesnake Roundup
Whigham
(229) 377-3663
whighamrattlesnakeroundup.com

FEBRUARY

Thomasville Antiques Show and Sale
Thomasville, Exchange Club Fairgrounds
(229) 236-8273
thomasvilleantiquesshow.com

APRIL

Thomasville Rose Festival
Thomasville
(229) 227-7001
thomasvillega.com

Callaway Gardens Spring Celebration
Callaway
(800) 852-3810
callawaygardens.com

National Mayhaw Festival
Colquitt
(229) 758-3757
colquitt-georgia.com

MAY

Riverfest Weekend
Columbus Riverwalk
(800) 999-1613
visitcolumbusga.com

Cotton Pickin' Country Fair
Gay
(706) 538-6814
cpfair.com

Andersonville Antiques, Crafts and Civil War Artifacts Fair
Andersonville
(229) 924-2558
Andersonvillegeorgia.com

JULY

Watermelon Festival
Cordele
(229) 273-168
cityofcordele.com

SEPTEMBER

Peanut Festival
Plains
(229) 824-7477
friendsofjimmycarter.org

NOVEMBER

Mule Day
Calvary
(229) 872-3612
calvarylionsmuleday.com

Swine Time
Climax
(229) 4160-2511
swinetimefestival.com

DECEMBER

Christmas in Thomasville
Thomasville
(229) 226-7977
thomasvillega.com

Christmas Festival of Lights
Callaway Gardens
(800) 225-5292
callawaygardens.com

Trade Ya My Apple for That Baloney Sandwich

It used to be that kids carried their sandwiches and cookies to school in a metal lunch box. Take a trip back in time at Allen Woodall's collection of thousands of metal, plastic, and vinyl boxes with images from the *A-Team* to *Zorro*, and scenes from popular radio and TV shows like *Hopalong Cassidy, Howdy Doody, The Green Hornet, Lost in Space, Little Lulu,* and *The Jetsons.* Originating in the 1890s, metal boxes were replaced with plastic and vinyl in the 1980s, when parents argued that the metal type were potential weapons. Woodall's 2,000 lunch boxes, and collections of furniture, glassware, military items, and other collectibles, are displayed at *River Market Antiques and Art Center* (3226 Hamilton Rd., Columbus; 706-653-6240; therivermarketantiques.com).

Those looking for real adventure may want to tackle Columbus's **Whitewater** course on the Chattahoochee River. Listed as one of the Top 12 Man-Made Adventures in the world, the exhilarating 2.5-mile course goes through the heart of the city. For pricing, contact (706) 321-4720 or visit chattahoochee .whitewaterexpress.com.

Oxbow Meadows Environmental Learning Center (3535 S. Lumpkin Rd., Columbus; 706-687-4090; oxbow.columbusstate.edu) is a fun and fascinating place to get out in the countryside and learn something about the world around you. Start your visit to the 1,600-acre site in the Chattahoochee River floodplain in a 2,000-square-foot building where you can observe live, mounted, and re-created plant and animal life. Two nature trails will let you stretch your legs in the wetlands and woodlands and come face to face with the creatures that live there. Open Tues through Fri from 9 a.m. to 4 p.m.; Sat 10 a.m. to 3 p.m.; and Sun from noon to 5 p.m. Free admission.

Even if you're not a war buff, don't miss the **National Infantry Museum** (101 4th Ave., Columbus; 706-685-5800; nationalinfantrymuseum.org) on the mammoth Fort Benning Army compound (1775 Legacy Way, Fort Benning). The museum's 3 floors and 12 spacious galleries exhibit more than 6,000 items from the French and Indian War and the American Revolution, through the world wars, to Vietnam and the Persian Gulf conflict and Iraq. You'll see a porthole from the battleship *Maine*, 16th-century English armor, the wing of a World War II Japanese Zero, ancient Korean and Chinese weapons and armor, gas masks worn by World War I horses, and wartime documents signed by 20 US presidents. A 5-story-high IMAX theater will put you right into the action. Open Tues through Sat from 9 a.m. to 5 p.m. (except for major national holidays); Sun from 11 a.m. to 5 p.m. Free admission, although a $5 donation is encouraged. The Giant Screen Theater is $10 for adults; military, seniors, and students, $9; and children ages 4 to 13, $8.

The **Port Columbus National Civil War Naval Museum** (1002 Victory Dr., Columbus; 706-327-9798; portcolumbus.org) covers the war on the high seas, from blockade runners to conventional wooden gunboats, the new age of ironclads, and Union and Confederate amphibious operations. Visitors to the 40,000-square-foot museum witness simulated battles from inside an ironclad and view naval artillery pieces, weapons, uniforms, personal effects, flags, interpretive exhibits, and artwork. The Confederate iron ram CSS *Jackson* is the museum's star attraction. Built at the Columbus Shipyards, less than a mile from the museum, the *Jackson* was within a few weeks of completion when Union raiders crossed the Chattahoochee River from Alabama in December 1864, and burned it to the waterline. The hull drifted 30 miles downriver and sank to the bottom, where it was salvaged in the 1960s. Visitors view the *Jackson*'s 225-foot hull from a platform above the bow and at floor level. A steel "ghost" superstructure over the hull helps viewers appreciate the ship's enormous size. Fully operational, it would have been sheathed in two layers of iron plate, been armed with six big cannons weighing about 700,000 pounds, and would have sat only 7 feet deep in the water. Other exhibits include a partial replica of the USS *Hartford*, the flagship that Union Admiral David Farragut rode into Mobile Bay, shouting, "Damn the torpedoes, full speed ahead. An 87-foot reconstruction of the ironclad CSS *Albemarle* gives visitors an "inside" audiovisual look at a Union surprise attack. A little-known fact: During the Civil War, a young man named Isidor Strauss was the overseas agent for a Columbus group, which financed construction of Confederate blockade runners in England. After the war, Strauss went to New York, where he built Macy's Department Stores; he died on the *Titanic* in 1912. Open Tues through Sat 10 a.m. to 4:30 p.m.; Sun and Mon 12:30 to 4:30 p.m. Admission is $8 for adults; $7 for military and seniors age 65 and older; $6 for students; age 6 and under free.

The **RiverCenter for the Performing Arts** (900 Broadway, Columbus; 706-256-3612; rivercenter.org) is a spectacular downtown Columbus cultural complex, with 5 interconnected buildings joined by a dramatic 4-story atrium lobby and glass curtain exterior wall. The 245,000-square-foot center's components include the 150-seat Studio Theater; 430-seat Legacy Hall, with a 4,000-pipe organ; and 2,000-seat Bill Heard Theater. Performances range from classical and country music to touring Broadway musicals, ballet, and contemporary dance. It also houses **Columbus State University's Schwob School of Music** (music.columbusstate.edu).

The **Columbus Museum** (1251 Wynnton Rd., Columbus; 706-748-2562; columbusmuseum.com) is a peaceful place to spend a few hours browsing.

Permanent exhibits include a hands-on discovery gallery for youngsters and adults, a fine arts decorative gallery, a regional history gallery, and changing exhibits of regional art. The museum is open Wed through Sun. Admission is free, but donations are invited.

The small town of **Lumpkin**, south of Columbus, offers an opportunity to step back through time by walking through **Historic Westville** (3557 S. Lumpkin Rd.; 706-940-0057; westville.org). The town offers a blend of European, African, and Native American history as it relates to the 19th-century South. There are antebellum and pioneer sections. Live interpreters explain everyday life, foods, and crafts of the time. Open Thurs through Sat. Admission is $10 for adults and $5 for children.

With its redbrick courthouse, granite Confederate soldier, and 1-story buildings flanking the quiet square, Lumpkin could be moved, intact, into a museum as an exhibit of 19th-century Americana. The **Bedingfield Inn on the Square** (Cotton Street on the Square; 229-838-6419; bedingfieldinn.word press.com) was built in 1836 as a doctor's residence and stagecoach inn. This museum is open Tues through Sat from 10 a.m. to 5 p.m. Admission is $5 for adults, $2 for children.

Nearby, **Providence Canyon State Park** preserves the scenic beauty of an area often referred to as "Georgia's Little Grand Canyon." More than a dozen canyons in the 1,108-acre park have been chiseled out over the past 50 million years by the slow, relentless process of soil erosion due to poor farming practices during the 1800s. As deep as 150 feet, the canyons offer a geological primer and a stunning visual display of stratified soil layers. Many fascinating formations stand alone in the midst of the canyons.

During spring and fall, those making the easy hike to the canyon floor are rewarded by multicolored wildflowers, which complement the pinks, purples, and whites of the Providence soils. From July to Sept, the rare plumleaf azalea blooms in shades from light orange to salmon and various tones of red and scarlet.

Stop first at the park's interpretive center (GA 39C, Lumpkin; 229-838-6202, 800-864-PARK; gastateparks.org) for an overview. A day-use park, Providence has picnic tables, shelters, and restrooms. It's 7 miles west of Lumpkin, and open daily from 7 a.m. to dark. There is a $5 per visit parking fee. Backcountry and pioneer campsites are available in the park by reservation at a cost of $9 a night.

You can also stay overnight and fish and boat in the Chattahoochee River at **Florence Marina State Park** (Route 1, Omaha; 229-838-6870, 800-864-PARK; gastateparks.org/FlorenceMarina). Campgrounds have electricity, water, restrooms, and showers. Furnished efficiency apartments, sleeping up to 5,

AUTHOR'S FAVORITES

Cecil B. Day Butterfly Center, Callaway Gardens, Pine Mountain

Chattahoochee Riverwalk

Climax Swine Time

FDR's Little White House Parks at Chehaw

Flint RiverQuarium

Jimmy Carter National Historic Park

Lamar Dodd Art Center and LaGrange Art Museum

Hills and Dales Estate

National Prisoner of War Museum, Andersonville National Cemetery and Historic Site

Pebble Hill Plantation

Providence Canyon State Park and Historic Westville Village

Rattlesnake Roundup

River Market Antiques' Lunch Box Museum

Windsor Hotel

with kitchenettes, are available. Six 2-bedroom cabins are completely furnished and have fully equipped kitchens. Call (800) 864-PARK or visit gastateparks.org for rates and reservations. The park also has a swimming pool, tennis courts, a playground, and a small grocery store. It is on GA 39C, 10 miles west of Providence Canyon. There is a $5 per visit parking fee.

George T. Bagby State Park, fronting the Chattahoochee River's 48,000-acre Lake Walter F. George (also known as Lake Eufaula), is a resort-style getaway. The 60-room George Bagby Lodge and Conference Center has all the modern comforts and a full-service restaurant. Call (800) 864-PARK for lodge and cottage rates and reservations or go to georgebagbylodge.com. Around it you'll find boat ramps and marinas, swimming pools, tennis courts, an 18-hole championship golf course, and hiking and picnic areas. You can also stay in furnished cottages. There's a $5 per visit parking fee. Contact 330 Bagby Pkwy., Fort Gaines; (229) 768-2571. Phone (800) 864-7275 or visit georgetbagby.com for campsite reservations. For tee times at the golf course, call (800) 434-0982.

At *Frontier Village* in neighboring Fort Gaines, a one-third-scale replica of the original fort, built in 1816, has Civil War cannons and authentic log cabins that reflect the area's frontier heritage. Most of the buildings are over a century old. The village is open to the public to explore and is located in Bluff Park which has scenic view from the bluffs of the Chattahoochee River and overlooks Alabama plains. Phone (229) 768-2248 or visit fortgaines.com.

Kolomoki Mounds State Historic Park (Route 1, Blakely; 229-724-2150, 800-864-PARK; gastateparks.org) is an important archaeological site, as well as a recreation area. Within the 1,294-acre park you can climb some of the 7 burial mounds and temple mounds built by Creek Indians in the 12th and 13th centuries. These are among the largest and earliest Woodland period mound groupings in the Southern US and the largest in Georgia. Dating back to between 350 and 750 AD, the largest mound is 57 feet high. The small museum has artifacts unearthed from the mounds and the excavated burial mound of a tribal chief. Also in the park, you're invited to swim in two pools, fish and boat in a pair of lakes, have a picnic, and play miniature golf. The park's 35 camping sites have group shelters, water and electricity, hot showers, and restrooms.

While you're tempted to just look at the beautiful 1853 neoclassical building when you're driving around the **Early County Courthouse** (also called the Grand Ole Lady) in Blakely, look for the stone monument to the counties' biggest agricultural crop—the peanut.

If ever a body of water were created with anglers in mind, it's got to be **Lake Seminole.** Formed by an impoundment of the Chattahoochee and Flint Rivers, the 37,500-acre lake, with a 250-mile shoreline, is especially bountiful grounds for bass fishing. Largemouth routinely weigh in at upward of 15 pounds. Anglers also snare a wealth of bodacious black bass, white bass, hybrid bass, and stripers, as well as bream, chain pickerel, catfish, yellow perch, and many other varieties.

Yet the marshy, reedy lake—afloat with thousands of acres of grass beds and lily pads and spiked with the ghostly trunks of cypress and live oak trees—is so far off the beaten path, down where Georgia's southwestern corner bumps against Alabama and Florida, that when more than 50 boats appear on a single day, old-timers grumble that "Ol' Sem" is turning into a waterbound I-75.

The lake's largest public recreational area is **Seminole State Park,** off GA 39, 16 miles south of Donalsonville (229-861-3137; gastateparks.org). Activities include fishing, boating, swimming, waterskiing, picnicking, and camping; furnished cottages are available. Check their website for scheduled activities such as Dewberry picking or craft shows. Call (800) 864-PARK for camping and cottage rates and reservations. There is a $5 per visit parking fee.

Peaches, Pecans & FDR

President Franklin Delano Roosevelt left his everlasting imprint on the hills and piney woodlands of Meriwether County. The future president was governor of New York when he first came to this isolated rural county, 85 miles southwest of Atlanta, in 1924 to immerse his polio-afflicted limbs in the mineral waters of Warm Springs. His **Little White House,** secluded in a wooded grove, became his sanctuary from the monumental pressures of World War II. Now maintained by the Georgia Department of Natural Resources, the comfortable little house remains as he left it when he died there on April 12, 1945.

In the kitchen, simple dishes, pots and pans, a hand-cranked ice-cream maker, and other utensils are neatly stacked. In the woodwork, FDR's cook penciled this touching message: "Daisy Bonner cooked the first meal and the last one in this cottage for President Roosevelt."

The **FDR Memorial Museum** emphasizes Roosevelt's life at Warm Springs and his impact on Georgia, the South, and the rest of Depression-ravaged rural America. Connected to the entrance plaza and visitor center, the 12,000-square-foot museum's hundreds of exhibits include his 1938 Ford convertible equipped with hand controls; his wheelchair, leg braces, and canes; photos of his life at Warm Springs; a 1930s kitchen with his "Fireside Chats" playing on a radio; and displays featuring the Rural Electrification Administration, the Tennessee Valley Authority, and other New Deal programs, which brought modern conveniences into millions of homes for the first time.

A welcome film includes historic footage of FDR swimming in the Warm Springs pools, visiting with neighbors, having picnics, playing with his Scottie dog, Fala, and his funeral procession, when he left his Little White House for the last time. While posing in the living room for a portrait by Madame Elizabeth Shoumatoff on April 12, 1945, he suffered a stroke and died. The famous *Unfinished Portrait* is in the museum, with a *Finished Portrait* Madame Shoumatoff painted after World War II. FDR's Little White House State Historic Site (US 27-A, Warm Springs; 706-655-5870; gastateparks.org/littlewhitehouse) is open daily. Adults $12, seniors and ages 6 to 18 $7, 5 and under free. Special observances on April 12 commemorate FDR's extraordinary presidency.

The adjacent village of **Warm Springs** (population 443) has been revived with visitors in mind. More than 60 stores along the main street are stocked with antiques, collectibles, and Georgia-made arts and crafts. The **Warm Springs Welcome Center** (1 Broad St.; 800-FDR-1927, 706-655-3322; warm springsga.com) is open every day for information and brochures.

The **Hotel Warm Springs Bed & Breakfast Inn** (47 Broad St., Warm Springs; 706-655-2114 or 800-366-7616; hotelwarmspringsbb.org) once housed the press, Secret Service, and visitors to FDR's Little White House. Now the 3-story 1907 hotel receives bed-and-breakfast guests who come here to see the FDR shrines and shop at Warm Springs' dozens of handicraft stores. Fourteen guest rooms with 2 full beds are furnished with original oak Val-Kill furniture. The Presidential Suite has 2 separate rooms with a connecting bath. The lobby has original ceramic tile floors, a vintage Stromberg-Carlson cord switchboard, stenciled walls, and 16-foot ceilings. The hotel has a restaurant and an old-fashioned soda shop with ice cream (homemade Georgia peach is innkeeper

Lee Thompson's special treat). A bountiful Southern "Breakfast Feast" is included in the inexpensive to moderate rates.

Franklin D. Roosevelt State Park, about 5 miles west of Warm Springs, on GA 190, is ideal for a mini-vacation. On the wooded crest of Pine Mountain, the 9,480-acre park has a lake for swimming, fishing, and boating; hiking trails; horseback riding; and picturesque picnic spots. Many of the fieldstone buildings in the park were the product of the Depression-era Civilian Conservation Corps. Campsites ($10 a night) have water, electricity, hot showers, and restrooms. Cottages have fireplaces and fully equipped kitchens for standard state fees. Call (800) 864-PARK or log on to gastateparks.org/FDRoosevelt for rates and reservations. There is a $5 per visit parking fee. The park office, Box 749, Pine Mountain, (706) 663-4858, is open daily from 8 a.m. to 5 p.m.

A life-size seated statue of FDR overlooks the Pine Mountain Valley, at *Dowdell's Knob*, a rocky 1,395-foot spur of the Pine Mountain ridge. One of FDR's favorite picnic and contemplation sites, it's off GA 190, inside FDR State Park. Hikers in your crowd can lace up their boots and hit the scenic 23-mile *Pine Mountain Trail.* Starting at the Callaway Gardens Country Store on US 27, the trail winds past rock formations, waterfalls, big stands of trees, and lush vegetation on its way to its terminus at the TV tower on GA 85W near Warm Springs. One of the country's southernmost mountain trails, it has 12 access points, so you can get on and off with ease. Pick up a trail map at the FDR Park office.

If you'd like to spend some time canoeing on a scenic, unspoiled river, get in touch with *Flint River Outdoor Center* (4429 Woodland Rd., Thomaston; 706-647-2633). Guided and self-guided trips on the river begin at GA 36, 15 miles south of Warm Springs. You pass through mostly mild rapids, waterfalls, hills and valleys, wildflowers, ferns, and animal habitats. Canoe, kayak, and equipment rentals are available. If you have your own, the shuttle to the put-in point is $20 to Sprewell Bluff or further upstream to Goat Mountain for $28. The center features campsites ($20) and 5 RV hookups ($22) for those who would like to overnight.

The 7-acre *Pasaquan Folk Art Compound* (238 Eddie Martin Rd., Buena Vista; pasaquan.columbusstae.edu) would probably seem extraordinary even in the Land of Oz. In rural Marion County, near the tiny county seat of Buena Vista, this outdoor ensemble of toothy totem faces, smiling snakes, whirling pinwheels, suns, moons, and stars—all painted in brilliant primary colors—is positively otherworldly. It was the product of the late Eddie Owens Martin, who spent 30 years creating it. Born here in 1908, Martin moved to New York where, while sick with a fever, he claimed to have been instructed by three people from the future to come home and create this fabulous legacy, which he did in

Albany's Ray Charles

The **Ray Charles** statue and plaza honors the entertainment icon born in Albany on September 23, 1930. He went with his family to Florida when he was a small child, became blind at age 6, and overcame his disability to become one of the world's most beloved musicians. He died in California in 2004. Dedicated in 2007, his illuminated bronze statue, slowly revolving around Ray Charles Plaza on the downtown Albany riverfront, depicts him with his signature dark sunglasses, seated at a piano, perhaps playing "Georgia On My Mind," "I Can't Stop Loving You," "What'd I Say," or another of his many classic gold and platinum hits. Along with the main statue, surrounded by a fountain, the plaza also features a "maquette," a miniature version that visitors can touch. In 1979, Charles performed "Georgia On My Mind" for the state legislature, which named it Georgia's official state song.

1950. To finance his creativity, he came to town in a turban and robes, renamed himself St. EOM, and told fortunes and sold jewelry around the courthouse.

Since Martin's death in 1986, his "Land of Pasaquan" has been meticulously restored and is now managed by the Kohler Foundation and Columbus State University. Open Apr through Nov, from Thurs to Sat. Call (229) 649-9444 to verify times.

The *Sign of the Dove Bed & Breakfast and Restaurant* (108 N. Church St., Buena Vista; 888-690-3663, 229-649-3663; sign-of-the-dove.com) has 3 large guest rooms in a 1905 neoclassical home and a 4-bedroom cottage. The restaurant serves Southern food, steaks, and seafood. Inexpensive to moderate.

Approaching *Albany* from any direction, you'll pass symmetrical groves of papershell pecan trees. Pecans are available year-round, still in the paper-thin shell or roasted and boxed. Some groves invite you to come in and pick your own. The attractive city of 75,000 has other pleasant surprises as well.

While Atlanta boasts one of the world's largest aquariums with the world's largest fish, Albany is just as proud of its *Flint RiverQuarium* (117 Pine Ave., Albany; 877-463-5468; flintriverquarium.com). Although the 175,000-gallon RiverQuarium would be a drop in the fish tank compared to the 10-million-gallon Georgia Aquarium in downtown Atlanta, it is a centerpiece for the city Albanians call "All-benny."

The Flint RiverQuarium was the linchpin in the redevelopment of the city after Albany suffered catastrophic flooding from the Flint River in 1994.

As visitors enter the lobby, they go up a ramp to a room called Skywater, the Creek Indian name for Blue Hole Springs. A re-creation of a natural river spring, the 22-foot-deep hole is open to the outside. Viewed through a 25-foot window, the Blue Hole teems with life. Snapping turtles, sliders, cooters, and other turtles swim through the clear water and sun themselves on logs just above the spring. Largemouth bass, 5-foot-long gar, 50-pound catfish, and dozens of other species drift through underwater caves and partially submerged cypresses and live oak trees, whose above-water branches house native birds, herons, and egrets. Juvenile and 6-foot-long gators have their own portioned-off habitat. Divers go into the Hole every day to feed the fish and amphibians.

A large tank in the gallery area showcases the sometimes ornery Flint River, which is born in a spring near Atlanta's Hartsfield-Jackson International Airport and twists more than 300 miles across middle and southwest Georgia, through Albany down to Lake Seminole. There it joins the Chattahoochee to form the Apalachicola, which flows through the Florida Panhandle into the Gulf of Mexico.

The aquarium's star and mascot is Big Al, a 150-pound, 100-year-old alligator snapping turtle. His lovably homely image graces mugs, T-shirts, and other souvenir items. If you have never seen an albino alligator, the pink-eyed "Moonshine" is easy to spot in the dark waters of Cypress Creek. Cypress is also home to the only native bird aviary in Georgia. There, you will find over 40 native birds flying around the 35-foot-tall enclosure.

Fish, reptiles, and other creatures from the Amazon, Ganges, and other world rivers populate the "World of Water" exhibit.

In Discovery Caverns, kids can play interactive games that focus on stewardship of natural resources. They make their own weather, change a river's flow, and crawl through a cave to find creatures that live underground.

The Flint RiverQuarium is open Tues through Sat from 10 a.m. to 5 p.m.; Sun 1 to 5 p.m. Adult RiverQuarium admission, $9; seniors 62 and over, $8; ages 4 to 12, $6.50.

Playgrounds, benches, and picnic tables are in Riverfront Park outside the aquarium. Festively decorated fiberglass turtles are goodwill ambassadors. Visitors can stay at the neighboring *Hilton Garden Inn.*

At *Parks at Chehaw* (105 Chehaw Park Rd.; 229-430-5275; chehaw.org), African black rhinoceros and zebra, Andean llamas, North American black bears, bobcats, elk, bison, and deer roam in 700 acres of natural habitats designed by the late naturalist, Jim Fowler. You view the animals from protected, elevated walkways. Admission to the zoo and a companion recreational park with play areas, jogging, hiking, and biking trails, a re-created Creek Indian village, miniature train rides, a boat dock, and picnic areas for adults is $7, age 62 and over $5, military $6, and ages 4 to 12 $5. The *Chehaw National Indian Festival,* held in the park the second weekend in April, is one of the Southeast Tourism Society's top 20 yearly events. The park is open from 9 a.m. to 5:30 p.m. daily. The zoo is open 9 a.m. to 5 p.m.

Thronateeska Heritage Foundation (100 Roosevelt Ave., Albany; 229-432-6955; heritagecenter.org) is a delightful, hands-on science experience for young and old alike. Its name is an homage to its location and is Muskogee Creek, meaning "flint picking up place." The science complex is adjacent to an early 1900s "prairie style" train depot, a 1910 steam locomotive, and an 1840s house, and includes the *Wetherbee Planetarium, Science and History Museum* where you can witness a variety of live astronomy presentations. It's open Thurs through Sat 10 a.m. to 4 p.m. Admission is free during normal operating hours.

The *Albany Museum of Art* (311 Meadowlark Dr., Albany; 229-439-8400) has both permanent and changing displays of regional and national artists. The African Art Center collection is one of the nation's most outstanding. Open Wed through Sun from 10 a.m. to 5 p.m. Admission is $6 for adults; $5 for senior, military, and college students; first- through fourth-graders $3.

Albany Civil Rights Institute (326 Whitney Ave., Albany; 229-432-1698; albanycivilrightsinstitute.org) is the restored Mount Zion Baptist Church, where Dr. Martin Luther King Jr. preached during the 1961 civil rights demonstrations. Photos and exhibits illustrate Dr. King's pivotal part in the "Albany movement." He was arrested and jailed for his civil disobedience activities, and freed through the intervention of US Attorney General Robert Kennedy. Open Tues through Sat, 10 a.m. to 4 p.m.; Sun 2 to 5 p.m. Adults $6, seniors and students $5, first- through fourth-graders $3, and preschoolers $2.

Considered one of Georgia's Seven Natural Wonders, *Radium Springs* (2501 Radium Springs Rd.; 229-430-6120) is a beautiful park on the outskirts of Albany. Here 70,000 gallons of clear, 68-degree water pumps each minute from an underground cave and spills Into the Flint River. Until the early 1990s, the area was home to a casino, but now, it's a nature park that includes trails, flora, and fauna. The park is free and open Tues to Sat 9 a.m. to 5 p.m.; Sun 1 p.m. to 5 p.m. You can also contact the Albany CVB & Welcome Center at 112 Front St., Albany; (800) 475-8700; visitalbanyga.com.

Every spring in the swamps and bogs of southwestern Georgia, a thorny, scrubby, rather homely tree called the mayhaw produces an apple-like fruit prized by gourmets and homemakers. The small, coral-hued fruit is gathered in fishing nets and by hand, then turned into a delectable sweet-tart jelly that's sold in stores around the small Miller County seat of Colquitt. The fruit is the star of *Colquitt's Mayhaw Festival,* the third weekend of April. Phone (229) 758-3757.

While you're in the Colquitt area, try to catch a performance of *"Swamp Gravy,"* an entertaining folklife play about the comedies and tragedies, tall tales, music, dance, and songs of Miller County and rural Georgia. Sponsored by the Colquitt/Miller Arts Council, it's performed in Jan, Mar, Apr, Oct, and Nov at the Cotton Hall Theater, 166 E. Main St. Call (229) 758-5450 for more information, or visit swampgravy.com.

"If walls could talk" isn't wishful thinking in Colquitt. Walk around the town square and 5 bigger-than-life murals, created by the Colquitt/Miller County Arts Council's Millennium Mural Project, "speak" about events that shaped the lives of the peanut farming community of 2,500. The 4 panels of *Saturday on the Square*, by Alabama artist Wes Hardin, capture the excitement when "The Circus Comes to Town"; when a runaway "Bull Comes to Colquitt"; "When a Young Soldier Leaves Colquitt"; and "Hanging Out on the Square." Other murals depict neighbors helping neighbors; Saturday morning in Colquitt's black community; and the story of the South's three dominant cultures: Native American, black, and white. Contact Colquitt/Miller County Chamber of Commerce at 166 S. 1st St., Colquitt, (229) 758-1000, colquittga.com.

The *Tarrer Inn* (155 S. Cuthbert St., Colquitt; 229-758-2888; thetarrerinn .com) is considered the Grand Dame on the Colquitt town square. Built in 1861 as a boardinghouse, the inn has been refurbished as a comfortable small hotel. Twelve guest rooms are decorated with antiques and modern amenities. A lunch buffet is served Tues, Wed, Thurs, Fri, and Sun; dinner on Fri and Sat. Inexpensive to moderate rates include breakfast.

If you're a fan of country fairs and enjoy good, old-fashioned fun, put *Climax Swine Time* (229-246-0910) on your post-Thanksgiving calendar. Held the Friday and Saturday after Thanksgiving in the Decatur County community of Climax, many of the activities are pig-related: a hog-calling contest, best-dressed pig competition, a greased-pig chase, and a "chitlin" (chitterling) eating contest. Also on the agenda are a parade, country and gospel music, a 10K race, cane grinding and syrup making, and barbecue and fried chicken for

Plain Nuts for Peanuts

The annual *Plains Peanut Festival* pays tribute each September to the legume that put this tiny town on the map long before local boy Jimmy Carter became the 39th president of the United States. A true small-town experience, the festival features a fun run, arts and crafts, music, and dance as well as a parade that is almost longer than the town itself. The peanut is highly celebrated in both food options (try a grilled peanut butter and jelly sandwich!) and in agricultural demonstrations. The most crowded location will be the Peanut Pavilion where free samples abound. You can usually spot Carter himself in attendance along with his wife Rosalynn. For information call (229) 824-5373 or friendsofjimmycarter.org.

those who care not for "chitlins." Contact Bainbridge/Decatur County Chamber of Commerce at 100 Boat Basin Rd., Bainbridge; (229) 246-2511; swinetime-festival.com.

The **Rattlesnake Roundup,** the last weekend of January, is the social event of the year at the small Grady County town of **Whigham,** 6 miles east of Climax. The event began a couple of decades ago when Whigham residents, tired of being accosted by the hissing reptiles every time they walked through their fields and farms, decided to do something about it and have some sport at the same time. On the big day each January, visitors pack tiny downtown Whigham as snakes by the hundreds are brought in and displayed. Contact Cairo-Grady County Chamber of Commerce; (229) 377-3663; whighamrattle-snakeroundup.com.

Mule Day, in **Calvary**, the first Saturday of November, salutes the stalwart workhorses of the fields. Hundreds of jacks and jennies parade through Calvary, on US 11 in Grady County, just north of the Florida border. Contestants are judged on beauty, poise, congeniality, and mulish cussedness. They go haunch to haunch in a plowing contest and other events. Humans exhibit their skills at cane grinding, corn shucking, quilting, and syrup making. And of course, there is always food and arts and crafts. For information phone (229) 872-3128 or visit calvarylionsmuleday.com.

Carter Country

Peach County leaves little doubt that it's the heart of Georgia's most luscious industry. Traveling on I-75 at night, you can't miss "The Big Peach," an enormous illuminated rendition of the fruit on a 100-foot-pole at the Byron/Fort Valley exit. During the summer, visitors have plenty of opportunities to go into the orchards and pick their own or to buy fresh peaches at packing houses and roadside stands. The Byron/Fort Valley exit 49 is the northern end of the Andersonville Trail, which leads through Fort Valley to Plains on GA 49 and US 280.

In early June, you're invited to the **Georgia Peach Festival** in Byron and Fort Valley (gapeachfestivalcom). This weeklong event includes parades, street dances, peach pie cookoffs, peach-eating contests, and a king-and-queen coronation.

At **Lane Southern Orchards** (50 Lane Rd.; 478-825-2891; lanesouthernor-chards.com) you can tour the orchards and take home bushels or bagsful of the succulent fresh fruit, peach jam, and other peachy products (pecans and strawberries, as well). The family owned business and been in operation since 1908! Open daily 9 a.m. to 6 p.m. Free tours.

Six miles south of Fort Valley, at the Peach/Macon County line, look for a left turn off GA 49 into Massee Lane Gardens, home of the **American Camellia Society** (100 Massee Ln.; 478-967-2358; americancamellias.com). Between Nov and Mar, pink and white blossoms in every known variety bloom in the society's more than 100-acre botanical gardens. Year-round, you're invited to the society's Williamsburg-style headquarters to admire the 170 porcelain birds and flowers created in the studios of the late American artist Edward Marshall Boehm. The pieces are so lifelike they appear to be on the verge of flight. Some were created as gifts of state for presidents and kings. Open year-round, the gardens have other blooming plants but camellia season is from Jan through Mar, Tues through Sat from 10 a.m. to 4:30 p.m.; Sun from 1 to 4:30 p.m. Free to the public.

Part of the Presidential Pathways of the Andersonville Trail, **Macon County** is the home of Georgia's largest Mennonite community. You can admire antebellum white columns in the small towns of Marshallville and **Montezuma**. which is also the county seat.

Originally called Traveler's Rest, it was renamed Montezuma by returning Mexican War veterans. It sits on the banks of the Flint River and the entire downtown is on the National Historic Register. Check out the **Macon County Historical Museum** in a Victorian train depot (E. Railroad Street). Pick up a driving tour map from the Macon County Chamber of Commerce, 109 N. Dooly St., Montezuma; (478) 472-2391; maconcountyga.org.

Nearly 100 Mennonite families give the little town some of the appearance of the Pennsylvania Dutch country. Drive east of Montezuma on GA 26 past the neat barns and silos and the contented herds of the Mennonite dairy farms.

Three miles from Montezuma—and 14 miles west of I-75 exit 127—look for a black buggy parked in front of **Yoder's Deitsch Haus,** (5252 GA Hwy. 26 E; 478-472-2024) a sparkling clean cafeteria where Mennonites in traditional dress prepare truly admirable Southern cooking, spiced with such Pennsylvania Dutch specialties as shoofly pie and pot roast. Before leaving, stop by the bakery for a sackful of cakes, cookies, breads, and strudel. It's open for breakfast, lunch, and dinner Tues through Sat. Handmade Mennonite dolls, afghans, coverlets, garden ornaments, and other items are on sale in the adjacent gift shop.

Neighboring **Sumter County,** the epicenter of Georgia's peanut industry, is home of the world's most famous peanut farmer, our 39th president, Jimmy Carter. The southern anchor of the Andersonville Trail, Sumter is also the site of the Civil War's most notorious prisoner-of-war camp, Camp Sumter military prison.

These days, all is green and peaceful at the **Andersonville National Cemetery and Historic Site,** GA 49, Andersonville, (229-924-0343; nps.gov/

ande). Stop first at the National Park Service Visitors Center to view the film and exhibits, then take the self-guided driving tour of the 514-acre site.

Built in 1864 as confinement for 10,000 Union prisoners of war, the 26.5-acre stockade soon became a charnel house for upward of 33,000 captives. With the Confederacy barely able to feed and clothe its own forces, about 12,000 of the Andersonville inmates perished of disease and starvation. As park rangers point out, however, Southern prisoners in the more well-off North often fared no better than the Union prisoners at Andersonville. After the war, the camp commander, Swiss-born Captain Henry Wirz, was found guilty of war crimes and hanged. The self-guided tour leads you past thousands of graves and impressive memorials erected by states whose sons died here. Tunnels testify to the prisoners' usually failed attempts to escape the horrors.

The **National Prisoner of War Museum** (nps.gov/ande), on the Andersonville grounds, honors the 800,000 American soldiers, sailors, and airmen who've endured the horrors of capture and imprisonment from the American Revolution to the Persian Gulf conflict and the Iraq War. The 10,000-square-foot museum was built in partnership by the American Ex-Prisoners of War (AXPW), a national organization of 20,000 former POWs, and Friends of the Park, local citizens who support the National Park Service at Andersonville. Funds were raised by the sale of 270,000 commemorative coins created by the US Mint. More than 10,000 donors and corporations gave about $700,000, and the Georgia Department of Transportation built a new entrance road and parking areas. Andersonville was chosen for the museum in recognition of the site's tragic history as the nation's most infamous POW camp. During the tour, you "experience" the terror of being captured by enemy troops and taken to prison. One room highlights the horrors of World War II's Bataan Death March and the forced marches to North Korean POW camps. Another room displays drawings, poetry, carvings, and clandestine radios POWs created to help them keep their sanity. The tour ends with a full-scale replica of POWs digging an escape tunnel under a Nazi prison camp. The museum's courtyard opens onto the remains of the Civil War Andersonville stockade. A fountain gushing water into a stream symbolizes the lack of fresh water prevalent in most POW camps.

A granite springhouse marks the site of **Providence Spring,** which legend says flowed from barren ground in answer to prisoners' prayers for water.

Across Highway 49, the Civil War village of **Andersonville** (229-924-2558; andersonvillegeorgia.com), population 227, has been returned to its 1860s appearance. The quaint little town welcomes visitors with antique and craft stores, picnic groves, and antebellum churches and homes. Stop by the Welcome Center, which is located in the lobby of the **Drummer Boy Museum** right on Church Street. The museum houses an extensive collection of guns,

Peanuts! Fresh Roasted Peanuts!

Jimmy Carter, Georgia's peanut farmer–president, drew the world's attention to the state's most bountiful crop. His native southwest Georgia is the heart of this tasty industry, and it produces most of the more than 2 billion pounds of goobers grown in the state every year.

Breaking it down, there are about 200 peanut pods to a pound, and usually 2 pea-nuts per pod. They would make a mountain of about 800 billion peanuts. Laid end to end, they'd extend for more than 6 million miles, about 25 times the distance from the Earth to the Moon. "Goober" is believed to come from an African word, *nguba,* which, of course, means "peanut."

swords, battle flags, and documents signed by Jefferson Davis and Abraham Lincoln. The village's major yearly happening is the **Andersonville Camp and Battlefield Portrayal** in early October, which features battle reenactments and scores of craftspeople and musicians.

A charming bed-and-breakfast called **A Place Away** (229-924-1044) has 2 bedrooms in a comfortable, rustic-looking cottage with private baths, refrig-erators, and coffeemakers. Guest rooms and a sitting room are decorated in kick-off-your-shoes casual country style. The inexpensive rate comes with a bountiful Southern breakfast.

At nearby **Americus,** stop at the Americus/Sumter County Tourism Council Welcome Center (123 W. Lamar St., Americus; 229-928-6059; visitamericusga .com) for a driving guide to the historic showplaces around the pleasant city of 15,300.

The world acclaimed charity and nonprofit housing ministry **Habitat for Humanity International** was founded in Americus in 1976 by Millard and Linda Fuller, Habitat for Humanity has partnered with more than 22 million people to build simple, affordable houses in every state and more than 70 countries. The **Global Village and Discovery Center** in downtown Americus has model homes and exhibits about the organization's history. It's open Mon through Sat. Adults are $4, students/seniors $3. Habitat for Humanity Interna-tional is at 721 W. Church St., Americus, (229) 410-7937, (800) HABITAT, habitat .org/gvdc. Two of Habitat's biggest supporters are former President Jimmy Carter and his wife Rosalynn from neighboring Plains.

If you love old movie palaces, try to be in Americus for a performance at the gorgeously restored **Rylander Theater** (310 W. Lamar St.; 229-931-0001; rylander.org). Opened in 1921, the ornate theater was the setting for 30 years of vaudeville, silent movies, stellar attractions like bandmaster John Philip Sousa, the Ziegfeld Follies, political speeches, graduations, dance recitals and concerts, and films from Hollywood's golden era. The theater closed in 1950 and was forgotten until 1992, when a restoration movement began. Reopened in 1999, the venerable house, with 630 seats on 3 levels and a 1928 "Mighty Mo" Möller pipe organ, hosts touring musicals, plays, concerts, and festive events of all sorts.

In 1923, four years before he captured the world's imagination with his historic transatlantic solo flight, an unheralded barnstormer named Charles A. Lindbergh made his first-ever solo flight at **Souther Field**, a US Army aviation training camp at Americus which dates to 1918. "The Lone Eagle" made his flight in the first plane he ever owned, a single-engine WWI surplus, Jenny. It was obviously love at first flight. His feat is remembered on a plaque at what's now Jimmy Carter Regional Airport: "I had not soloed up to the time I bought my *Jenny* at Americus, Georgia [signed] Charles A. Lindbergh." Contact the airport at (229) 924-3090; souther-field.com.

For contemporary comforts wrapped in a splendid turn-of-the-century package, check into the **Windsor Hotel** in downtown Americus. This is no doubt the fanciest Best Western Hotel you will ever see. Built in 1896, the redbrick, turreted-and-towered Italianate landmark reopened in 1991 to rave reviews. The 53 large guest rooms are beautifully furnished and decorated. The Grand Dining Room serves high-Southern and continental cuisine, and there's a full bar and an open veranda with wicker rockers. The private Lindbergh Dining Room was named for "Lucky Lindy," who purchased his first plane and made his first solo flight from nearby Souther Field. Lindbergh used to stay in the Windsor and would play pool across the street from the hotel. The Windsor is at 125 W. Lamar St., Americus. Call (229) 924-1555 or (888) 297-9567 or visit bestwestern.com. Inexpensive to moderate.

More than four decades after Jimmy Carter left the White House, the 39th president's sleepy little Sumter County hometown of Plains treasures the legacy of the quiet-spoken peanut farmer who made it world-famous. Visitors still come to town to visit the simple, unassuming places included in the *Jimmy Carter National Historic Park.* The National Park Service Visitor Center in the former Plains school is the best place to start. In the late 1930s and early 1940s, when Carter sat in the classrooms and walked its corridors, the brick school housed grades 1 through 11. There was no 12th grade in those days. Today the school is a museum, showcasing life in the rural South during the Great Depression. Stiff-backed wood and metal school desks are lined up like rows of peanuts in a red clay field. On an audiotape, today's Carter talks fondly of Julia Coleman, his teacher and school principal, who advised him and fellow students to "accommodate changing times, but cling to unchanging principles." When students got out of hand, a wooden paddle, legal in those days, was there to get them back in line. Wouldn't Julia Coleman be proud to know her former pupil became president and won the 2002 Nobel Peace Prize? That Peace Prize is on display at the school site, along with a replica of his Oval Office where visitors can sit at his desk and pose for photographs. The Visitor Center (300 N. Bond St., Plains; friendsofjimmycarter.org) is open daily from 9 a.m. to 5 p.m. Admission is free.

Elsewhere in town, the old railroad depot, made famous by the 1976 presidential campaign, is now the **Depot Museum,** dedicated to that historic campaign.

Also part of the National Historic Park, the **Jimmy Carter Boyhood Home,** in the Archery community (402 Old Plains Hwy.), 2 miles from the heart of town, includes the farmhouse, barns, outbuildings, and the farm store where Carter grew up in the 1930s. In push-button audios around the site, Carter describes the no-frills life on his father's farm. The house had no electricity until the early 1940s, and the family's day usually began before dawn and ended not long after dark. A battery-operated radio with newscasts and popular shows like *Amos 'n Andy* and *Fibber Magee and Molly* was one of the family's few sources of entertainment.

The **Plains Inn and Antique Shop,** a 2-story building on Main Street, has a 24-booth antiques mall on the street floor and 7 luxury suites on the second floor, each decorated in the style of a decade from the 1920s to the 1980s. Inexpensive to moderate. Phone (229) 824-4517 or visit plainsinn.net.

A peanut with a famous toothy grin welcomes visitors to Plains. Made of wooden hoops, chicken wire, aluminum foil, and polyurethane, the 13-foot-tall goober was a gift to the town from Carter's friends. When termites took a liking to "Mr. Peanut," townsfolk came to the rescue with patches of cement. It's just up the street from the Visitor's Center and before the Carter family's home church, **Maranatha Baptist Church** (mbcplains.org).

The Carters' current home, a modest ranch-style house, will eventually be included in the National Historic Park. Carter and his wife, Rosalynn have slowed down due to age and health but can often be seen around town. Visitors are welcome when the former president teaches Sunday school at Maranatha Baptist Church but be prepared to get there early to clear the secret service screening. For information about the National Historic Park, write National Park Service, Plains 31780 (229-824-4104; nps.gov/jica). All sites are open daily, and admission is free. Plains is on US 280 about 40 miles west of I-75 exit 101. Shops on Plains' main street are stocked with Carter memorabilia and peanuts in many different guises.

Carter's mother, Miss Lillian, was born 20 minutes further west on Hwy. 280 in tiny **Richland** but you'll want to make the journey to visit the **Richland**

Distilling Company (355 E. Broad St.; 229-887-3537; richlandrum.com). Dutch-born and professed rum connoisseur Erik Vonk has built a rum empire in what was virtually a deserted downtown. RR is the only single-estate, single-barrel rum in the US and voted "America's Best Rum." Tour the distillery daily except Sunday or just relax in their tasting room.

Hello, Central! The ***Georgia Rural Telephone Museum*** (135 Bailey Ave., Leslie; 229-874-4786; grtm.org) in the small Sumter County town of Leslie recalls the bygone era when the telephone hung on the wall and not your back pocket. Tommy Smith, who owns the local Citizen's Telephone Company, opened the museum in 1995 in a 1911 cotton warehouse he saved from destruction. His 2,000 pieces of telephonia include hand-cranked wooden voice boxes, early telephones of every size and description, and life-size dioramas of switchboard operators in period dress. You'll also see a re-creation of Alexander Graham Bell's workshop, phone booths, and an early 1900s Model A Ford service truck. Open Mon through Fri from 9 a.m. to 3:30 p.m. Adults $5, seniors $4, children $3.

Georgia Veterans Memorial State Park is a tranquil haven 9 miles west of Cordele. A museum and vintage aircraft honor the state's military veterans. The park sits on Lake Blackshear, an 18-mile-long waterway renowned for catfish, black bass, bream, pickerel, and other delicious catches. Visitors can also enjoy boating, an 18-hole golf course, swimming in a freshwater pool, and a nature interpretive center and playground. The 100 camping and trailer sites have electricity, water, restrooms, and hot showers. Ten 2- and 3-bedroom cottages, with fireplaces and fully equipped kitchens, are available. There is a $5 per visit parking fee. The park office (US 280, Cordele; 229-276-2371, 800-864-PARK; georgiaveteransstatepark.org) is open daily from 8 a.m. to 5 p.m. The ***Lake Blackshear Resort & Golf Club*** is a deluxe resort inside Georgia Veterans Park. Looking more like a modern art museum than a state park lodge, the retreat's 88 smartly furnished guest rooms and villas are moderately priced. Amenities include a stunning restaurant in the resort, as well as a casual grill located lakeside, indoor and outdoor pools, fitness center, conference center, golf, marina, fishing, and water sports. Moderate to expensive. Call (800) 459-1230, (229) 276-2004, or visit lakeblackshearresort.com.

Daphne Lodge (on US 280 West; 229-273-2596; daphnelodge.com) is a pleasantly rustic, family-owned restaurant famous for its fried catfish and hush puppies. They also serve shrimp, steaks, quail, country ham, and fried chicken at dinner Tues through Sat, 5 to 9:30 p.m.

If you're down this way in late June, join in the fun of Cordele's annual **Watermelon Festival.**

Calling all train nuts! The ***Savannah-Americus-Montgomery Shortline*** is now accepting passengers for its 36-mile daily run between Cordele and

Plains. Opened in late 2002, the state-operated excursion train, dubbed "The Rolling State Park," glides through pecan groves, peanut fields, and small towns and makes a scenic crossing of Lake Blackshear. It stops at the Jimmy Carter National Historic Park and the Georgia Rural Telephone Museum and also gives riders time to tour Habitat for Humanity's Tour Center and Museum in Americus. The SAM Shortline gets its name from a historic route that dates back to 1888 and these days goes nowhere near Savannah. Fares range from coach class (adults $39.99; ages 3 to 12, $29.99) to the Chairman class in the restored 1925 Pullman car the Dearing at $119 per person. Phone (229) 276-0755 or (877) GA-RAILS for pricing, or visit samshortline.com.

Roses & Pine Trees

The *Georgia Museum of Agriculture and Historic Village* (or *Agrirama* for short) is an off-the-beaten-path experience less than 0.25-mile off the well-beaten path of I-75 exit 63B. About three dozen vintage farm buildings make up the state's 95-acre agricultural heritage center. Inside the gates of this 19th-century time warp, youngsters may go nose to nose with friendly farmyard animals and take a trip on a steam-powered logging train. Cotton is planted in the old-fashioned way by a farmer in bib overalls commanding a mule and a plow. The village blacksmith hammers out nails and utensils over a white-hot forge. Sugarcane is harvested by hand and reduced into syrup and corn into grits and meal at a picture-postcard gristmill. A country store sells handmade quilts, preserves, cookbooks, toys, and corn shuck dolls.

The *Agrirama* (1392 Whiddon Mill Rd., Tifton; 229-391-5205; gma.abac .edu) is open year-round Tues through Sat, 9 a.m. to 4:30 p.m. All-inclusive admission Tues through Fri is $7 for adults, $6 for senior citizens 55 and over, $4 children 5 to 16; free for children under 4. Saturday is when the train runs so admission is $10 for adults, $8 for seniors, and $5 for children.

Downtown Tifton, bustling with about 30 shops and eateries, attracts visitors to a complex of restored 19th- and early 20th-century buildings. The 1906 Myon Hotel now houses City Hall (130 1st St. E), a permanent collection of regional art, shops, offices, and a restaurant. Contact the Tifton/Tift County Tourism Association, 115 W. Second St., Tifton; (229) 382-8700; tiftontourism.com.

From 1870 to the turn of the new century, *Thomasville* was a Southern Newport, the forefather of Palm Beach and Miami. Encouraged by reports of the area's healthy climate, wealthy Northerners came by private train to spend the winter at grand hotels, which brought chefs and orchestras all the way from New York and Europe. Many regular visitors built their own lavish homes and purchased surrounding plantations for grouse and quail hunting. In the early

1900s, the rich and famous discovered Florida, and Thomasville's "Golden Age" was over. Left behind was a remarkable heritage. Presidents, aristocrats, and "commoners" still flock to the city of 20,000 to hunt game birds and antiques, tour homes and plantations, and participate in late April's *Thomasville Rose Festival.*

Stop first at the Thomasville/Thomas County Convention and Visitors Bureau (144 E. Jackson St., Thomasville; 229-228-7977, 866-577-3600; thomas villega.com) where you can load up on maps, brochures, and self-guided walking and driving tour information. Guides can be arranged for tour groups. The Welcome Center is open Mon through Fri from 8 a.m. to 5 p.m.; Sat from 10 a.m. to 3 p.m.

On your own, stop at the *Thomas County Historical Museum* (725 N. Dawson St., Thomasville; 229-226-7664; thomascountyhistory.org) where you'll see hundreds of photos and souvenirs of the "Golden Age." It's open Mon through Sat from 10 a.m. to 5 p.m. Self-guided admission for adults is $5, for students $1. Guided tours are $8 for adults, $3 for students.

Nearby, the *Lapham-Patterson House State Historic Site* (626 N. Dawson St., Thomasville; 229-225-7664, 800-864-PARK; gastateparks.org) is an outlandish Victorian mansion built for Chicago shoe manufacturer C. W. Lapham. Maintained as a state historical museum, the tri-winged, mustard-yellow mansion is highlighted by cantilevered interior balconies, double-flue chimneys, and fish-scale shingles. It's open Fri 1 to 5 p.m.; Sat from 10 a.m. to 5 p.m.; Sun from 2 to 5 p.m. Admission is $5 for adults, $2.50 for children 6 to 18; free for children 5 and under.

Pebble Hill Plantation (229-226-2344; pebblehill.com) is a "must-see." The 28-room Georgian and Greek Revival main house and the gardens, stables, and kennels were left as a museum by the late Pansy Ireland Poe. Inside the house are 33 original John James Audubon bird prints and extensive collections of silver, crystal, and antique furnishings. Five miles southwest of Thomasville, on US 319, it's open Tues through Sat from 10 a.m. to 5 p.m. and Sun from 12 to 5 p.m. Admission fee for the self-guided tour of the grounds is $5 for adults and $2 for children; the guided main house tour is $16 for adults and $6.50 for children ages 6 to 12; children under 6 not permitted in main house.

The *Thomasville Black Heritage Trail* was created by retired Air Force officer James "Jack" Hadley to give visitors an opportunity to learn about the city's rich African-American history. The 2.5-hour "step-on, step-off" tour includes churches, historic sites, schools, cemeteries, businesses, parks, and a black-owned bed-and-breakfast. More than a half-dozen sites focus on the life of Lt. Henry Ossian Flipper, who was born a slave on a Thomasville area plantation in 1856 and 21 years later became the first black graduate of the

Lieutenant's Scrambled Dogs

Lieutenant Stevens started cooking up something he called a "scrambled dog" decades ago at Columbus's Dinglewood Pharmacy. Lieutenant retired and passed away in 2019, but the staff still prepares it Lieutenant's way—splitting and splaying 2 hot dogs on a bun in a banana split dish and dressing them with cheese, mustard, pickles, and a rich coating of Lieutenant's secretrecipe chili, topped with a shower of oyster crackers. Betcha can't eat more than one! Incidentally, Lieutenant is Stevens's real name. He was born on Armistice Day, 1931, and his parents wanted their son to honor America's armed forces. *Dinglewood Pharmacy* is at 1939 Wynnton Rd., near downtown Columbus. Call (706) 322-0616.

United States Military Academy at West Point. For information on the Thomasville Black Heritage Trail contact (229) 228-6983; jackhadleyblackhistory museum.com. The *Jack Hadley Black History Museum*'s (214 Alexander St.; 229-226-5029; jackhadleyblackhistorymuseum.com) 2,000 artifacts and pictorial exhibits highlight Thomasville's black achievers and also commemorate state and national black leaders. It's open Tues through Sat from 10 a.m. to 5 p.m. Adults $5; students $3.

Several of Thomasville's most beautiful old homes welcome bed-and-breakfast guests. All take pride in their antique furnishings and traditional South Georgia hospitality. They include the AAA Four Diamond *1884 Paxton House Inn* (445 Remington Ave.; 229-226-5197; thepaxton1884.com), *Dawson Street Inn* (324 W. Dawson St.; 229-226-7515), the *Magnolia Leaf* (501 E. Washington St.; 229-226-4499; themagnolialeaf.com), and *Thomasville Bed and Breakfast* (429 North Crawford St.; 229-227-1749; thomasvillebedandbreakfast.com). All have private baths, antiques, and personable hosts. Rates range from inexpensive to expensive.

You can't leave town without stopping by the corner of Crawford and Monroe Streets to see "The Big Oak." It's estimated this giant Southern live oak was planted around 1685. Its limb span is over 165 feet. President Dwight Eisenhower was so impressed that he took photos of it himself during a visit to Thomasville. For a bit of fun, go to the Big Oak Cam sign, stand in front of the tree, and dial (229) 236-0053. You'll get instructions for what to do, but basically you'll strike a pose while looking at the camera on the pole across the street. Your photo will show up on rose.net/plogger/index.php.

If you'd like to enjoy a bit of Thomasville's sporting life, shoot some skeet, and hunt birds and game, contact *Myrtlewood Plantation* (3081 Lower Cairo

Rd.; 229-228-6232; myrtlewoodplantation.com). There are four lodges on the plantation where you can stay individually or as a group.

Thomasville's really big annual event is the late-April **Rose Festival**, a week of parades, pageantry, home tours, and rose judgings that attract visitors from many countries. The **Thomasville Rose Garden** displays scores of varieties of blooming plants around the shores of Cherokee Lake, at the corner of Covington and Smith Avenues. Admission is free.

Places to Stay in Southwest Georgia

ALBANY

Hilton Garden Inn
101 S. Front St.
(229) 888-1590
hiltongardeninn.com
Moderate to expensive
125-room hotel, fitness center, pool, full-service restaurant and bar

AMERICUS

Americus Garden Inn
504 Rees Park
(229) 931-0122
(888) 758-4749
americusgardeninn.com
Inexpensive to moderate
Eight guest rooms with plush antique furnishings, large private baths

Windsor Hotel
125 W. Lamar St.
(888) 297-9567
(229) 924-1555
bestwestern.com
Inexpensive to moderate
See p. 64 for details

BUENA VISTA

Sign of the Dove Bed & Breakfast and Restaurant
108 Church St.
(229) 649-3663
Inexpensive to moderate
Three guest bedrooms in a neoclassical home and a guest cottage

COLQUITT

Tarrer Inn
155 S. Cuthbert St.
(229) 758-2888
Thetarrerinn.com
Inexpensive to moderate
Thirteen guest rooms; includes full country breakfast

COLUMBUS

Gates House
802 Broadway
(800) 891-3187
Moderate to expensive
1880 Colonial Revival house

Marriott Columbus
800 Front Ave., at the Riverwalk
(888) 228-6290
(706) 324-1800
marriott.com
Moderate
177-room hotel has an outdoor pool, restaurant and bar, and meeting rooms

Rothschild-Pound House
201 7th St.
(706) 322-4075
thepoundhouseinn.com
Moderate to expensive
Second Empire–style showplace has 10 guest suites and cottages with private baths; full breakfast and evening cocktails

CORDELE

Lake Blackshear Resort & Golf Club
(229) 276-2004
(800) 459-1230
lakeblackshearresort.com
Moderate to expensive
See p. 66 for details

HAMILTON

Holly House of Hamilton
127 Barnes Mill Rd.
(706) 628-5634
hollyhouseofhamilton.com
Moderate
Five guest rooms and 2
family suites

HOGANSVILLE

**Hogan's House at
Rosehill**
804 E. Main St.
(706) 415-1874
hoganhousebandb.com
Moderate
Victorian home with
two small suites and a
double room; includes full
breakfast

PINE MOUNTAIN

Chipley Murrah Bed
and Breakfast
207 W. Harris St.
(888) 782-0797
(706) 663-9801
chipleymurrah.com
Moderate
Victorian home built in
1895; 3 spacious cottages
on the property

PLAINS

Plains Inn
106 E. Main St.
(229) 824-4517
plainsgeorgia.com
Inexpensive to moderate
See p. 65 for details

THOMASVILLE

1884 Paxton House Inn
445 Remington Ave.
(229) 226-5167
1884paxtonhouseinn.com
Moderate to expensive
Queen Anne–style home
has 3 suites and a room in
the main house, carriage
house, pool house, and
cottage; breakfast included

TIFTON

**Shalom House Bed and
Breakfast**
7 Ross Rd.
(229) 386-0513
shalomhousebnb.com
Inexpensive to moderate
Three guest rooms in the
main house and fully-
equipped cabin known
as "The Pond House";
breakfast included

Places to Eat in
Southwest Georgia

COLUMBUS

The Black Cow
115 12th St.
(706) 321-2020
theblackcowga.com
Moderate
Southern

The Cannon Brewpub
1041 Broadway
(706) 653-2337
thecannonbrewpub.com
Inexpensive
Pub fare and pizza

Country's BBQ
1329 Broadway
(706) 596-8910
countrysbarbecue.com
Inexpensive
Chattahoochee Valley–style
BBQ

**Minnie's Uptown
Restaurant**
104 8th St.
(706) 322-2766
Inexpensive
Southern

Ruth Ann's
941 Veteran's Pkwy.
(706) 221-2154
ruthannsrestaurant.net
Inexpensive
Southern

GEORGETOWN

Michelle's of Georgetown
765 GA 50
(229) 334-5912
Inexpensive
Southern

PINE MOUNTAIN

**Carriage and Horses
Restaurant**
607 Butts Mill Rd.
(706) 663-4777
cometodagher.com
Moderate to expensive
International, Southern

Cricket's Restaurant
14661 GA 18
(706) 663-8136
cricketsrestaurant.com
Moderate
Cajun and Creole

HELPFUL WEBSITES

Americus-Sumter County Tourism Council
visitamericusga.com

Columbus Convention & Visitors Bureau
visitcolumbusga.com

Massee Lane Camellia Society Gardens
americancamellias.com

Pebble Hill Plantation
pebblehill.com

Eddie Mae's Kountry Kitchen
324 Main Ave. North
(706) 663-2640
Moderate to expensive
Southern

The Kitchen at Rose Cottage
111 E. Broad St.
(706) 663-7877
Inexpensive to moderate
English tea, sandwiches, soup, salads, desserts, wine

THOMASVILLE

The Billiard Academy
121 S. Broad St.
(912) 226-9981
Inexpensive
Hot dogs, beer

George & Louie's
217 Remington Ave.
(912) 226-1218
georgeandlouies.com
Moderate
Seafood, burgers, steaks

Jonah's Fish and Grits
109 E. Jackson St.
(229) 226-0508
jonahsfish.com
Inexpensive to moderate
Seafood

Liam's Restaurant
113 E. Jackson St
(229) 226-9444
liamsthomasville.com
Inexpensive to moderate
New American, cocktails

Mom & Dad's Italian Restaurant
1800 Smith Ave.
(912) 226-6265
momanddadsitalian.com
Moderate
Italian

The Plaza Restaurant and Oyster Bar
217 S. Broad St.
(912) 226-5153
thomasvilleplaza.com
Moderate
Steak, seafood

Sass Sweet and Savory Sisters
420 W. Jackson St.
(229) 236-6006
sassthomasville.com
Inexpensive
Southern

WARM SPRINGS

The Bulloch House
70 Broad St.
(706) 655-9057
bullochhouse.com
Inexpensive
Southern, buffet

Southeast Georgia

BBQ & Harness Horses

The pleasant little city of Perry, population 17,300, on I-75 exit 136, 25 miles south of Macon, is home to Georgia's largest fairgrounds, a former US senator, and a revitalized downtown that you'll wish was your own. Its nickname is the "crossroads of Georgia" and was once a major stagecoach stop for travelers making their way north or south pre-railroad days. Perry is also the seat of **Houston County** (pronounced "Howston"), population 157,000, home of Robins Air Force Base.

The 628-acre **Georgia National Fairgrounds & Agricenter** (478-987-3247; gnfa.com) hosts livestock and horse shows, fairs, concerts, rodeos, and sporting events year-round. The three biggest events are the **Georgia National Fair** in October; the **Georgia National Junior Livestock Show and Rodeo** in February; and the **"Big, Bang, Boom"** July Fourth celebration. A giant Ferris wheel, cotton candy, and other fun stuff to ride and gorge on give the fairgrounds the festive feeling of an old-time carnival.

Downtown Perry is part of **Main Street America**, a national project to help revitalize historic town centers. You

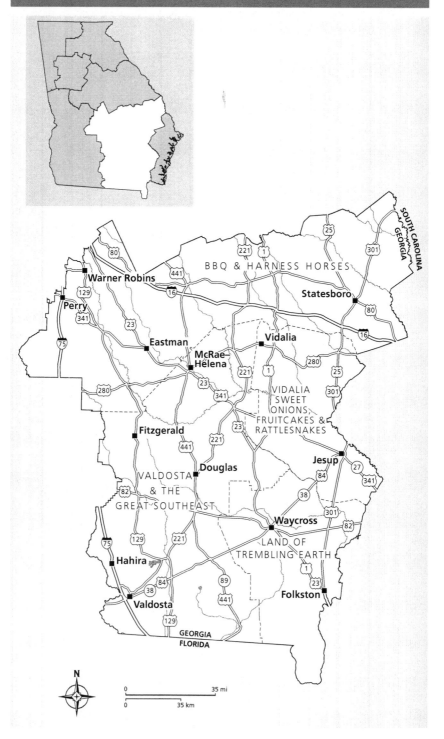

SOUTH CAROLINA
GEORGIA

25

301

221 1

BBQ & HARNESS HORSES

441

80

Warner Robins

129

16

Statesboro

Perry

80

341

23

16

75

Eastman

Vidalia

280

McRae–
Helena

25

221 1

301

280

23

VIDALIA
SWEET
ONIONS,
FRUITCAKES &
RATTLESNAKES

341

23

Fitzgerald

221

441

Douglas

Jesup

27

VALDOSTA
& THE
GREAT SOUTHEAST

82

84

341

38

301

129 221

Waycross

82

75

LAND OF
TREMBLING EARTH

Hahira

1

84

89

23

38

441

Folkston

Valdosta

129

GEORGIA
FLORIDA

N

0   35 mi

0   35 km

can have a fun time shopping for antiques, gifts, and home decor, or dine at a tearoom or Southern comfort food restaurant on Carroll Street which stretches through the heart of town.

You'll no doubt notice the stately **New Perry Hotel** at 800 Main Street. This landmark hotel served travelers from the 1920s until 2017, when it was sold to be converted to apartments. Take time to visit the lobby which has been restored to reflect that by-gone era.

The **Sen. Sam Nunn Library** in the 1925 former Perry High School building, now the Houston County Board of Education (1100 Main St., Perry; 478-988-6200) exhibits memorabilia, photos, documents, and videos about the life and political career of the Perry native and lifelong resident, who served as a Democratic US senator from 1972 to 1997. A classroom is like it was when Nunn pondered the "three Rs" here. Open Mon through Fri from 9 a.m. to 5 p.m. Free admission.

Even those who don't know a thing about fishing would enjoy the **Go Fish Education Center** (11255 Perry Pkwy.; 478 988-6701; gofisheducation center.com). Operated by the Georgia Department of Natural Resources and devoted to promoting fishing and mentoring young anglers, the center has a 200,000-gallon freshwater aquarium with native Georgian fish, interactive fishing and boating simulators, and allows you to even catch-and-release fish in the stocked pond. A visit isn't just about fishing, but also learning about Georgia's water ecosystems and the influence of pollution. Admission is $8 adults, $4 for seniors, and $3 children. Open Wed through Sat 9 a.m. to 5 p.m.; Sun 1 p.m. to 5 p.m.

The Retreat of Southern Bridle Farms (125 South Langston Cir.; 478-396-5947; theretreatofsouthernbridlefarms.com) is a luxurious country inn, event venue, and restaurant 10 miles south of Perry. Located on 8,000 acres of farmland, there are ten vintage Southern country houses and cottages which have been fully restored and help prove the perfect middle Georgia escape for a private event or wedding. Guests stay in 28 designer-decorated rooms and suites with deluxe private baths, feather beds, and fireplaces. The formal gardens have become a favorite place for weddings and outdoor events. Bridle Farms' **Carriage House Restaurant** and its bar are open to the public when there is not an event underway.

The **Museum of Aviation and Georgia Aviation Hall of Fame** (1942 Heritage Blvd., Robins AFB; 478-926-6870; museumofaviation.org), 2 miles south of Warner Robins Air Force Base is the second largest US Air Force museum and a tribute to our winged military might. In four huge buildings you can admire more than 100 military aircraft and missiles. You can also see a film on the history of the Air Force and numerous exhibits and displays. The

Aviation Hall of Fame honors men and women who have made significant contributions to aviation in Georgia. Take I-75 exit 146 (Centerville/Warner Robins) and follow the signs through the city of Warner Robins. Open Tues through Sat from 10 a.m. to 4 p.m.; Sun noon until 4 p.m. Free admission.

Barbecue is dear to Georgians' hearts, celebrated in song and story, and exalted at annual festivals such as the **Big Pig Jig** the first weekend of November at the little middle Georgia town of Vienna (pronounced "VIGH-enna"). Dubbed the "Cadillac of Barbecue Contests" and proclaimed the state of Georgia's official barbecue cooking contest by the state legislature, this is serious business indeed. The winning team takes home prize money, trophies, bragging rights, and the honor of representing Georgia at the annual World Championship Barbeque Cooking Contest in Memphis, Tennessee—and just maybe coming back as world champion of the barbecuing arts.

Of course, there's a fun side to all this serious business. Judges sample the secret sauces, which, according to the rules, may include "any nonpoisonous substances," and the flavors and textures of ribs, shoulders, and other succulent portions of the porkers. Famished festivalgoers also get their chance to savor the entries in a "People's Choice" competition and take part in a host of other activities. There's always plenty of bluegrass and country music, square dancing and clog dancing, arts and crafts, a 5-kilometer "Hog Jog," and a "Whole Hog Parade," featuring handsome porkers, still not ready for the grill, decked out in all manner of zany costumes.

For information, contact Dooly County Chamber of Commerce, 117 E. Union St., Vienna; (229) 268-8275; doolychamber.com and bigpigjig.com.

Cotton may no longer be king, but it's still important to the economy of Dooly and other southeastern Georgia counties. At harvest time in September and October, the white bolls cover the ground like fresh-fallen snow. The **Georgia Cotton Museum** (1321 E. Union St., Vienna; 229-268-2045; cityof vienna.org), created by farmers and other Dooly Countians, looks at "white gold's" past, present, and future with artifacts, displays, and tools that planted, plowed, and harvested the cotton in the days before mechanized farming. It also looks at the dark side, the slave labor that was vital to its production. Open Mon through Fri from 9 a.m. to 4:30 p.m.; Sat 10 a.m. to 2 p.m. Admission is free.

Hawkinsville, the Pulaski County seat, is Georgia's harness racing capital. The **Harness Racing Festival** (hawkinsville-pulaski.org/visitors/festivals), the first weekend of April, celebrates this sport, which has been a part of Pulaski County's life since the late 1800s, when the county's mild climate made it a popular winter training grounds for harness horses from the Midwest, the Northeast, and Canada.

SOUTHEAST GEORGIA'S TOP HITS

Big Pig Jig	Lake Grace
Blue and Gray Museum	Laura S. Walker State Park
Center for Wildlife Education and Lamar Q. Ball Jr. Raptor Center	Little Ocmulgee State Park
	Magnolia Springs State Park
Douglas's public golf courses	Museum of Aviation
Edwin L. Hatch Nuclear Plant Visitors Center	Okefenokee Swamp Park
General Coffee State Park	Rattlesnake Roundup
George L. Smith State Park	Reed Bingham State Park
Georgia Cotton Museum	Statue of Liberty
Georgia Southern University Museum	Stephen C. Foster State Park
Go Fish	Suwannee Canal Recreation Area
Hahira Honeybee Festival	The Crescent, Valdosta
Harness Racing Festival	Vidalia sweet onion
Jefferson Davis Memorial State Historic Site	Wild Adventures Theme Park, Valdosta

Nowadays, more than 350 of the sleek, high-stepping trotters and pacers come to the town of 4,000 between October and April. On the 2-day festival weekend, more than 10,000 spectators crowd the grandstand at the festival grounds to watch the races and enjoy the country fair atmosphere that surrounds the red clay track. For those not familiar with the sport, the horses have two decidedly different gaits. Pacers wear plastic leg hoops (called hobbles) that cause the legs on each side of their body to move in tandem: left front and left rear, right front and right rear. Trotters navigate with a diagonal gait: left front and right rear legs move together, likewise right front and left rear. They seem to effortlessly pull the colorfully silked jockeys riding behind them in light two-wheeled sulkies.

After the festival the horses pack up and head for the big-money tracks up north. One thing missing from the event is parimutuel betting. Georgia law prohibits it, but that doesn't mean you can't find some friendly unofficial wagers around the track. On any given day, though, you could likely go out to the track and watch the trotters doing their thing. For information, call the city-owned ***Hawkinsville Harness Training Facility*** (290 Abbeville Hwy., Hawkinsville; 478-783-1717; hawkinsville-pulaski.org).

Away from the track, Hawkinsville's main attraction is its restored early-20th-century opera house. Built in early 1907 as a stop on the vaudeville circuit between New York and New Orleans, the ***Old Opera House*** (42 Lumpkin St.; 478-783-1884; hawkinsvilleoperahouse.com) was abandoned in the 1950s and was about to fall totally into ruins when a group of Pulaski County businesspeople came to its rescue. Now it hosts touring concerts and local productions. If you're here when an event is scheduled, come and spend a nostalgic evening in the restored horseshoe-shaped auditorium at 100 N. Lumpkin St., Hawkinsville.

Several antiques shops are on Broad Street, Hawkinsville's main street. For other information contact ***Hawkinsville-Pulaski County Chamber of Commerce*** (108 N. Lumpkin St., Hawkinsville; 478-783-1717; hawkinsville-pulaski .org).

Lovers of finely crafted cemetery art should have a "Kodak moment" at ***Orphans Cemetery*** south of Hawkinsville in Eastman. It's the legacy of the late Albert G. "A. G." Williamson. Born in North Carolina in the mid-1800s, Williamson and his five brothers were orphaned by the Civil War and moved to Dodge County, where they were collectively known as "The Orphans." A. G., the oldest, became a wealthy landowner. In 1887 he learned of the untimely death of a neighbor's 3-year-old son and deeded land for Orphans Cemetery, across from Orphans Christian Church. He planted a magnolia tree by the boy's grave that still blooms every summer. Before his own death, Williamson commissioned a sculptor in Carrara, Italy (where Michelangelo found the right stuff for David), to carve the cemetery's masterpiece, a marble-columned canopy with life-size statues of himself, his wife, Martha, and nephew, Jay Gould Williamson, for the family mausoleum. The sculptor created the realistic images with only photos to work from.

University of Georgia fans can find a tribute to the first official bulldog mascot, Mr. Angel, in Eastman as well. Mr. Angel and all of his successors are known officially as "Uga" (get it? U-GA) as they walk the sidelines in Athens at sporting events. Mr. Angel served 1944 until 1946 and a monument to the dog is located in front of the Bank of Eastman at 130 Oak St., Eastman. Contact the Eastman/Dodge County Chamber of Commerce Welcome Center: 116 9th Ave., Eastman; (478) 374-4723; eastman-georgia.com.

The Lauren County city of Dublin's 19th-century Irish heritage is reflected in its annual month-long ***St. Patrick's Day Festival*** (dublinstpatricks.com), a lively round of parades, beauty pageants, arts and crafts, square dancing, softball, and golf tournaments. Along the emerald-green lawns of the city's

Bellevue Avenue, many photogenic Greek Revival and Victorian showplaces parade year-round. Stop by the Dublin-Laurens Tourism Council (118 S. Monroe St.; 478 272-4002; visitdublinga.com) and pick up a brochure for a self-guided walking tour through the historic downtown. It includes a beautiful Victorian home that is now the Dublin Laurens County Museum & Cultural Heritage Center which is known for its genealogical research center (702 Bellevue Ave.; 478-272-5710).

George L. Smith State Park, off US 23, 4 miles southeast of Twin City, is a quiet retreat with 21 fully equipped camping sites, furnished cottages, picnic areas, and a fishing lake with rental boats. An 1880s covered bridge with a working gristmill is the park's scenic landmark. Cornmeal from the mill is sold in the park office. Call (478) 763-2759 or (800) 864-PARK for camping reservations or visit gastateparks.org/georgelsmith. For an on the water view of the cypress-lined Watson Mill Pond at George L. Smith as well as the Ogeechee River, take a kayak tour offered through Mill Pond Kayak (478-299-6616; mill pondkayak.com). Two very nice bed-and-breakfasts are in the Emanuel County seat of Swainsboro: ***Coleman House*** (323 N. Main St.; 478-237-9100; coleman houseinn.com) and ***Edenfield House Inn*** (426 W. Church St.; 478-237-3007; edenfieldhouse.com). Both are inexpensive and located in the heart of this scenic little Southern town.

Guido Gardens (600 Lewis St., Metter; 912-685-2222; sowerministries.org) is a lush little oasis 2 miles from I-16 exit 104 at Metter and one of the reasons the town's motto is "It's better in Metter." "God's Three Acres," as it is known, is planted with shade trees, flowers, Biblical topiaries, and a topiary of garden founder Michael Guido, the late televangelist. Fountains and waterfalls splash, birds sing, and a brook winds past gazebos, benches, and a 24/7 chapel. In December the gardens are illuminated with Christmas lights and Nativity scenes. Visitors can tour the broadcast studios Mon through Fri and meet the Sower in person. The gardens are open 24 hours daily, free of charge. They are adjacent to Sower Studios, where for years Guido produced his national "Seeds from the Sower" broadcasts and where his ministry continues.

If you enjoy the outdoors, you may also consider visiting the ***Charles Harrold Preserve.*** The 73-acre preserve was Georgia's first ecological sanctuary. It includes two distinct habitats: a sandhill community and a mixture of flatwoods and alluvial swamp. Charles Harrold is home to gopher tortoises, a number of rare plants, and is a prime location for birding. You may get lucky and spot one of the endangered state gopher tortoises who find sanctuary there (Salem Church Road, Metter; 404-253-7216). As you exit I-16, stop at the Metter Welcome Center, in a former lumber company commissary at 1210 Lewis St.

For information on Guido Gardens and other area attractions call (912) 685-6988 or visit everythingsbetterinmetter.com.

Magnolia Springs State Park, US 25, 5 miles north of Millen, is one of the prettiest and quietest in the whole park system. Huge old trees bend their limbs over crystal clear springs flowing at an estimated 9 million gallons a day. With more than 1,000 acres to explore, it's a lovely spot to spread a picnic. You can also swim, dabble your bait for fish, and walk along nature trails. There are also some archeological remnants of the Civil War–era Camp Lawton Prison, at the time considered the world's largest. You may even want to camp out overnight or stay in a furnished cottage. There is a $5 per visit parking fee. For camping and cottage reservations contact Magnolia Springs State Park: 1053 Magnolia Springs Rd., Millen; (478) 982-1660 or (800) 864-PARK; gastateparks .org/MagnoliaSprings.

Tree-shaded *Statesboro* (population 32,000) is the Bulloch County seat and home of 20,000 Georgia Southern University students. The *University Museum* (2142 Southern Dr.; 912-681-5444; academics.georgiasouthern.edu/ museum) has a fascinating collection of dinosaur fossils, do-touch exhibits, and revolving scientific and technological displays. The "star" attraction is the *Plant Vogtle Whale*, a 45-million-year-old leviathan that scientists believe walked on sturdy legs. It was discovered at Georgia Power Company's Plant Vogtle in neighboring Burke County. The museum is open Mon through Fri, 9 a.m. to 5 p.m.; Sat and Sun, 2 to 5 p.m. Admission is $2 per person.

GSU is also home to the *Center for Wildlife Education* and *Lamar Q. Ball Jr. Raptor Center* (1461 Forest Dr.; 912-681-0831; academics.georgia southern.edu/wildlife) which is its most popular attraction. Visitors follow a self-guided nature walk through 6 natural habitats that house 14 birds of prey native to Georgia. They include bald eagles, falcons, ospreys, hawks, and several types of owls. They were rescued after being injured and can't return to the wild. Look up and you'll see a bald eagle camped in a hot tub–size aerie in the forks of a live oak tree, an osprey perched on a limb overlooking a cypress swamp, and a barred owl roosting in the rafters of an old barn strung with sheaves of drying tobacco. The center was designed by the late naturalist Jim Fowler, who also designed Albany's Chehaw Wild Animal Park. The center is open Mon through Fri from 9 a.m. to 4:45 p.m.; Sat and Sun from 1 to 4:45 p.m. It is closed Saturdays during summer months (June, July, and Aug). Admission is $4 for adults and $2 for children. A special program is held daily at 3:30 p.m. and is free with admission.

Near the campus, the 11-acre *Botanic Gardens* (1503 Bland Ave.; academics .georgiasouthern.edu/garden) grow around a restored 19th-century farmhouse and outbuildings. The gardens and its trails are open daily from dawn to dusk;

free admission. After trekking around the gardens, bring your best boarding-house reach to the ***Beaver House Inn & Restaurant*** (121 S. Main St., Statesboro; 912-764-2821; thebeaverhouseinn.com). The dining room table groans under a delicious family-style buffet that includes fried chicken, fish, baked ham, roast beef, and numerous vegetables, relishes, and desserts. It's open for lunch daily, dinner daily except Sun. ***Vandy's Barbecue*** (22 W. Vine St., Statesboro; 912-764-2444; vandysbbqstatesboro.com) has been around since 1929 and is another culinary landmark.

The Victorian/Federal-style ***Statesboro Inn and Restaurant*** (106 S. Main St., Statesboro; 912-489-8628; statesboroinn.com), built in 1872, is a lovely bed-and-breakfast near downtown Statesboro and the Georgia Southern campus. Architectural features include a spacious veranda, Palladian windows, and numerous brass and wood treatments. Guests stay in the main house or the adjacent Craftsman-style Brannen House. All 19 rooms have private baths, antiques, and wi-fi. The dining room's upscale fare features duck, chicken, seafood, beef, and elegant desserts. Dinner Mon through Sat. Moderate.

Statesboro is a short drive north of I-16 exit 116, 60 miles west of Savannah. Contact the Convention and Visitors Bureau: 332 S. Main St., Statesboro; (912) 259-9555; or go to visitstatesboro.org.

Vidalia Sweet Onions, Fruitcakes & Rattlesnakes

The sandy soil of Toombs, Treutlen, and neighboring southeastern Georgia counties yields a favorite gourmet delicacy. The well-known ***Vidalia sweet onion*** takes its name from the Toombs County town of Vidalia. During the summer, you can buy 'em by the sackful or carload at roadside stands in and around the town of 10,000. For information on farm tours, phone (912) 538-8687 or visit vidaliaga.com. The ***Sweet Onion Festival*** (vidaliaonionfestival .com), the third weekend of April, is the chance to sample the "fruit" in many tasty ways.

Claxton, seat of Evans County, a short drive south of I-16 exit 116, is famous for fruitcakes and rattlesnakes. As you drive into the small town in late summer, you're very nearly intoxicated by the sweet aroma of baking fruitcakes. More than 6 million pounds of the holiday treats are produced annually in Claxton's modern bakeries making the town the self-proclaimed "Fruitcake Capital of the World." You can get information on ***fruitcake plant tours*** and other area attractions at the Claxton Welcome Center, 1 N. Duval St., Claxton; (912) 739-1391; claxtonevanschamber.com.

If you're here in mid-March, you can take part in the festivities surrounding the annual **Rattlesnake and Wildlife Festival** (evanscountywildlife.com). Begun simply in 1968 as an effort to reduce the venomous reptile's threat to man and beast, the roundup has grown into a major 2-day happening, with a parade, wildlife demonstrations, hundreds of arts and crafts booths, home cooking, and such rattler-related events as awards for the most snakes brought in, the longest, the fattest, and so on. A reptile expert "milks" the snakes of their deadly venom, which is used in antivenom serums and other medicines.

Ever wonder what 25 million crickets sound like? The answer is at **Armstrong's Cricket Farm** (306 Gordon St., Glennville; 912-654-3408; armstrong crickets.com) in Glennville. Purportedly the world's largest cricket farm, Armstrong's sells and ships buckets full of the chirping insects, as well as worms, to anglers and reptile farms, where they're fed to snakes, frogs, and lizards. Demand for crickets was so large, they even opened another farm in Monroe, Louisiana. Owner Jeff Armstrong says, "One cricket in a room will drive you crazy, but 25 million sound like a big humming engine." Find out for yourself at the cricket farm, which is open Mon through Sat.

In neighboring Tattnall County, the 662-acre **Jack Hill State Park** (162 Park Ln., Reidsville; 912-557-7744) has 5 cottages, 29 tent and trailer sites with water and electricity, hot showers, and restrooms, as well as a swimming pool, a boat dock, and plenty of good fishing places on its 12-acre lake. You can rent aqua-cycles to take out on the lake or look for beaver dams from the observation deck. There's also an 18-hole golf course. Call (800) 864-PARK or log on to gastateparks.org/JackHill for camping reservations.

If you're a fishing family, you may come close to nirvana in Wayne County. One county removed from the Atlantic Coast, Wayne includes 60 miles of the **Altamaha River,** a waterway rich with several varieties of bass, bream, and perch. It's considered one of the premier catfish rivers in the Southeast.

Morgan Lake Wilderness Campground and RV Park offers a great getaway on scenic Morgan Lake, which feeds into the Altamaha. There are wilderness camping possibilities as well as RV hook ups, two boat ramps, and hiking, biking, and equestrian trails. The 140,000-acre lake is protected through the Nature Conservancy (300 Boat Landing Rd., Ludowici; 912-545-9026; morgan lakecampground.com).

Talk about off-the-beaten-path, **Adamson's Fish Camp and Beard's Bluff Campground** (Beards Bluff Rd., Glennville; 912-654-3632) just west of Jesup is located on the Altahama River bluff and has reportedly operated here since before the Revolutionary War when it was known as Ft. James and was a trading post. Untouched and unspoiled, it features cabins, as well as tent and RV sites.

Jaycee Landing Bait and Tackle Campground (230 Jaycee Landing Rd.; 912-588-9222; jayceelanding.com) on US 301 North, has a number of boat ramps in the Altamaha River, as well as a general store with food and all your favorite kinds of fishing bait. Campsites have water, electricity, restrooms, and showers.

For more information on recreational lakes and rivers, working farm tours, golf courses, fairs, and festivals, contact the Jesup-Wayne County Chamber of Commerce, 124 NW Broad St., Jesup; (912) 427-2028, (888) 224-5983; wayne tourism.com.

When you've bagged your limit, enjoy a large sample of Southeast Georgia cooking at *Jones' Kitchen* (526 N. Cherry St., Jesup; 912-427-4100). The all-you-can-eat daily luncheon spread includes fresh local fish, chicken, meat loaf, vegetables, several kinds of salads, and a peach or apple cobbler for less than you'd pay for lunch at a fast-food outlet.

Jesup, population less than 10,000, has a number of beautifully maintained Victorian homes, which you can drive past with a brochure provided by the chamber of commerce.

The *Edwin I. Hatch Nuclear Plant Visitors Center,* on US 1 (11036 Hatch Pkwy., Baxley), 14 miles north of the center of Baxley, will tell you all you ever wanted to know about this controversial source of energy. The story is told with films, hands-on exhibits, and animated displays. Tours can be scheduled by calling (706) 724-5197.

A one-of-a-kind treasure is the *Moody Forest Natural Area* (912-366-9549) on East River Road. Moody is one of the nation's last remaining old growth forests and its 4,426 acres contains old growth long leaf pines upward of 300 years old and massive Tupelo cypress trees estimated to be about 600 years old. It is also home to many rare birds, plants, and animals. Open dawn to dusk. Trail maps are available at baxley.org/tourism.

You can unwind at 170-acre *Lake Mayers* (319 Williams Dr.; 912-367-8190; baxley.org), a locally popular resort with fishing, boating, swimming, waterskiing, and picnic areas. Lake Mayers is off US 341, 8 miles west of Baxley.

Nonmembers may play the *Appling Country Club*'s 9-hole golf course (4628 Hatch Pkwy., Baxley; 912-367-3582). Contact Baxley-Appling County Tourism Board, 305 W. Parker St., Baxley; (912) 367-7731; baxley.org.

Land of Trembling Earth

Three gateways lead you into the primeval mysteries of the 402,000-acre *Okefenokee Swamp National Wildlife Refuge* (fws.gov/refuge/okefenokee .com) known as "Land of Trembling Earth." That name given to the swamp by

Native Americans because of the instability of the peat and saturated ground in parts of the swamp. The entrances are the **Suwannee Canal Recreation Area** and **Stephen C. Foster State Park** in Charlton County, and the Okefenokee Swamp Park is near Waycross, in Ware County.

The **Okefenokee Swamp Park,** off US 1, 8 miles south of Waycross, is the most popular of three entrances. Although most of the park is actually outside the boundaries of the 935-square-mile refuge, guided boat tours and cypress boardwalks lead you well into this fascinating world. The Swamp Park is the most casual, visitor-oriented of the three entrances—the others are in neighboring Charlton County—with numerous exhibits, interpretive centers, wildlife shows, and other visual displays.

Stop first at the cedar-roofed welcome center adjacent to the paved parking areas. Mounted wildlife exhibits and the real thing viewed through one-way windows, along with a 20-minute film, are an excellent orientation. From there, climb the 90-foot observation tower, peer into the dark tannic waters from the boardwalk, and see some of the Okefenokee's 3 dozen varieties of reptiles at the Serpentarium.

Gate admission $18 for adults, $17 for seniors and children 3 to 11, free for children under age 2—includes all exhibits and shows. The Low Water boat tour ($30 for adults, $25 children) takes you through some of the original Seminole Indian waterways and includes an even more extensive look at the hundreds of species of birds, otter, armadillo, black bear, deer, and other critters that inhabit the swamp. You'll also see some of the 15,000 gators as they cruise among the reeds and cypresses like ironclad gunboats.

Or hop aboard the "Lady Suwannee" steam engine and the Okefenokee Railroad. The 1.5 mile ride takes you through key parts of the swamp that make up the headwaters of the Suwannee River immortalized by songwriter Stephen Foster.

Okefenokee Swamp Park (US 1 South, Waycross; 912-283-0583; okeswamp.com) is open daily year-round from 9 a.m. to 5:30 p.m.

Two other attractions also mirror the swamp's colorful heritage. **Obediah's Okefenok** (5115 Swamp Rd., Waycross; 912-287-0090; okefenok.com), on a small island at the swamp's southwestern edge, was the early 1800s home of the Obediah Barber family. Their restored cabin and outbuildings are filled with authentic tools and household necessities. With boardwalks snaking through the wetlands, Obediah's is open daily. Admission is $6.50 for adults, $5.50 for seniors 55 and older, and $5 for children 3 to 17.

The **Okefenokee Heritage Center** (1460 N. Augusta Ave.; 912-285-4260; okefenokeeheritagecenter.org) near downtown Waycross, is an indoor/outdoor museum with historical displays, artwork, a 1912 locomotive and depot, an

Mummified Dog

Pity poor "Stuckie," the hound that chased a rabbit up a hollow tree and ended up as mummified and as immortalized as Old King Tut. Displayed at the **Southern Forest World Museum** (1440 N. Augusta Ave., Waycross; 912-285-4056; southern forestworld.com), the unfortunate 4-year-old brown-and-white doggie was discovered, years after his demise, by loggers who were cutting his "tomb" into pulpwood. A chimney effect in the hollow tree created upward drafts of air that kept his scent from insects and predators. The tree also provided a relatively dry environment, and its tannic acid leatherized Stuckie's skin and even preserved his last, terrified howl for help. While you're here, you can walk through a giant loblolly pine, listen to a talking tree, and view exhibits on forest management by the timber companies that support the museum. Open Tues through Sat 9 a.m. to 4:30 p.m. Adults $3; children under 5 are free.

1840s farmhouse, a print shop, and antique vehicles. Open Tues through Sat 10 a.m. to 4:30 p.m. Admission is $7 for adults, children 6–18 are $5.

Nearby **Laura S. Walker State Park and the Lakes Golf Course** (5653 Laura Walker Rd., Waycross; 912-287-4900) is a 626-acre park located near the northern edge of the Okefenokee. It has RV sites and campsites with water, electricity, showers, and restrooms ($25 to $35 per night); a swimming pool; a playground; fishing; and picnic tables. Cabins that sleep up to six are available for $125. There is a $5 parking fee. **The Lakes Golf Course** (5500 Laura Walker Rd.; 912-285-6154; thelakesgc.com) is a coastal Georgia course designed by Steve Burns. It features native sand in its sand traps. Course fees are $31. For reservations call (800) 864-PARK or visit gastateparks.org, or contact the Waycross Tourism Bureau, 417 Pendleton St., Waycross; (912) 287-2969; waycrosstourism.com.

Administered by the US Fish and Wildlife Service, **Suwannee Canal Recreation Area** is what remains of one man's frustrated efforts to drain the Okefenokee back in the 1880s. He left behind an 11-mile-long waterway that now provides an easy avenue for boaters, anglers, and sightseers. **Okefenokee Adventures** (4150 Suwannee Canal Rd., Folkston; 912-496-7156, 866-THE-SWAMP; okefenokeeadventures.com) is the US Fish and Wildlife Service's concessionaire. It offers 1- and 2-hour daytime, nighttime, and overnight guided boat tours through the swamp, where you'll see many of the swamp's thousands of gators, turtles, fish, egrets, heron, and other bird species, and learn a great deal about this primordial environment. The tour boats are covered with a canopy, but be sure to bring sunscreen, insect repellent, and bottled water. Tickets are $34 and they even offer a sunset tour for when the swamp really comes to life. You can also rent motorboats, canoes, kayaks, and bicycles. But be aware that getting lost in the swamp's many tributaries is very easy. The Concession Building stocks groceries, cold drinks, fishing gear, bug spray, and other necessities. The Camp Cornelia Cafe prepares sandwiches and salads. Open daily.

The nearby **Richard S. Bolt Visitors Center** is the refuge's official welcome center and has a 15-minute orientation film and interpretive exhibits on the swamp's plant and animal life, some of which you can see from nature trails, a boardwalk, and an observation tower. A short drive from the concession building and museum, **Chesser Island Homestead** is the pine and cypress cabin once home to several generations of the Chesser family.

Suwannee Canal Recreation Area (2700 Suwanee Canal Rd., Folkston; 912-496-7836) is open daily 1/2 hour before sunrise to sunset. A $5 gate fee is charged at the Folkston entrance by the Okefenokee Swamp National Wildlife Refuge. Drive on GA 121/US 23 for 8 miles south of Folkston, then turn right (west) at the Okefenokee Refuge sign and continue 3 miles.

Stephen C. Foster State Park (17515 GA 177, Fargo; 912-637-5274), is so far off Georgia's beaten path that the shortest way to get there from Suwannee Canal is a loop detour through northeastern Florida. From Suwannee Canal, drive 15 miles south on US 23 to St. George, 37 miles west on GA 94 and GA 2 in Florida, and back into Georgia at Fargo. From Fargo, go right on GA 177 and for 18 miles cross a domain of sentinel pines and palmetto thickets, swampy canals, egrets, great blue heron, deer, gators, armadillos, opossum, raccoons, reptiles, and amphibians. Beyond a sign warning that the gates close between sundown and sunup, you arrive at Stephen Foster's compound.

The state park is an 80-acre island entirely within the Okefenokee Swamp National Wildlife Refuge. Rangers conduct boat tours, replete with swamp legends and lore, practical lessons in fauna and flora, and lots of hilarious tall tales. You're bound to see plenty of gators, exotic birds and plants, turtles, and trees. You may also rent boats and canoes and venture forth on your own. There are also a 0.25-mile hiking trail, picnic shelters, a playground, and a small museum.

Staying overnight, serenaded by the symphony of the swamp, is an unforgettable experience. Campsites with electricity, water, hot showers, and restrooms are available, as are 2-bedroom cottages completely furnished with full kitchens and fireplaces, heat, and air-conditioning. There is a $5 per visit parking fee. The park's small grocery has minimal supplies, so be sure to stock up before leaving Fargo.

The park is open from 7 a.m. to 7 p.m. from mid-Sept to the end of Feb, and from 6:30 a.m. to 8:30 p.m. from Mar 1 to mid-Sept. For cottage and camping reservations call (800) 864-PARK or log on to gastateparks.org. When the gates are locked at night, only a dire emergency will open them before sunrise. This is done to protect you from roaming critters and the critters from roaming poachers. Also, bear in mind that a swamp is full of mosquitoes, other biting pests, and uncomfortable summer heat and humidity. Bring insect repellent and dress comfortably. In addition to the Folkston route, you may get to the park on US 441 to Fargo.

If you're wondering where everybody in **Folkston** is most any time of day, check out the covered platform that overlooks the **"Folkston Funnel,"** twin sets of tracks that carry more than 70 trains a day through the town of 4,700. Day and night, hundreds of Folkston folks and out-of-towners gather on the 32-foot-long, 15-foot-wide platform 2 blocks west of US 301. Train-spotting passion was sparked by Marvin "Cookie" Williams, an avid model-train collector whose enthusiasm for the real thing attracted others to the sport and led to a tourism development grant that funded the platform. While they're spotting passenger trains, coal trains, refrigerator cars, orange juice trains from Florida, military transports, and trains carrying chemicals and timber, the "spotters" enjoy the platform's camaraderie, picnic tables, grill, ceiling fans, and floodlights that illuminate trains that pass in the night. The **Folkston Railroad Museum** (3765 Main St.; 912-496-2536; charltoncountyga.us/239/Museum) located in the old depot across the streets form the platform gives you an insight into the towns' railroad heritage. For information about viewings contact Folkston City Hall (912-496-2536; okefenokechamber.com). If you want to stay awhile, try the **Inn at Folkston** (3576 Main St.; 912-496-6256; Innatfolkston.com). There are four rooms to choose from and guests can enjoy a hearty breakfast to fortify themselves for train spotting. The Inn is a 5-minute walk to the depot.

Valdosta & the Great Southeast

Depending on your perspective, **Lowndes County** is either the jumping-off place for Florida or your reentry point to Georgia. With 117,000 residents, Lowndes is Georgia's 16th most populous county. Valdosta, the county seat and self-proclaimed "Heart of South Georgia," with close to 56,500 residents, is the state's 10th largest city. With so much traffic flowing back and forth from Florida on I-75, much of the city is devoted to chain motels, fast-food strips, and factory outlet malls. Behind these contemporary distractions, under canopies of live oaks and palm trees and banks of azaleas and camellias, the city has many historic homes, churches, and public buildings.

Stop for free information and the Historic Tours self-guided map at the Valdosta-Lowndes County Convention and Visitors Bureau's Tourism

Information Center off I-75 exit 16 (One Meeting Pl., Valdosta; 229-245-0513; valdostatourism.com). Among the noted 26 landmarks, the most outstanding is *The Crescent.* Built in 1898 at a cost of $12,000 by Valdosta educator Colonel William S. West, the grand 23-room neoclassical mansion is graced by 13 Doric columns (one for each of the original colonies) supporting a crescent-shaped portico. In 1913 President Woodrow Wilson attended a gala dinner in the ballroom. Now maintained by the Valdosta Garden Center, the mansion has been restored to its original grandeur and appointed with many original furnishings and period antiques. Guided tours Mon through Fri, 2 to 5 p.m. Donations accepted. The gardens are always in bloom. It's at 904 N. Patterson St., Valdosta; (229) 244-6747; thecrescentatvaldosta.com.

Valdosta is largely an agricultural community and if you want to see what a real working farm looks like, visit *Raisin' Cane* (3350 Newsome Rd.; 229-259-2000; raisincanevaldosta.com) for a tour. They also have a great produce market with local gift items and some good Southern home cooking with *Kim's Kitchen.*

You're driving through South Georgia on a hot summer day. The kids are cranky, and you can't wait to see Orlando. Outside of Valdosta, a billboard advertises *Wild Adventures Theme Park,* "Over 100 Rides & Attractions." Stop for the day or a couple of days—you might forget all about Florida. True to its billing, Wild Adventures (Old Clyattville Rd., Valdosta; 229-219-7080; wild adventures.com) has 100 things to see and do, without the crowds and lines at the Florida theme parks. Nine roller coasters and 11 water rides range from wild to mild. A tram puts you up close and personal with elephants, antelopes, zebra, lions, tigers, kangaroos, wallabies, birds, monkeys, and reptiles. You can pet small animals and hand-feed giraffe. A yearly concert calendar, included in gate admission, features top-name celebrities like Sugarland, Trisha Yearwood, Alabama, Foreigner, and Shawn Mendes. Daily general admission is $49.99 for adults, and $44.99 for ages 3 to 9, and those age 55 and over save $10 if you buy online. Season passes start at $79.99 (save $15 if you buy online).

Before heading on, relax awhile at Valdosta's parks, boating and fishing lakes, and public golf courses and tennis courts.

The small Lowndes County town of *Hahira* (pronounced hay-hi-ruh), north of Valdosta at I-75 exit 84, is a center of Georgia's tobacco industry. From July to Oct you can witness the age-old ritual of tobacco auctioning at the town's warehouses. If you're here the first week of October, drop by the *Hahira Honeybee Festival* (229-794-3097; hahirahoneybeefest.com). To get the buzz on what's happening in town, and enjoy good home cooking, take a seat for breakfast or lunch at *Church Street Coffee* (107 S. Church St.;

229-794-3383; cschahira). The Hahira Chamber of Commerce (102 S. Church St., Hahira; 229-794-2567) offers tobacco and honey tours.

At **Reed Bingham State Park,** off GA 37 (542 Reed Bingham Rd., Adel; 229-896-3551), the Cook County seat, you can go boating, fishing, waterskiing, and swimming on a 375-acre lake. The park also has a nature trail, campsites, and picnic grounds. Sign up for a ranger-led canoe trip that is a real treat. If you are there in the winter, you have the chance to see a strange migration of thousands of black vultures and turkey vultures who come here to roost in the trees. Pontoon boats take visitors out to see the homely creatures. If you are a runner, you may choose to take part in the 10K "Road Kill Run" each April. For campsite reservations call (800) 864-PARK or log on to gastateparks.org.

The **Jefferson Davis Memorial State Historic Site** (338 Jeff Davis Park Rd., Fitzgerald; 229-831-2335) in the small community of Irwinville, commemorates the site where the Confederate president was captured by Union troops on May 10, 1865. The museum has Civil War artifacts and part of the tree where Davis was standing when captured. A 13-acre park around the museum has nature trails and picnic areas. Open Wed through Sun from 9 a.m. to 5 p.m. Admission is $4 for adults, $2.75 for children.

Worth a visit in **Douglas** is the historic **Ashley-Slater House** (211 S. Gaskin St.; 912-384-4555 and 888-426-3334). The neoclassical 1914 mansion is furnished with original antiques, a 70-foot pastoral mural in the dining room, and (some say) ghosts of the original owners, who can't bear to depart from their lovely home. The Douglas-Coffee County Welcome Center at 114 N. Peterson Ave. (912-384-6304; visitdouglasga.org) can help arrange a tour.

Railroad buffs will enjoy the **Heritage Station Museum**'s exhibits in the old Georgia & Florida train depot in downtown Douglas (219 E. Ward St.; 912-389-3461). Other exhibits highlight Coffee County's abundant agriculture. Open Thurs through Sat 10 a.m. to 4 p.m. Admission $1. Several antiques shops and gift shops are in the vibrant downtown or the town known as "Main Street City."

Broxton Rocks Preserve, 778 pristine acres north of Douglas, contains some of the most dramatic outcrops of ancient sandstone in the southeastern United States. Formations sculpted by rivers millions of years ago, and dense woodlands and swampy bogs, are home to more than 530 species of plants, birds, and animals, many of them threatened and endangered. Entrance to the Rocks is by appointment with the Nature Conservancy of Georgia, which owns the property (404-253-7210), or the City of Douglas Tourism Office (912-384-4555).

General Coffee State Park (46 John Coffee Rd., Nicholl; 912-384-7082), 6 miles east of the center of Douglas, offers a wealth of recreational opportunities. You can fish the lake and streams for catfish, gar, and bream, and swim in the outdoor pool. A nature trail winding through the wooded 1,490-acre park puts you in photo range of many species of birds, reptiles, deer, and other critters. There are also playgrounds and picnic shelters. Heritage Farm has nature trails, wildlife habitats, antique farm equipment, a cane mill, and barnyard animals. There are also almost 13.5 miles of equestrian trails for horse lovers. You can stay overnight in full-service campsites and in a group cabin sleeping 36. For camping and cabin reservations call (800) 864-PARK or log on to gastateparks.org/GeneralCoffee.

During World War II, Douglas was home of the *63rd AAF Flying Training Detachment* where young men would come to train to become pilots. Some of the base buildings still remain and the *WWII Flight Training Museum* (3 Airport Cir.; 912-383-9111; wwiiflighttraining.org) commemorates the air cadets' contributions to the war efforts. The grounds are always open, but the museum is open Thurs through Sat 11 a.m. to 4 p.m. The hanger onsite is a great place to see an old warbird being restored.

Douglas, home to South Georgia College and a pretty college town of 11,600 folks, is one of Georgia's Main Street Program cities. The First Friday of every month is celebrated with carnival activities as the historic downtown comes to life. You may want to enjoy dinner Tues through Sat at *Fern Bank Bar & Grill* (235 Peterson Ave. South, Douglas; 912-384-4385), a historic brick-walled building with good steaks, seafood, and Southern dishes and many relics from the city's past.

The small town of *Fitzgerald* (population 9,000) is a living memorial to the nation's post–Civil War reunification. In the 1890s Indiana newspaper publisher P. H. Fitzgerald envisioned a place where he and other Union veterans could live in peace with their former Southern foes. When Ben Hill County farmers sent trainloads of food in response to a Midwestern drought, it became the chosen place. The town was laid out on a grid, with streets on the west side named for Confederate generals, those on the east side for Union generals. Other streets were named for Northern and Southern trees and flowers.

The *Blue and Gray Museum* in the former train depot at 116 N. Johnston St., Fitzgerald, displays thousands of Civil War artifacts, including uniforms, weapons, newspaper articles about Lincoln's assassination, and the history of this unique town. *Marching As One*, a professionally produced documentary film, tells the story of Fitzgerald's founding with rare archival photographs of the city's early years. The Colony Days Gallery exhibits clothing, china, glassware, cooking utensils, and other items that tell the story of women in the city's first struggling years. There are also displays honoring Fitzgerald's veterans from all wars. The museum is open Tues through Sat from 10 a.m. to 4 p.m.; Sun from 1 to 5 p.m. Adults $5, students $2. Phone (229) 426-5069, or visit fitzgeraldga.org.

TOP ANNUAL EVENTS

MARCH

Peaches to Beaches Yard Sale
220 miles along US 341
between Barnesville & Jekyll Island
(912) 367-8300
baxley.org/peaches-to-the-beaches/

St. Patrick's Day Festival
Dublin
(912) 272-5546
visitdublinga.org/events

Fire Ant Festival
Downtown Ashburn
(229) 567-9696
Fireantfestival.com

Wild Chicken Festival
Fitzgerald
(800) 386-4642
wildchickenfestival.com

APRIL

Harness Racing Festival
Hawkinsville
(912) 783-1717
exploregeorgia.org/hawkinsville/events

Perry Dogwood Festival
Downtown Perry
(478) 987-1234
perrygachamber.com

Okefenokee Art Festival & Earth Day Celebration
Okefenokee National Wildlife Refuge,
Folkston
(912) 897-1184
okefenokeeadventures.com

Vidalia Onion Festival
Vidalia
(912) 538-8687
vidaliaonionfestival.com

SEPTEMBER

Gopher Tortoise Festival
downtown Douglas
(912) 384-1873

OCTOBER

Big Pig Jig
Vienna
(912) 268-4500
bigpigjig.com

Georgia National Fair
Georgia National Fairgrounds &
Agricenter, Perry
(912) 988-6483
georgianationalfair.com

DECEMBER

Celebration of Lights and Winter Wonderland
Baxley
(912) 367-7731
Baxley.org

All those chickens crossing the roads in Fitzgerald are the result of an experiment gone "afowl." In the 1960s, the Georgia Department of Natural Resources released flocks of Burmese junglefowl, with brilliant orange, yellow, and black plumage, on the Ocmulgee River, a few miles from the city. They were supposed to be a new kind of game bird, but many of them migrated into town and liked it so well they stayed and raised families. They now number about 2,500 to 5,000. Although the chickens' messy manners rile some home-owners and businesses, the city bows to a no-win situation and makes them the honored guests at the **Wild Chicken Festival** in late March (wildchicken festival.com).

Seventeen miles west of Fitzgerald in the town of Ashburn you'll find what looks like a castle that is anything but. Currently closed to the public, the **Crime and Punishment Museum** is located in a former jail that housed inmates upstairs and the jailers and their families downstairs. The fortress was built in 1906 at a cost of $10,000 and was known to inmates and Turner Countians as "Castle Turner" for its ornate Romanesque architecture. Jailers and their families kept the grounds so attractively landscaped, travelers sometimes mistook it for a hotel. The museum contains original draconian cells, the death cell, the hanging hook, and the trapdoor, where, in the interest of time and economy, two felons could be dispatched at a time.

When it was open to the public, visitors were ushered into the cheerful Last Meal Cafe, where Southern-style comfort meals "to die for" were served in the jailers' former living quarters. The Crime and Punishment Museum (jail museum.com) is closed for repairs for the foreseeable future. It is uncertain when they will open again, but visit their website to learn more about this fascinating attraction.

Before leaving Ashburn, take a gander at "The World's Largest Peanut," standing a majestic 20 feet tall, along I-75. Take exit 82/GA 107 into Ashburn and follow the signs to the Peanut and a gazebo, where you can have a tree-shaded picnic.

If you're around here the fourth weekend of March, join the fun of the annual **Fire Ant Festival** (fireantfestival.com). One of the highlights is the Fire Ant Calling Contest. "You can call 'em any way you want," festival sponsors say, "but if they answer, you're in a whole heap o' trouble."

No need to travel to New York City or Philadelphia. The State of Liberty, the Liberty Bell, and the Declaration of Independence can all be found in the little Telfair County seat of **McRae-Helena,** 25 miles north of Fitzgerald. Right in the middle of town, where US 341, US 441, US 280, US 23, and US 319 come together, there are replicas of all of these patriotic symbols. "Miss Liberty" stands 35 feet tall—a 1/12-scale reproduction of the original in New York Harbor. And she's entirely homemade: Her head is carved from a black gum tree stump from a nearby swamp, her torch is actually an insulated electrician's glove, and her fiberglass coating was created by a McRae boat manufacturer. McRae and Helena were two separate towns standing side by side for more than a century. They voted to merge and in 2015 became McRae-Helena. Contact the Telfair County Chamber of Commerce at 120 E. Oak St., McRae-Helena; (229) 868-6365; telfairco.org. The town also participates in the **Peaches to Beaches** (peachestobeaches.com) yard sale. Held the second Friday and Saturday in

March, a giant yard sale takes place across 220 miles from Barnesville in North Georgia to the Golden Isles along Highway 341.

Little Ocmulgee State Park and Lodge, off US 441, 2 miles north of McRae-Helena (80 Live Oak Trail), is a resort park with lots of things to keep you happily occupied. The well-maintained 18-hole, par-72 Wallace Adams Golf Course has both carts and clubs available to rent at the pro shop, as well as its Fairway Grill to grab a bite. You can also swim, play tennis, and hike nature trails. The Little Ocmulgee Lodge has 60 modern guest rooms, an outdoor pool, a full-service restaurant, and meeting rooms. You can also pitch your tent or park your RV in full-service campsites and stay in furnished cottages. For camping and cottage reservations, phone (800) 864-PARK or log on to gastateparks.org. Reservations for the lodge can be made through little ocmulgeelodge.com or (877) 591-5572. For general information, contact the Park Superintendent: 80 Live Oak Trail, McRae-Helena, (229) 868-7474.

Places to Stay in Southeast Georgia

DUBLIN

Dublin Farm Come Home to the Country
875 James Currie Rd.
(478) 275-8766
dublinfarm.com
Moderate
Four large rooms available and a full restaurant; breakfast included

EASTMAN

Peacock Place
5207 W. Main St.
(478) 231-3788
peacockplacebnb.com
Inexpensive
Victorian home with modern amenities in 4 guest rooms; full breakfast is offered

FITZGERALD

Dorminy-Massee House Bed and Breakfast
516 W. Central Ave.
(228) 423-3123
dorminymasseehouse.com
Inexpensive
Six large bedrooms in a historic home; includes full breakfast

FOLKSTON

The Inn at Folkston
509 W. Main St.
(888) 509-6246
innatfolkston.com
Inexpensive
1920s bungalow with 4 spacious guest rooms and private baths; includes full breakfast

JESUP

Trowell Historic Bed and Breakfast
256 E. Cherry St.
(912) 559-2456
trowellhistoricinn.com
Inexpensive
Queen Anne–style home with four beautiful suites; full homemade breakfast

MCREA-HELENA

Parker House Inn
51 W. Huckabee St.
(229) 868-0067
Inexpensive
Built in 1901, this gorgeous inn offers 6 suites

HELPFUL WEBSITES

Baxley–Appling County Tourism Board
baxley.org

Dublin-Laurens County Welcome Center
visitdublinga.com

Folkston/Okefenokee Chamber of Commerce
okefenokeechamber,com

Statesboro Tourism Office
visitstatesboro.org

Valdosta–Lowndes Convention & Visitors Bureau
visitvaldosta.org

Waycross/Ware County Tourism Bureau
waycrosstourism.com

STATESBORO

Statesboro Inn and Restaurant
106 S. Main St.
(912) 489-8628
statesboroinn.com
Moderate
See p. 81 for details

VIENNA

Fruits of Vienna Bed & Breakfast
509 N. 3rd St.
(229) 947-3401
fruitsofvienna.com
Moderate
Four guest rooms with private baths; includes full breakfast

Places to Eat in Southeast Georgia

DOUGLAS

Fern Bank Bar & Grill
235 Peterson Ave. South
(912) 384-4385
Moderate
See p. 90 for details

DUBLIN

Jo Jo's Biscuits and Burgers
1010 Telfair St.
(478) 272-6478
Inexpensive
Burgers, steak

FOLKSTON

Okefenokee Restaurant
1507 3rd St.
(912) 496-3236
Inexpensive to moderate
Southern, seafood, buffet

METTER

Jomax BBQ
GA 121
(912) 685-3636
Inexpensive
BBQ

PERRY

Oil Lamp Restaurant
401 General Courtney Hodges Blvd.
(478) 988-2643
theoillamprestaurant.com
Moderate
Southern, cafeteria-style

The Swanson
933 Carroll St.
(478) 987-1938
theswanson.com
Inexpensive to moderate
Southern

STATESBORO

Beaver House Inn & Restaurant
121 S. Main St.
(912) 764-2821
thebeaverhouserestaurant
.com
Moderate to expensive
See p. 81 for details

Vandy's Barbecue
22 W. Vine St.
(912) 764-2444
vandysbbq.com
Inexpensive
BBQ

Northwest Georgia

Cloudland Canyon to Georgia's Rome

Cloudland Canyon State Park, in far northwest Georgia's remote and rugged Dade County, contains one of the Southeast's most awesome natural sights. The park's namesake and centerpiece is a steep canyon cut into the western flank of Lookout Mountain by ***Sitton Creek Gulch.*** You can stand by the rim and peer into misty reaches 1,800 feet deep. Better still, lace up your hiking boots, follow woodland trails down to 3 waterfalls on the canyon floor, and get really off the beaten path on 6 miles of backcountry trails.

After you hike, unwind with a swim in the park pool or a few quick sets of tennis. Also, in the heavily forested 3,488-acre park are 16 completely furnished cottages, a group lodge, and 72 tent and trailer sites, with electrical and water connections, showers, and restrooms, as well as 11 backcountry camps. For camping and cottage reservations call (800) 864-PARK. Contact the park superintendent at 122 Cloudland Canyon Park Rd., Rising Fawn; (706) 657-4050; gastateparks.org/CloudlandCanyon.

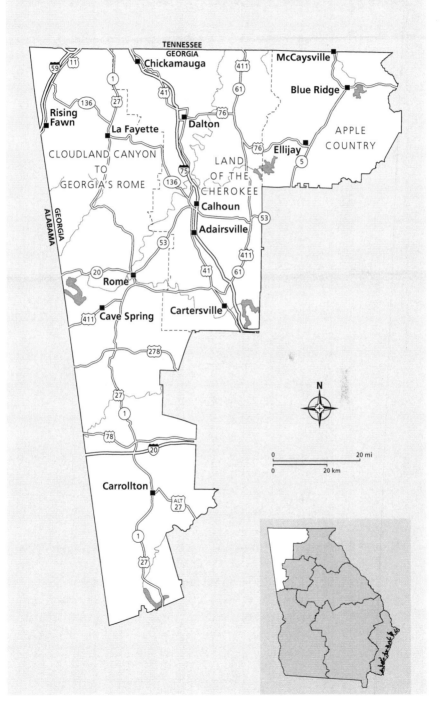

NORTHWEST GEORGIA'S TOP HITS

Berry College	Funk Heritage Center
Booth Western Art Museum	Gordon Lee Mansion
Capitoline Wolf	James H. (Sloppy) Floyd State Park
Chattanooga and Chickamauga National Military Park	John Tanner State Park
	Lock and Dam Park
Chieftains Museum	Martha Berry Museum and Art Gallery
Cloudland Canyon State Park	New Echota State Historic Site
Cohutta National Wilderness	Prater's Mill Country Fair
Col. Oscar Poole's Pig Hill of Fame	Red Top Mountain State Park
Dalton carpet outlets	Rome Clock Tower
Ellijay's Georgia Apple Festival	Tellus: Northwest Georgia Science Museum
Etowah Indian Mounds State Historic Site	Vann House
Fort Mountain State Park	

According to tradition, Cherokee Indians named their children for symbolic signs that caught their eye after birth. So the Cloudland community of *Rising Fawn* owes its poetic name to a chief who legend says looked out of his lodge on the happy morning his son was born and saw a newborn fawn wobble to its feet by its mother's side.

After a vigorous day in the park, make tracks for *Cornerstone Restaurant* (4356 US-11; 423-718-2065; cornerstonerestaurant.com). Just south of the Cloudland entrance, this amazing eatery is the eating-meeting-greeting destination for folks from miles around. At breakfast, lunch, and dinner, country cooking just doesn't get any better.

Hidden Hollow Country Inn, 5 miles down the mountain from Cloudland Canyon, is one of those discoveries you can hardly wait to tell your best friends about. Tommy and Bonnie Jean Thomas preside over a gaggle of rustic but very comfortable family-size cabins around a small lake full of Canada geese. Cabins are filled with well-worn furniture, cards, board games, dog-eared magazines, and coffee, but there are no TVs or phones to ruffle your peaceful ruminations. For entertainment snag a fish in the lake, hike in the woods, and watch the sun come up and go down. The Lodge is available for workshops and events and is popular for "hoedowns." Inexpensive to moderate. No meals are served, but Geneva Wooten's and other restaurants are close by. The inn is at 463 Hidden Hollow Ln., Chickamauga. Call (706) 539-2372 or visit hidden hollowresort.com.

Be sure to bring your fishing gear when you head for *James H. (Sloppy) Floyd State Park.* Off US 27, 3 miles southeast of the Chattooga County seat of Summerville, the 561-acre park is renowned as one of the state's finest fishing places. Two stocked lakes—30 and 35 acres—offer excellent bass-fishing opportunities from the banks. Only boats with trolling motors are allowed.

Area anglers say you can expect to reel in impressive largemouth bass, as well as big catches of catfish and bream. Youngsters can learn some of the fine art of fishing during the park's annual fishing rodeo in mid-May. Admission is free, and prizes are awarded for the first, largest, and most fish caught.

Floyd State Park's 25 tent and trailer sites have water and electrical hookups and convenient showers and restrooms. You'll also find a playground, picnic areas, and hiking trails in the neighboring Chattahoochee National Forest. Contact Park Superintendent at 2800 Sloppy Floyd Lake Rd., Summerville, (706) 857-0826. Call (800) 864-PARK or log on to gastateparks.org/JamesHFloyd for camping reservations.

Like its Italian counterpart, Georgia's **Rome** spreads over 7 green hills, in the foothills of the state's northwestern Appalachian Mountains. In the rivers department, the Georgia city of 30,000 has the edge. Instead of one mere Tiber, the Floyd County seat has three: the Etowah and Oostanaula, which join up downtown and form the Coosa. It may not have personages to match the Caesars, but a dramatis personae of Cherokee Indian chieftains, Southern aristocrats, cotton traders, Civil War soldiers, and riverboat paddle wheelers have made a rich and colorful cast, all the same. The city got its name quite by chance. In 1834 two traveling salesmen and a cotton planter put their choice of names in a hat. "Rome" was the fortuitous choice; otherwise, the city might be known today as Warsaw or Hamburg. A revitalized downtown, focusing on the three rivers, ensures Rome of a future as exciting as its past.

Begin your Roman holiday at the Greater Rome Visitors Center (706-295-5576; romegeorgia.org), a rejuvenated Southern Railway passenger depot, circa 1900, and a retired caboose at 402 Civic Center Dr., off GA 20 and US 27 near downtown. Information is available Mon through Fri 9 a.m. to 5 p.m., Sat 10 a.m. to 3 p.m., and Sun noon to 3 p.m.

The Rome Selfie Tour—it can also be driven, of course—leads you past 38 historic downtown landmarks and encourages you to take and share selfies at each. If you've been to the Italian Rome, you'll probably recognize the statue in front of City Hall here on Broad Street, downtown. The *Capitoline Wolf,* a replica of the Etruscan sculpture on ancient Rome's Capitoline Hill,

Root, Root, Root for the Rome Team

If you've forgotten how much fun a night at the ballpark can be, a night of minor league baseball with the Rome Braves will bring it all back. So, buy some peanuts and Cracker Jacks, hot dogs, nachos, and ice cream and find a seat in the *Rome Braves' State Mutual Stadium*. While the Atlanta Braves Class A farm hands take their first steps toward the big show, the 5,200 seats in the retro-style ballpark will put you so close you can practically reach out and pat them on the back. And all for ticket and hot dog prices that won't require you to take out a second mortgage on your homestead. For tickets, phone (706) 368-9388 or visit romebraves.com.

depicts the city's mythical founders, Romulus and Remus, being nurtured by a she-wolf. It was a 1929 goodwill gift from Benito Mussolini, a gift that was a tad embarrassing to the townspeople. In small-town Georgia, 1929, people were unaccustomed to seeing babies suckling their mother's bare breast in public, even if the mother was a wolf.

The *Town Clock,* on Clock Tower Hill, is the city's symbol and one of its most beloved landmarks. Built in Waltham, Massachusetts, in 1871, the four 9-foot-diameter clock faces rest upon a handsome 104-foot-tall brick and cypress water tower. So many people wanted to climb the 104-foot tower that the city opened it as the *Clock Tower Museum* (706-236-4430). You can walk up the spiral staircase and take in panoramic views of the city's hills and rivers. The museum is open by appointment only or on the first Sat of each month at noon. Free admission.

Myrtle Hill Cemetery, on another of the city's 7 hills, is a beautiful tree-shaded sanctuary where the first Mrs. Woodrow Wilson, 377 Confederate soldiers, and other notables are buried. You're welcome to stroll and admire the panoramic views of Rome's rivers and green hills. Phone (706) 295-5576.

Until recently the Etowah, Oostanaula, and Coosa had to flood before Romans would pay them any attention. Nowadays the 4-mile *Heritage Trail* walking, biking, and hiking route, shaded by big trees, takes inhabitants and visitors along the Oostanaula from the *Rome–Floyd County Public Library* downtown to the Chieftains Museum and connects 4 smaller trails within the city for a total of 13.5 miles of sightseeing and hiking. If you'd like to get out on the water, the visitor bureau can direct you to a canoe rental.

You can also unwind at *Lock and Dam Park,* a publicly owned camping/ RV/fishing/boating park in a mountain setting beside a 1910 lock on the Coosa River. Facilities include 25 fully equipped RV campsites, a fishing pier, canoe rentals, boat ramp and docks, a bait shop, and a snack bar. Located at 181 Lock and Dam Rd. SW; call (706) 234-5001 for information.

Rocky Mountain Recreation and Public Fishing Area is a joint venture of the Georgia Department of Natural Resources and Oglethorpe Power Corporation. The 5,000-acre retreat in northern Floyd County has 2 recreational lakes (357-acre Antioch Lake and 202-acre Heath Lake) for swimming, fishing, and boating. You can also enjoy picnic pavilions, hiking trails, and other outdoor activities and camp out at 39 RV sites and 9 wooded tent sites. For information, call the Greater Rome Visitors Bureau at (706) 295-5576.

Rome Area History Museum (305 Broad St., Rome; 706-235-8051; romeareahistorymuseum.org) covers nearly two centuries of northwest Georgia's past. Exhibits focus on the Civil War, the Cherokees, cotton, and commerce. Original documents include maps, photographs, letters, and even business records that paint a picture of Rome's history. They have a great gift shop that also includes items made by local artists. Open Wed through Fri from 10 a.m. to 4 p.m. General admission is free, but tours are $3 for adults, $2 for seniors, and students.

If golf's your game, check out the **Stonebridge Golf Club** (706-236-5046 and 800-336-5046; romestonebridge.com). Owned by the city of Rome, the 18-hole, par-72, 6,800-yard layout is at the base of Lavender Mountain, on the Berry College grounds. Rolling fairways, water, and big stands of hardwoods and pines are scenic to look at and challenging to play. The course is named for an old stone bridge over a lake on the ninth fairway. Greens fees won't handicap your budget.

The **Chieftains Museum/Major Ridge Home** is Rome's oldest historical landmark. Built as a frontier log cabin in 1794, Chieftains was the home of Major Ridge, the Cherokee leader who signed a treaty with the US government that partially contributed to the expulsion of the Cherokees from Georgia and the tragic "Trail of Tears." Along with Cherokee history, the museum's artifacts tell the story of Rome as a river town and its role in the antebellum South and the Civil War. An open archaeological dig and a 19th-century riverboat are on the grounds. It's at 501 Riverside Pkwy., Rome, off US 27. Call (706) 291-9494 or log on to chieftainsmuseum.org. Hours are Wed through Sat from 10 a.m. to 5 p.m. Adults $5, seniors $3, students $2.

When in Rome, shoppers from across northwestern Georgia; neighboring Alabama; Chattanooga, Tennessee; and Atlanta (65 miles north and south, respectively) do as savvy Romans do: They pass up the shopping center same-old-same-olds and hunt for unique treasures on downtown Rome's Broad Street and the Berry College campus, 10 minutes from downtown. While downtown, check out the **Historic DeSoto Theater** (530 Broad St.; 706-295-7171;

John Wisdom's "Midnight Ride"

Boston has its Paul Revere, and Romans remember their own courageous rider who saved the day (and their necks). Learning that Union troops were approaching the city in May of 1863, mail carrier John Wisdom rode off in a desperate attempt to mobilize defenders. He abandoned his mail buggy after 20 miles, begged and borrowed horses, which he changed 6 times, and galloped 65 miles in less than 9 hours.

The approaching Union troops saw Rome's defenders armed with shotguns, squirrel guns, and muzzle-loading rifles and retreated into captivity under Confederate General Nathan Bedford Forrest. Rome's grateful citizens gave Wisdom $400 and a silver service.

---

thedestor.org). Built in 1929, it was the first theater in the south to exclusively show "talkies." Beautifully restored, it is always hosting an event worth attending. At **Old Havana Cigar Company** (327 Broad St.; 706-295-0546; oldhavana cigar.com) enjoy a glass of wine, a beer, or a cup of coffee while you choose among 230 types of cigars from Honduras, the Dominican Republic, Nicaragua, and Puerto Rico.

Born to privilege, the remarkable and very determined Miss Martha Berry founded the Berry School in 1902. Her original small school is now **Berry College,** a 4-year liberal arts college set among 28,000 acres of woodlands, forests, and fields. Automobile magnate Henry Ford funded the English Gothic–style Ford Buildings complex in 1924. As you're driving around the campus, watch out for deer impulsively crossing the roads—there are said to be 8.4 whitetails for each of the college's 2,000 students. About 90 percent of the students still work for part of their tuition.

The Miracle of the Mountains, as the school's story is called, is chronicled at the **Martha Berry Museum,** across from the campus on US 27. Exhibits, photos, and a 28-minute film trace Miss Berry's life and her numerous honors. It is located on the grounds of **Oak Hill,** a classic, white-columned Old South Greek Revival mansion built in 1847, which was the Berry family's home. Students lead tours through rooms filled with antiques, art, and family memorabilia. An easygoing nature trail loops through gardens and woodlands. Oak Hill and the Martha Berry Museum (24 Veterans Memorial Hwy., Rome; 706-291-1883; berry.edu/oakhill) are open Mon through Sat from 10 a.m. to 5 p.m. Admission $5, $3 ages 6 to 12.

If you love the Berry campus, you may want to also visit the scenic campuses of **Shorter College**—a Christian college founded in 1877 (315 Shorter

Ave. NW; su.shorter.edu) and *Darlington School*—an exclusive college prep boarding school founded in 1905 (1014 Cave Springs Rd.; darlingtonschool .org), neighbors on Shorter Avenue west of downtown.

If you'd like to get a little lost in the woods, make an appointment to visit *Marshall Forest,* on Horseleg Creek Road, Rome, off GA 20, 4 miles west of downtown. The lush 311-acre preserve is the only virgin forest in the US that is located within city limits. Administered by the Georgia Chapter of the Nature Conservancy, Marshall includes 90 acres of fields and 80 acres of forests where northern red and chestnut oaks mingle with long-leaf southern pines. About 300 species of wildflowers and other plants grow on the Flower Glen Trail. The Big Pine Braille Trail offers blind visitors the opportunity to stop at 20 stations describing 53 plant species, 31 species of trees, and 19 species of vines and shrubs. Contact the Rome Visitor Center for information, (800) 444-1834, romegeorgia.com/attraction/marshall-forest-interpretive-trail; or the Nature Conservancy, (404) 873-6946, nature.org/Georgia.

Cave Spring, a village of 1,000 residents and 1 traffic light 16 miles south of Rome (via US 411), is pure Norman Rockwell. The *Hearn Inn* (13 Cedartown St. SW; 706-381-2060), a comfy community-owned inn in an 1840s schoolhouse, features 5 guest rooms with private bath and breakfast at inexpensive rates. When you're well rested, lace up your walking shoes and head across *Rolater Park* to the limestone cave that gave the town its name. The spring water flows out of the cave into a tree-shaded pond. Around the pond and the park are picnic tables and pavilions, restrooms, and a spring-fed 1.5-acre swimming pool shaped like the state of Georgia. The pool has bathhouses, snack bars, and plenty of room to spread your towels.

Built in 1810, the *Cherokee Vann Cabin* (24 Broad St.) is one of the oldest houses in North Georgia. For years, the two-story structure was the site of a local hotel. Residents knew it was old but had no idea just how old. In 2016, a restoration crew found the hotel had been built around the cabin of Cherokee Avery Vann, brother of the legendary Chief James Vann. The family lived here until they were vanquished on the "Trail of Tears."

The Cave Springs Historical Society runs tours from Apr through Oct between 10:30 a.m. and 1:30 p.m. leaving from the Visitor's Center at 4 Rome Rd. Call (706) 777-9608 or visit cshistoricalsociety.weebly.com. The tour is $15 if you would like a meal included; otherwise it is $10.

Antiques, home decor, and gift shops and family-owned restaurants are around the square. More than 100 artists and craftspeople come for the *Cave Spring Arts Festival* the second weekend of June. For information, contact the Visitor's Center or City of Cave Spring, 4 Rome Rd.; (706) 777-8608.

John Tanner State Park, off GA 16, 6 miles west of Carrollton, is a popular getaway for west Georgians and east Alabamians. Six furnished 1-bedroom cottages, a group lodge, and 31 full-service campsites surround a lake with a sandy swimming beach, rental fishing boats, and tree-shaded picnic shelters. There is a $5 parking fee. Contact Park Superintendent: 354 Tanner Beach Rd., Carrollton; (770) 830-2222. For campsite and cottage reservations, call (800) 864-PARK, gastateparks.org/JohnTanner.

The area of North Georgia is known for its textiles and there's no better place to get a sense of this than at the ***Southeastern Quilt and Textile Museum*** (306 Bradley St.; 770-301-2187; southeasternquiltmuseum.com). The museum is located in an old cotton museum and is dedicated to the restoration and preservation of quilts and textiles, open Thurs to Sat, 10 a.m. to 4 p.m. Admission is $5.

Fans of Oscar-winning actress ***Susan Hayward*** (Oscar for *I Want to Live*, 1959) can visit her gravesite at Our Lady of Perpetual Help Catholic Church (210 Centerpoint Rd., Carrollton). In 1957, Hayward married businessman Eaton Chalkley and moved with him to Carrollton, where they raised horses and cattle. When Chalkley died in 1966, Hayward moved back to California. When she died of brain cancer in 1972, she was buried beside him in the church cemetery across from their former home. Open daily, no admission fee. For information contact Carrollton Area Convention and Visitors Bureau at 102 N. Lake Shore Dr., Carrollton; (770) 214-9746; carrolltonga.com.

Land of the Cherokee

In the hellish heat of September 19 and 20, 1863, nearly 130,000 Americans engaged in one of the bloodiest battles of the entire Civil War. When it was over, Confederate forces under the command of General Braxton Bragg had a costly and dubious victory. They had repulsed the outnumbered Union armies under General William Rosecrans but were too weakened to pursue the Federals as they fled to safety around Chattanooga, Tennessee. Subsequent Union victories at Chattanooga's Lookout Mountain and Missionary Ridge and the capture of the city's vital railway hub opened General William T. Sherman's route to Atlanta and the sea.

The 5,500-acre Chickamauga battlefield is now part of the ***Chattanooga and Chickamauga National Military Park.*** The major sites are adjacent to US 27, near Chattanooga and Chickamauga. Stop first at the National Park Service Visitors Center for the audiovisual orientation and the many exhibits. The Fuller Collection of Military Arms has more than 400 weapons from the French and Indian Wars through present-day conflicts. Park rangers demonstrate cannon and rifles and there's always a special program planned to check their event calendar (nps.gov/chch/planyourvisit).

From the visitor center, follow US 27 for 3 miles through the park. Battle sites are marked by earthworks, cannon batteries, and farm buildings. Impressive monuments have been placed by states whose sons in blue and gray died here more than 125 years ago. The park is open all the time. The visitor center is open daily from 8 a.m. to 5:45 p.m. Contact Park Superintendent at 3370 LaFayette Rd., Fort Oglethorpe; (706) 866-9241; nps.gov/chch.

The *Gordon-Lee Mansion,* on the edge of the battlefield park, was built in 1847 by James Gordon. The white-columned Greek Revival residence sits on 7 acres of gardens and grounds and served as Union headquarters and a hospital during the battle. The home was purchased from the Lee family in 1974 by Dr. Frank Green who restored it to its splendor. Furnished entirely with 18th and 19th century antiques, it is now owned and operated by the City of Chicakmauga and is used for events. Tours of the mansion are given each Sat from Memorial Day through Labor Day and are $5 for adults and $1 for children 12 and under. Contact Gordon-Lee Mansion at 217 Cove Rd., Chickamauga; (423) 488-0861; friendsofthegordonleemansion.com.

Before leaving the area, see *Lookout Mountain, Missionary Ridge,* and other major parts of the Chattanooga and Chickamauga National Military Park.

If you've been planning to recarpet your home or cover your pool deck or patio with Astroturf, put off that major purchase until you've been to Dalton. Seat of northwest Georgia's green and hilly Whitfield County, industrious *Dalton,* with a population of 33,500, is the long-reigning "Carpet Capital of the World."

About 90 percent of the functional carpet produced worldwide is made within a 25-mile radius of Dalton in the more than 150 modern carpet plants. If you're in a buying frame of mind or would just enjoy browsing the latest styles and colors, dozens of *Dalton carpet outlets* offer a full range of floor coverings at greatly reduced prices. The Dalton Convention and Visitors Bureau (305 Depot St., Dalton; 706-270-9960; visitdaltonga.com), open Mon through Sat, can provide you with an up-to-date outlets directory. You can also find out about guided tours of area mills, Civil War and Native American sites, restaurants, and lodgings.

Dalton's $15 billion carpeting industry was born around 1900, when a Whitfield County farm girl named Catherine Evans produced a hand-tufted chenille bedspread, copied from a family heirloom, and promptly sold it for the handsome price of $2.50. Encouraged by her success, she made more of the brightly colored cotton bedspreads, and these, too, were eagerly snapped up by tourists and local homemakers. Other homebound women began following her lead, and by the early 1920s, tufted bedspreads had grown into a major "cottage industry."

The bedspreads usually featured flowers and other patterns, but the brilliantly plumed male peacock was such a runaway favorite that US 41, the major highway leading into Dalton, became popularly known as "Peacock Alley."

In the 1920s, a machine invented in Dalton was able to mass-produce the cotton bedspreads. Another wizard soon realized that by tufting more densely and adding a sturdy backing the same machinery could be adapted to the manufacture of carpeting. Dalton—and households the world over—were never again the same.

The original "cottage craft" of chenille bedspreads is still alive. You can find a practical souvenir with a peacock, Elvis Presley, Jesus Christ, the Confederate battle flag, and other designs at stores around Dalton and along US 41—the original "Peacock Alley"—between Dalton and the Tennessee border. Figure on paying a bit more than $2.50, however!

Some of the early chenille bedspreads are among the exhibits at Whitfield-Murray Historical Society at **Crown Gardens and Archives,** in the original Crown Cotton Mill (715 Chattanooga Ave., Dalton; 706-278-0217; whitfield-murrayhistoricalsociety.org). The museum also has historical displays, a Black Heritage room, an outdoor spring, and picnic areas. It's open Tues through Fri 10 a.m. to 4 p.m.; Sat 9 a.m. until 1 p.m. Admission is free.

With its influx of executives and workers from across the nation and several countries, this surprisingly cosmopolitan little city is very active in the fine arts. The **Creative Arts Guild** (520 W. Waugh St., Dalton; 706-278-0168; creativeartsguild.org) is a tastefully contemporary complex with 2 art galleries and a forum for live theater, dance, and other cultural programs. It's open daily. Admission is free.

Dalton is also a festive city. The **Downtown Dalton Beer Festival** each June draws thousands to sample local, American, and international brews as well as local foods. The **BBQ and Bluegrass Festival** each July is a bit more family friendly with arts, crafts, and music to go along with an impressive array of barbecue chefs vying for the Kansas City Barbecue Championship. Contact Downtown Dalton Development Authority in the Historic Freight Depot, 305 S. Depot St.; (706) 278-3332.

On the second weekends of May and October, the **Prater's Mill Country Fair** (pratersmill.org/fair) centers on Benjamin Franklin Prater's circa 1859 gristmill. While the huge millstones turn out silky cornmeal, 185 artists and craftspeople sell their wares to the tune of bluegrass fiddlers, clog dancers, and gospel singers. There are pony rides and other special treats just for the youngsters.

Carpet Shopping Tips

If you're planning to do serious carpet shopping, do your homework ahead of time. Have a good idea of what you're looking for, how much you'll need, the color and style, and what you can afford to pay. Do comparison shopping in your local stores— the more than 100 outlet stores in Dalton and neighboring towns like Calhoun and Chatsworth offer prices up to 70 percent less than you'll pay in a retail store. You can get a list of the Carpet & Rug Institute member stores online at carpet-rug.org/ about-us and get guidance from the Dalton-Whitfield Chamber of Commerce, (706) 278-7373, and the Dalton Convention and Visitors Bureau, (706) 270-9960 or (800) 331-3258.

Most outlets deal in "seconds," that is, those with some problems that exclude them from the "A list." It's often just a small tear or a color that doesn't match the mill's specifications. Be sure to examine it thoroughly. Having your carpet shipped will be much easier than trying to take it home yourself.

One of the most popular sports bars in the region, **Crescent City Tavern** (324 S. Deport St.; 706-529-0467; crescentcitytavern.com) always has some game on its many TVs. But come for the camaraderie and the food. There's live music and always something going on.

Mexican and Hispanic carpet workers make up about half of Dalton's population, which accounts for the city's many Latino cafes and stores, a Spanish-language newspaper and radio station, and other services. For great Mexican food, try **Alondra's** (314 Glenwood Ave.; 706-529-3562). The food is authentic, plentiful, and very affordable.

The **Tunnel Hill Heritage Center & Museum** (215 Clisby Austin Rd.; 706-876-1571; civilwarrailroadtunnel.com) is a must-see for train enthusiasts. The area gets its name from the 1,477-foot Western & Atlantic Railroad Tunnel, built through the mountains in 1848–1850 to connect the port of Augusta, on the Savannah River in east Georgia, with the Tennessee River Valley. It was the focus of Civil War battles and remained in use until 1928. In the 1990s, it was restored and opened to the public. Along with the tunnel, the heritage center includes the 1848 Clisby Austin House, Civil War artifacts, and original chenille bedspreads. It's open Mon through Sat from 9 a.m. to 5 p.m.; closed Sun. Admission is $8 for general admission and $12 for a guided tour.

The **Chief Vann House** was a showplace of 19th-century Cherokee accomplishment. At the junction of GA 52-A and GA 225, 3 miles west of modern-day Chatsworth, the sturdy 3-story house, with brick walls 2 feet thick, was built in modified Georgian style in 1804–1805. Owner James Vann was a half-Cherokee, half-Scot who helped create a Moravian mission for the

AUTHOR'S FAVORITES

Barnsley Gardens	Fort Mountain State Park
Blue Ridge Scenic Railroad	Hidden Hollow Country Inn
Booth Western Art Museum	Martha Berry Museum and Art Gallery
Cave Springs	New Echota State Historic Site
Cloudland Canyon State Park	Tellus Museum
Cohutta National Wilderness	

education of young Cherokees. When Vann was murdered in 1809, his son Joseph inherited the house and surrounding farmlands. He prospered until 1830, when the state of Georgia confiscated his lands for violating a law forbidding white men to work for Indians.

The Georgia Department of Natural Resources has restored the house and refurnished and redecorated the rooms in early 19th-century style. An intricately carved "floating staircase" is one of Georgia's earliest surviving examples of cantilevered construction. Elsewhere are Bibles, dinnerware, and dining room and bedroom furnishings. Vann House, at the intersection of GA 52-A and GA 225, 82 GA 225 North, Chatsworth, is open Tues through Sat from 9 a.m. to 5 p.m.; Sun from 2 to 5:30 p.m. (706-695-2598, 800-864-PARK; gastate parks.org/ChiefVannHouse). Admission $6 for adults, $3.50 for children 6 to 18; free for children under 6.

On GA 52, 7 miles east of Chatsworth, *Fort Mountain State Park* is a super-scenic park on a forested, 2,800-foot peak of the Blue Ridge Mountains' Cohutta Range. The park's namesake is a puzzling rock wall, or foundation, that winds nearly 900 feet around the mountainside. Whether it was an ancient Indian fortress, a bastion built by 12th-century Welsh explorers, or part of some other inscrutable mission is a matter of speculation. The stone observation tower nearby is no mystery. It's a legacy of the Depression-era Civilian Conservation Corps.

History lessons aside, you can relax in Fort Mountain's lake, go horseback riding, hike nature trails, play miniature golf, and set the kids loose on the playground. The 70 campsites have water, electricity, hot showers, and restrooms. Fifteen 2- and 3-bedroom cottages come with kitchen appliances, towels, sheets, and logs for the fireplace. Contact Park Superintendent at 181 Fort Mountain Park Rd., Chatsworth; (706) 422-1932. For reservations, call (800) 864-PARK or log on to gastateparks.org/FortMountain.

The 40,000-acre **Cohutta National Wilderness** in northwestern Georgia is a favorite of backpackers who really like to get away from it all. The parking area at Dally Gap, near McCaysville, is near the trailhead for Jack's River Trail, which winds through the eastern side of the wilderness. At 17 miles, Jack's River is longer than many trails in the wilderness and is one of the most scenic, with big stands of trees, ferns, and wildflowers. The Cohutta Mountains themselves rise to 4,200 feet and offer more than 87 miles of remote hiking within the wilderness area. You'll probably see white-tailed deer, beaver, and many species of birds. Be alert for black bears. Those who don't care to hike can still see a lot on the scenic drive from Fort Mountain along GA 52 towards Ellijay. The Fannin County Chamber of Commerce has a brochure with scenic drives and #2 takes you through the heart of the Cohutta (Blue Ridge Welcome Center, 152 Orvin Lance Dr., Blue Ridge; 706-632-5680; blueridgemountains.com/things-to-do/scenic-drives/cohutta). For additional information contact Cohutta Wildlife Management Area at (707) 295-6041.

The Cherokee assimilated themselves into the way of life established by the white settlers, then were ruthlessly crushed at **New Echota State Historic Site,** near modern-day Calhoun. In the 1820s New Echota was laid out as the capital of the Cherokee Nation that included parts of Georgia, the Carolinas, Tennessee, and Alabama. Here, the Cherokee legislature formulated laws, enforced by a series of district courts and a supreme court. The Indians wore European-style dress, used the farming methods of the white settlers, and lived in stone and frame houses with the most modern conveniences of the day. The more affluent owned black slaves. The first North American tribe to formulate its own written alphabet, the Cherokee published a bilingual newspaper, circulated as far as Europe.

Gold discovered on Cherokee lands in the late 1820s brought it all to an end. Supported by President Andrew Jackson, the state of Georgia confiscated all Cherokee lands and in 1838 forced the Indians into exile in what is now Oklahoma. Thousands perished along this "Trail of Tears."

New Echota has been meticulously reconstructed as a state historic site. Stop first to see the orientation slide show and exhibits in the reception center. Then take a self-guided walking tour that includes the supreme court building, the printing presses of the *Cherokee Phoenix* newspaper, a tavern/general store, and the home of the Reverend Samuel Worcester, a Massachusetts minister who established a mission for the Cherokee. There are 12 original and reconstructed buildings at the site, including the Council House, print shop, Worcester's home, and a host of outbuildings. Park rangers frequently demonstrate arrowhead-making and hunting techniques. Books about the Cherokee civilization are on sale at the reception center. In late October the **Cherokee Fall Festival** is a weekend of Native American crafts, cooking, and storytelling.

New Echota State Historic Site (1211 GA-225, Calhoun; 706-624-1321, 800-864-PARK; gastatepark.org/NewEchota) is open Thurs through Sat from 9 a.m. to 5 p.m. Admission is $7 for adults; $5.50 for children 6 to 18; free for children under 6.

If you love sunflowers and/or pumpkins, then detour to **Copper Creek Farms** outside of Calhoun (1514 Reeves Station Rd.; 706-280-5592; copper creekfarm.com). Late spring into summer, you'll find acres of sunflowers with a **Sunflower Fest** held in June. Come fall, it's all about pumpkins, corn mazes and hayrides.

Barnsley Gardens Resort, off I-75 exit 306, 10 miles west of Adairsville, dates to 1841, when English cotton broker Godfrey Barnsley brought his wife, Julia, from Savannah and built an Italianate villa and formal gardens on 10,000 acres of former Cherokee land. More than 160 years later, Hubertus Fugger, a Bavarian prince, has complemented Barnsley's gardens with plush lodgings, a European spa, a stem-winding golf course, and other resort amenities. Thirty-three English-style guest cottages, with 1 to 4 bedrooms, have plush furnishings, private baths, wood-burning fireplaces, heart-pine floors, front porch rockers, and other luxuries. Along with the 18-hole championship golf course and multifaceted spa, guests can enjoy the outdoor pool, bratwurst and German brews in a Bavarian beer garden, fine cuisine in the formal dining room, and Godfrey Barnsley's restored gardens and the romantic ruins of his villa, where Godfrey and Julia reportedly still appear from time to time. Julia's image is on the tiered fountain in the formal gardens. The golf course, gardens, spa, and dining room are available to non-guests. Golf, tennis, romantic getaway, and other package plans are available. Barnsley also encompasses the 1,800-acre hunting estate called Springbank Plantation, where guests can participate in sport clay shooting as well as quail and pheasant hunting and horseback

Cassville

Just north of Cartersville on Cass White Road at Firetower Road, you'll find a handful of historic buildings and a granite monument marking what used to be the grand town of Cassville. With the original Georgia Supreme Court, 2 colleges, 4 hotels, and a newspaper, Cassville was the cultural center for North Georgia in the mid-1800s.

During the Civil War, the Union Army gave residents just 20 minutes' notice before burning the entire town. Only a handful of buildings survived and those who fled never came back. Cassville's Confederate Cemetery holds 300 graves.

riding. Barnsley Gardens Resort is at 597 Barnsley Gardens Rd., Adairsville. Call (770) 773-7480 or (877) 773-2447 or visit barnsleyresort.com. Expensive.

While you're in the area, browse the antiques shops around Adairsville's downtown square.

Between AD 1000 and 1500, the Etowah tribe migrated into the fertile Etowah River Valley, near today's Cartersville, and created a remarkably sophisticated culture. Beans, squash, corn, and fruit that the women cultivated complemented game trapped by the men in surrounding forests and the abundant fish in the Etowah. As part of a vast trading network, the Etowahs made tools, arrowheads, axes, and household implements from Great Lakes copper and Mississippi and Ohio Valley flint. Gulf Coast seashells were fashioned into ceremonial jewelry.

Surrounded by a deep moat and log stockade, a compact city of clay and wooden houses sheltered as many as 4,000 members of the tribe. The heart of the city was a half-dozen rectangular earthen mounds. The *Etowah Indian Mounds Historic Site* was the forum for religious rites conducted by chiefs and priests and the final resting place of these dignitaries.

Stop first at the excellent small museum and reception center, where dioramas and artifacts from the mounds tell the story of this mysteriously vanished tribe. The exhibits are highlighted by a priest's burial chamber and beautifully carved busts of a woman and a warrior. A film traces the history of the Etowah. With a diagrammed map, cross the moat and explore the grass-covered mounds. Ninety-two steps take you up 63 feet to the top of Mound "A," from which the priest conducted rituals for the townspeople assembled below in the plaza. Mound "C," one of the smallest, was a principal burial site and the source of most of the artifacts in the museum. Park rangers periodically lead moonlight walks around the site.

About a 15-minute drive west of I-75 exit 288, via GA 113/GA 61, *Etowah Indian Mounds Historic Site* (813 Indian Mound Rd. SE, Cartersville; 770-387-3747, 800-864-PARK; gastateparks.org/EtowahIndianMounds) is open Wed through Sat from 9 a.m. to 5 p.m. Admission is $6 for adults, $4 for children; free for children under 6.

For more insights into ancient Native American cultures, visit the *Funk Heritage Center* (7300 Reinhardt College Pkwy., Waleska; 770-720-5970; reinhardt.edu/funkheritage) at Reinhardt College, in Waleska, on GA 140 northeast of Cartersville. You'll enter the Funk's *Bennett History Museum* through a 50-foot-long structure that resembles an Iroquois longhouse, where several families would have lived communally. Historians believe the northeastern Iroquois traded with Cherokees and other southeastern tribes. The left and right wings of the museum were inspired by temple mounds built at Etowah, at Cartersville, and elsewhere in the Southeast during the Mississippian period, AD 1000–1500. The Rogers Gallery of Contemporary Indian Art exhibits some 400 paintings, sculptures, and other creative endeavors. A majority were created by descendants of southeastern Cherokees, Creeks, and other tribes that were removed west of the Mississippi during the 1830s "Trail of Tears." Also on permanent exhibit, the Sellars Collection of Ancient Hand Tools includes thousands of tools and implements dating back as far as the 17th century. Funk Heritage Center is open Tues through Fri 9 a.m. to 4 p.m.; Sat 10 a.m. to 5 p.m.; and Sun 1 to 5 p.m. Adults 18 and older, $7, seniors 65 and older, $6.50; age 18 and under, $5.

The **Booth Western Art Museum**, in downtown Cartersville (population 20,000), draws us into the once-upon-a-time America of cowboys and Indians, cowgirls and gunslingers, buffalo hunters and rodeo "bulldoggers," stagecoaches and iron horses, big skies and endless horizons, movie icons and pulp fiction heroes. Now affiliated with the Smithsonian, this 120,000-square-foot museum is one of the largest Western art museums anywhere in the United States.

The permanent collection's more than 350 paintings and sculptures are by some of America's leading contemporary Western artists. The Civil War Gallery's 25 paintings dramatize the conflict from the first shots at Manassas to surrender at Appomattox. The Reel West Gallery's vintage movie posters and illustrations bring back those thrilling days at the Saturday matinee, when Roy Rogers and Gene Autry quelled the bad guys and rode victoriously into the sunset just before the final credits. In the Presidential Gallery, all 45 US presidents are represented by a portrait or photograph and an original signed document. Two separate halls have life-size paintings of them standing beside one another. At Sagebrush Ranch, kids have a great time riding the make-believe range in a lifelike bouncing stagecoach, dressing up as cowboys and cowgirls, and creating their own Western masterpieces. The museum also hosts 6 to 10 temporary exhibits each year. Booth Western Art Museum (501 Museum Dr., Cartersville; 770-387-1300; boothmuseum.org) has a gift shop, cafe, and 60-seat multimedia theater with an orientation film about the collections. Open Tues, Wed, Fri, and Sat 10 a.m. to 5 p.m.; Thurs 10 a.m. to 8 p.m.; Sun 1 to 5 p.m. Adults, $12; seniors, $10; students and ages 13 to 18, $9; age 12 and under free.

Proudly known as the oldest restaurant in Georgia without a phone, **4-Way Lunch**, Main Street (corner of Gilmer Street), downtown Cartersville, has been a landmark of swift (not "fast") food and service for more than 90 years. This is not Burger King, a sign over the coffeepot advises, you don't get it your way, you get it our way, or you don't get it. Another cautions about the service: I can only please one person a day—and today ain't your day. Crowds line up every weekday morning for bacon, eggs, grits, and biscuits, and many come back at lunch for first-class burgers, hot dogs, chopped steak, and stew. With only 11 seats at the red Formica counter, there's no lollygagging—when you're done, it's time to move on and let other hungry patrons have their 4-Way fix. Cash only.

Red Top Mountain State Park, on exit 285 off I-75 south of Cartersville, is one of the nicest and prettiest in the whole system. A wealth of recreational opportunities, campsites, and cottages are spread over the wooded hillsides around 12,000-acre Lake Allatoona. During warm weather, you can sun on a sandy beach, swim, and waterski. The rest of the year, bring tennis racquets, fishing gear, picnic supplies, and hiking shoes. Boaters may bring their own or rent houseboats and pontoon boats at the park marina. A small grocery is at the reception center.

Red Top's twenty 2-bedroom cottages are completely furnished and include fireplaces. The 93 tent and RV camping sites have electricity, water, hot showers, and restrooms. There is also a yurt available. The park office is open daily from 8 a.m. to 5 p.m. Contact Park Superintendent at 50 Lodge Rd., Cartersville; (770) 975-0055. Call (800) 864-PARK for camping, cottage, and yurt reservations, or visit gastateparks.org/RedTopMountain for more information.

Tellus: the Northwest Georgia Science Museum (100 Tellus Dr., Cartersville; 770-606-5700; tellusmuseum.org) is a spectacular 125,000-square-foot science museum devoted to minerals, fossils, transportation technology, and hands-on science experiences. The 120-seat digital planetarium features a variety of astronomy programs, "Night at the Museum" stargazing events, and family activities. Discover how the earth was formed billions of years ago in the Weinman Mineral Gallery, which showcases more than 4,000 rocks, fossils, crystals, geodes, gemstones, and minerals. "Stan," a 40-foot T-rex, is the star of the Fossil Gallery. There's a constantly changing creative list of events available so check their schedule. Adults are $16, children ages 3 to 17, $13.

For information about other attractions, contact the Cartersville-Bartow County Convention & Visitors Bureau at 1 Friendship Plaza, Cartersville; (770) 387-1357; visitcaretersvillega.org.

Apple Country

Gilmer County, in the Blue Ridge Mountains about 90 minutes due north of Metro Atlanta, is "Georgia's Apple Capital." Dozens of orchards dotting the county's green mountainsides annually produce more than 600,000 bushels of Granny Smiths, Red and Golden Delicious, Yates, Jonathans, Stayman Winesaps, Rome Beauties, and exotic Asian varieties such as Fujis and Mutsus. In the fall, when the trees are loaded with fruit, visitors by the thousands are invited into the orchards to pick their own basketsful. Those who'd just as soon leave the labor to somebody else can buy all they can haul home at farm stores that line the highways leading to **Ellijay,** the Gilmer County seat. They also can take away freshly pressed apple cider, apple pies and cakes, and recipe books to prepare just about everything with apples.

To celebrate the harvest, **Ellijay's Georgia Apple Festival,** 2 weekends in mid-October, puts on parades, apple pie–eating and apple-cooking contests, arts and crafts, mountain music and dancing, and a host of other festivities. Ellijay is a delightful small town with 1,700 amiable inhabitants. It may remind you of Sheriff Andy Taylor's bucolic hometown of Mayberry.

When your appetite is worked up again, get ready for some serious barbecue. As you drive into town on the 4-lane Zell Miller Mountain Parkway (GA 515), you can't help but notice **Col. Oscar Poole's Pig Hill of Fame** (706-635-4100; poolesbbq.com). For $5 you, too, can have your name painted on one of thousands of little plywood piggies that graze on the hillside beside Col. Poole's yolk-yellow **Real Pit Bar-B-Q** establishment. (Col. Poole is also a Methodist minister, and your $5 goes to church missions.) Inside, the barbecue is seriously delicious.

Whitewater rafters, canoeists, and kayakers flock to the Ellijay and Cartecay Rivers that flow out of the mountains, right into Ellijay. Contact the Gilmer County Chamber of Commerce, 368 Craig St., Ellijay; (706) 635-7400; gilmer chamber.com.

Sasquatch exists! At least for the aficionados who run **Expedition Bigfoot** just north of tiny Cherry Log on Hwy. 515 (1934 Hwy. 515; 706-946-2601; expeditionbigfoot.com). The 4,000-square-foot facility has a massive array of Bigfoot photos and artifacts, as well as updated sighting maps and the world's only known Bigfoot Research and Tech vehicle. Open daily 10 a.m. to 5 p.m. Adults $8, children $6.

The mountain community of Blue Ridge has attracted an array of artists and artisans. Studio shops create museum-quality jewelry, stained and blown glass, pottery, paintings, wood, and fiber pieces eagerly sought by tourists and residents alike. You can also satisfy your hunger for antiques and collectibles in scads of shops on downtown Blue Ridge's Main Street. As you go from shop to shop, stop for a lunch-and-dinner pick-me-up at **Blue Jeans Pizza and Pasta Factory** (11 Mountain St.; 706-632-6503; bluejeansblueridge.com).

The **Blue Ridge Scenic Railroad** (241 Depot St., Blue Ridge; 706-632-9833, 877-413-TRAIN; brscenic.com) takes train enthusiasts in enclosed and open-air cars on a 26-mile round-trip through the mountains and along the Toccoa River between the Fannin County towns of Blue Ridge and McCaysville.

The excursion operates between Mar and Dec and is especially popular in Sept and Oct when the high country's fall foliage is at its colorful peak. The Christmas Express and Halloween Haunted Express are other popular special events and you can even pay a little extra and ride on the engine. Choices are coach or premier class. Adults, $38 to $73; senior citizens, $35 to $69; ages 3 to 12, $35 to $69.

Places to Stay in Northwest Georgia

CAVE SPRING

Cedar Creek Park
6770 Hwy. 411
(706) 777-3030
bigcedarcreek.com
Inexpensive
Fifty RV sites with full hookups; 24 tent sites with water, restrooms, and showers

Hearn Inn
Rolater Park
13 Cedartown St. SW
(706) 381-2060
Inexpensive
Five guest rooms in a 2-story Federal-style house; full breakfast included

Tumlin House Bed & Breakfast
38 Alabama St.
(706) 777-0066
tumlinhouse.com
Inexpensive
Victorian home with 3 queen-size bedrooms and one twin bedroom; full breakfast included

CHATSWORTH

The Overlook Inn
9440 GA-52
(706) 517-0300
theoverlookinn.com
Moderate
Mountain getaway with incredible views, 6 guest rooms; 3-course breakfast and evening cocktails included

CLOUDLAND CANYON

Hidden Hollow Country Inn
463 Hidden Hollow Dr.
(706) 539-2372
hiddenhollowresort.com
Inexpensive to moderate
See p. 98 for details

ROME

Claremont House Bed & Breakfast
906 E. 2nd Ave.
(706) 291-0900
(800) 254-4797
Moderate to expensive
Victorian Gothic mansion; full gourmet breakfast and evening cocktails included

Places to Eat in Northwest Georgia

CARTERSVILLE

Appalachian Grill
14 E. Church St.
(770) 607-5357
appalachiangrill.com
Inexpensive to moderate
American

Ate Track Bar & Grill
25 N. Wall St.
(470) 315-4369
thecitycellar.com
Moderate
American

City Cellar and Loft
110 N. Museum Dr.
(770) 334-3170
thecitycellar.com
Moderate
Seafood, steak, pasta

Ross's Diner
17 N. Wall St.
(770) 382-9159
Inexpensive
Southern

TOP ANNUAL EVENTS

MARCH

Native American Heritage Day
Etowah Indian Mounds State Historic
Site
(770) 387-3747

APRIL

Cedar Valley Arts Festival
Cedartown
(770) 748-0397
cedarvalleyartsfestival.com

Georgia Steeplechase
Kingston Downs, Rome
(855) 978-7856
georgiasteeplechase.org

MAY

Cherokee County Indian Festival
Canton
(770) 735-6275

Prater's Mill Country Fair
Dalton
(706) 275-6455
pratersmill.org

OCTOBER

Chiaha Harvest Fair
Rome
(706) 235-4542
chiaha.org

Georgia Apple Festival
Ellijay
(706) 636-4500
georgiaapplefestival.org

DECEMBER

Candles & Carols at Oak Hill
Martha Berry Museum, Rome
(800) 220-5504

Swheat Market Deli
5 E. Main St.
(770) 607-0067
swheatmarketdeli.com
Inexpensive
Sandwiches and soups

DALTON

Alondra's
314 Glenwood Ave.
(706) 529-3562
Moderate
See p. 107 for details

Crescent City Tavern
324 S. Depot St.
(706) 529-0467
Crescentcitytavern.com
Moderate
Burgers and beer

The Oakwood Cafe
201 W. Cuyler St.
(706) 278-4421
oakwoodcafe.net
Inexpensive to moderate
American

EAST ELLIJAY

**Oscar Poole's Real Pit
Bar B-Q**
Zell Miller Pkwy./GA 515
(706) 635-4100
poolesbbq.com
Moderate
See p. 114 for details

ROME

Harvest Moon Cafe
234 Broad St.
(706) 292-0099
myharvestmooncafe.com
Southern, burgers

**La Scala Restaurant
& Bar**
465 Broad St.
(706) 238-9000
lascalaromega.com
Moderate to expensive
Italian

HELPFUL WEBSITES

**Cartersville-Bartow County
Convention & Visitors Bureau**
visitcartersvillega.org

Dalton Convention & Visitors Bureau
visitdaltonga.com

Rome Convention & Visitors Bureau
romegeorgia.com

Middle Georgia

Cherry Blossoms & Fried Green Tomatoes

For travelers caught in the relentless grind of interstate traffic, Macon can be a quick and refreshing retreat to a slower, easier era. Only a few minutes from the major highways, **Downtown Macon Historic District** offers a glimpse at beautifully restored Greek Revival and Victorian homes, churches, and public buildings on quiet, tree-shaded streets. Three landmark houses are open year-round. Others invite guests during the late March Cherry Blossom Festival and September Jubilee.

Your first stop should be the **Macon-Bibb County Convention and Visitors Bureau** (450 Martin Luther King Jr. Blvd., Macon; 478-743-3401; maconga.org). You can pick up free maps, brochures, information, and self-guided tours.

Whether with a guide or on your own, the **Hay House** (924 Georgia Ave., Macon; 478-742-8155; hayhousemacon.org) will be a highlight. Taking five years to complete, the opulent Italian Renaissance palazzo was finished in April 1861 just as Macon and Georgia were marching off to the War Between the States. Behind the stately redbrick facade, the 24 rooms are a

MIDDLE GEORGIA

SOUTH CAROLINA
GEORGIA

Clarks Hill Lake

Savannah R.

MASTERS GOLF & BIG WATER

Waynesboro

Augusta

Harlem

Thomson

Washington

Crawfordville

Greensboro

ANTEBELLUM TRAIL

Milledgeville

Madison

Eatonton

Rutledge

Covington

CHERRY BLOSSOMS & FRIED GREEN TOMATOES

Juliette

Macon

N

25 mi

25 km

treasure trove of stained glass, statuary, European and American furnishings, silver and crystal, paintings, and silk and damask draperies and wall coverings. Long before air-conditioning, a cleverly concealed ventilation system kept the high-ceilinged rooms surprisingly cool even on the most torrid summer days. Hay House is open Mon through Sat from 10 a.m. to 4 p.m.; Sun 1 to 4 p.m. Admission is $12 for adults, $11 for senior citizens, $8 for students; free for children 6 and under. They also offer behind-the-scenes tours.

Just around the corner is a white-columned Greek Revival house that achieved lasting notoriety when a Union shell crashed through the facade and landed in the front hallway. Walk through the **Cannonball House** and adjoining **Macon Confederate Museum** (856 Mulberry St.; 478-745-5982; cannonballhouse.org) for a look at the stray missile, Civil War photos, artifacts, china, crystal, weapons, uniforms, and such rare treasures as Mrs. Robert E. Lee's rolling pin. It's open Mon through Sat from 10 a.m. to 4 p.m. Admission is $8 for adults, $6 for senior citizens, $4 for students, free for age 4 and under.

Walking into **St. Joseph's Catholic Church** rivals walking into an historical church in Europe. It's fitting because Catholic history in middle Georgia dates back to 1540 when the Spanish explorer Hernando De Soto came through the area. As Macon grew in the 1800s, the local Jesuits were determined that they should have a church worthy of worship. By all accounts, they succeeded. Started in 1889, it took fourteen years to complete the Romanesque, Neo-Gothic church. There are over 60 stained-glass windows depicting saints, angels, and Biblical scenes. White marble statues and altars from both Italian and Georgian quarries are throughout. Its twin cross-topped spires rise 200 feet above the Macon skyline. Open for visits at 830 Poplar St.; (478) 745-1631; stjosephmacon.wordpress.com.

Macon's modern musical heritage includes Rock 'n' Roll Hall of Famer "Little Richard" Penniman, soul singer Otis Redding (a life-size statue of Otis sitting on the dock of the bay can be found near the entrance of Gateway Park), and the Allman Brothers Band. Duane Allman and fellow band member Berry Oakley—both killed in 1970s motorcycle accidents—are buried in much-visited graves at **Rose Hill Cemetery.** Maconites from all the way back to the 1830s and 600 Confederate and Union soldiers are also in the historic cemetery at 1071 Riverside Dr., Macon. April and October weekends, local historians conduct "Rose Hill Rambles" or tours of the cemetery for $5. Call (478) 751-9119 or visit historicmacon.org/rose-hill-cemetery for information.

Allman Brothers fans can also make a pilgrimage to the place where many of their songs were created, **The Big House** (2321 Vineville St., Macon; 478-741-5551; thebighousemuseum.com). Home to the Allman Brothers Band

MIDDLE GEORGIA'S TOP HITS

A. H. Stephens State Historic Park & Confederate Museum	Milledgeville Trolley Tour
	Mistletoe State Park
The Big House	Morgan County African-American Museum
Blue Willow Inn Restaurant	
Callaway Plantation	Morris Museum of Art
Cannonball House	Ocmulgee National Monument
Downtown Macon Historic District	Old Governor's Mansion
Elijah Clark State Park	Old Market House
Flannery O'Connor Room	Piedmont National Wildlife Refuge
Hard Labor Creek State Park	Riverwalk Augusta
Hay House	Rock Eagle
High Falls State Park	Rutledge antiques and craft stores
Indian Springs State Park	Social Circle
Jarrell Plantation	The Tubman African American Museum
Kettle Creek Battleground	The Uncle Remus Museum
Madison–Morgan County Cultural Center	Washington Historical Museum
	Whistle Stop Cafe
Masters Golf Tournament	

Museum, this Tudor-style house was the place where the band lived just after they formed in 1969 and it was the center of all their early activity. The museum holds a vast array of their instruments as well as clothing, posters, and even gold records. Open Thurs through Sun 11 a.m. to 6 p.m.; tickets start at $8.

The **Tubman African American Museum** (310 Cherry St., Macon; 478-743-8544; tubmanmuseum.com) displays paintings, sculpture, and other creative endeavors by black American, African, and Caribbean artists and craftspeople. The **Resources Room** has available reference materials and books on black Americans. The museum's shop sells handcrafted jewelry, paintings, posters, recordings, and books. A mural depicting contemporary black personages features Colin Powell as a military hero. Open Tues through Sat from 9 a.m. to 5 p.m. Admission is $10 for adults, $8 for seniors and the military, $6 for children 3 to 17; free for children under 4.

Ocmulgee National Monument, a short drive from downtown, is a must-see for anyone fascinated by ancient Native American civilization. A dozen ceremonial and burial mounds, the highest nearly 45 feet, were built by Mississippian Indians between about AD 900 and 1100. They were succeeded at the site by Creeks, who remained here until their expulsion to Oklahoma in the 1830s.

Stop first at the National Park Service Visitors Center and see a short film, artifacts unearthed from the mounds, and dioramas on the cultures that flourished here. You can climb steep wooden stairs to the flat top of the 45-foot-high *Great Temple Mound* and to the crest of the surrounding smaller mounds. You may also see them from the comfort of your car. A sound-and-light presentation brings the circular *Earthlodge* back to life, as tribal elders discuss plans for a war, the effects of a drought, and other important issues. The monument is at 1207 Emery Hwy., Macon (478-752-8257; nps.gov/ocmu). Hours are (daily) 9 a.m. to 5 p.m. Free admission.

The *Georgia Sports Hall of Fame* (301 Cherry St., Macon; 478-752-1585; georgiasportshalloffame.com), a 43,000-square-foot museum, showcases heroes of golf, football, baseball, basketball, and other endeavors. You'll be able to test your skills on interactive and virtual reality games. Open Mon through Sat 9 a.m. to 5 p.m., Sun 1 to 5 p.m. Admission is $8 for adults; $6 for military personnel, college students with ID, and senior citizens 60 and older; $3.50 for children 6 to 16; free for children 5 and under.

Douglass Theatre (335 Martin Luther King Jr. Blvd., Macon; 478-742-2000; douglasstheatre.org) was built in 1921 by African-American businessman Charles Douglass. The downtown Macon theater hosted many of the country's most acclaimed performers. Among the talents that delighted audiences for more than three decades were Duke Ellington, Bessie Smith, Cab Calloway, Nat King Cole, Billie Holiday, James Brown, "Ma" Rainey, and Macon's own Otis Redding and "Little Richard" Penniman. Restored and reopened in 1996, the Douglass now has state-of-the-art facilities for movies and live performances and an archive of black history in music, film, and drama. Open for tours Mon through Sat from 9 a.m. to 5 p.m., Sun from noon to 5 p.m. Donations accepted.

To get in the proper antebellum spirit, make reservations at the *1842 Inn* (353 College St., Macon; 478-741-1842 or 877-452-6599; 1842inn.com). The 22 guest rooms in the circa-1842 Greek Revival showplace and an adjacent cottage are decorated with antiques, fresh flowers, fireplaces, and all the contemporary comforts. Some rooms have whirlpool baths. Double rates (expensive) include continental breakfast and afternoon wine and hors d'oeuvres.

During the last 10 days of March, more than 300,000 Japanese cherry trees set the stage for the city's annual *Cherry Blossom Festival* highlighted by

Harlem's Oliver Hardy

One of the silver screen's most popular and recognizable comedians was born in 1892 in the small eastern Georgia town of Harlem. Rotund fussbudget Oliver Hardy left home when he was 8 years old and joined a traveling show as a boy soprano. Weary of the road, he attended Georgia Military Academy and studied law at the University of Georgia.

But greasepaint was apparently in his blood. He opened Milledgeville's first movie house and was so intrigued by the films that he became a comic villain in a theater company. In the mid-1920s, he went to Hollywood and teamed up with his sidekick and foil, Stan Laurel. It was a match made in the stars. They appeared together in more than 100 pictures and performed on radio, stage, and TV.

Hardy died in 1957, and his memory lives on at Harlem's *Laurel and Hardy Festival* in early October. Visitors enjoy a Laurel and Hardy film fest and a look-alike contest (laurelandhardy.org). You can also visit the ever popular *Laurel and Hardy Museum* (250 N. Louisville St.; 706-556-0401; laurelandhardymuseum.com). Open Tues through Sat 10 a.m. to 4 p.m.

concerts, home and garden tours, parades, and other activities. You won't be in town very long before proud Maconites tell you that in sheer numbers of blossoming trees, if nothing else, their festival is bigger than Washington, DC's.

Cherry blossom season or not, you'll still enjoy a drive by the stately homes on north Macon's *"Cherry Blossom Trail,"* several miles of streets marked by pink and white signs. For information visit cherryblossom.com or call (478) 330-7050.

Hidden off-the-beaten path and built into a hillside of the woods in the 400 block of Forest Hill Road is a large, stone cave-like structure called the *Grotto.* Built by Jesuits as a shrine to Saint Bernadette and Our Lady of Lourdes around 1901, it stood on land granted to Ann Rich in 1821 after Native Americans were removed. Her family sold 10 acres to La Societe Cathloique Religieuse to build St. Stanislaus College. The college was destroyed by fire in 1921. For almost 100 years the Grotto was abandoned until the family of former Macon Mayor Robert Reichert purchased it and the surrounding land, restoring it and ensuring its safety. Limited tours are now conducted through the Museum of Arts and Sciences and can be arranged by calling (478) 477-3232.

Jarrell Plantation State Historic Site is a homespun juxtaposition to the romanticized Old South of Tara and Twelve Oaks, dashing beaux and ladies fair. At the end of a tree-shaded graveled road off GA 18 between Forsyth and Gray, you enter a world where unrelenting hard work—not flirtation and idle mint juleps—was the rule of society. From the early 1840s, when John Fitz

Jarrell built the first dwelling, until 1958, when the last direct heir died, the plantation was worked by three generations of Jarrells. They planted cotton, ran gins and gristmills, and battled boll weevils, depressions, and General William Tecumseh Sherman himself. Nowadays, the dwellings, work buildings, barnyards, and fields are maintained by the Georgia Department of Natural Resources as a living memorial to the state's agricultural heritage.

You'll enter the plantation through the scuppernong arbor, whose juicy fruit Jarrell women turned into pies and jellies. A flock of guinea fowl, squawking like so many feathered burglar alarms, alerted the family that visitors were approaching. These days, the guinea fowl still sound off, and an assortment of barnyard animals—a goat, a horse, a brown milk cow, a burro, a couple of sheep—press against the fence for the hay held out by children.

At the modern visitor center, you can watch a film on the plantation's history and pick up a self-guided walking-tour map.

At the 1847 plantation's plain first dwelling, you can visualize the womenfolk sitting in a circle, busily making quilts and clothes while hearty stews bubbled on the wood-burning stove. At the mill complex down the hill from the house, workmen get the steam engine ready to grind the sugarcane into syrup. The site was donated to the State of Georgia by his descendants.

Jarrell Plantation (Route 1, Box 40, Juliette; 478-986-5172, 800-864-PARK; gastateparks.org/JarrellPlantation) is open Thurs through Sat from 9 a.m. to 5 p.m. Admission is $6.50 for adults, $4 for children 6 to 18; free for children 5 and under. It's 18 miles south of I-75 exit 185 at Forsyth, 18 miles north of I-75 exit 171 at Macon.

The **Piedmont National Wildlife Refuge** (478-986-5441; fws.gov/piedmont) a 35,000-acre preserve 10 miles down the graveled road from the plantation, has a visitor center and hiking trails. A pristine area known for creek bottoms and loblolly pines, you can truly escape to this hidden gem. There's awesome birding and you can bring your fishing gear and try your luck in the Ocmulgee River.

If you saw the movie *Fried Green Tomatoes* or read the Fannie Flagg novel it was based on, you'll be glad to know it wasn't pure fiction. After the movie's highly successful 1991 run, enterprising folks in the almost-ghost town of *Juliette* bought up the store that served as the movie's cafe and reopened the "new" **Whistle Stop Cafe** (443 McCrackin St.; 478-992-8886; thewhistlestopcafe.com). Fried green tomatoes are served, along with barbecue, fried chicken, meat loaf, pork chops, and other home-cooked favorites. Southern-style breakfast is also served. The block of stores and the white frame depot around the cafe have also been revived as antiques and gift shops. Adding to the atmosphere, local kids dive off the dam near the textile mill, just as they did in the film. The Whistle

Stop Cafe is open every day but Wednesday, 11 a.m. to 4 p.m. It's in downtown Juliette, 10 miles off I-75 north and south exit 186. Inexpensive.

A quiet and peaceful recreation place now, *Indian Springs State Park,* near Jackson, has a long, colorful, and tragic history. For many centuries Creeks and other tribes gathered at a sulfur spring whose waters were believed to have magical powers to cure ailments and restore vitality. In the spring of 1825, Creek Chief William McIntosh signed an illegal treaty ceding all tribal lands to the state of Georgia. The fraudulent treaty so enraged the dispossessed natives that they murdered McIntosh and several of his followers. A valid treaty in 1828 finally ended Creek dominion, and the town of Indian Springs was founded, along with what's believed to be the oldest state park anywhere in the United States.

Nowadays people still flock to the sulfur springs and take home jugs of the strong-smelling water. They swear by its ability to restore health and vitality and offer advice to those who quail at the rotten-egg smell. Just let it sit for 2 to 3 days, and the aroma will vanish, but not the curative strength of the minerals.

The handsome fieldstone buildings in the park were built during the Great Depression by the Civilian Conservation Corps. Along with the mineral waters, artifacts and historical displays are on view at the *Indian Hotel/Museum* where McIntosh signed the ill-fated document. Around a 105-acre lake are a swimming beach, fishing, rental boats, nature trails, and picnic areas. Camp-sites with electrical and water hookups are $25 a night. Completely furnished 2-bedroom cottages, with log-burning fireplaces, are available. There is a $5 per visit parking fee. Contact Park Superintendent at 678 Lake Clark Rd., Flovilla; (770) 504-2277. For reservations, call (800) 864-PARK or log on to gastateparks .org/IndianSprings.

Fresh Air Bar-B-Que (1164 GA-42, Jackson; 770-775-3182; freshairbar bque.com), between Jackson and Indian Springs State Park, is one of the holy grails of this savory Georgia art form. Except for wooden planking that covered the old sawdust floor a few years ago, and one change of ownership more than 75 years ago, this rambling, wooden barbecue shack has changed only margin-ally since it served its first platter in 1929.

The pine board tables have been in place for more than 50 years. Pork is slowly cooked over hickory and oak coals right behind the ordering counter. It's sweet and succulent, with a tangy pièce de résistance provided by a secret sauce prepared by the family that has operated the place since the early 1940s. Along with barbecued pork, the simple menu includes only Brunswick stew, coleslaw, slabs of starchy white bread, soft drinks, and iced tea. It's open Mon through Thurs from 11 a.m. to 8 p.m.; Fri and Sat until 9 p.m.; and Sun until 8 p.m. During the summer, it usually remains open a half hour to an hour later.

High Falls State Park, off GA 36 (I-75 exit 198), about 12 miles south of Indian Springs, is another rustic off-the-beaten-path retreat. The centerpiece is a series of scenic whitewater cataracts of the *Towaliga River* rushing over mossy rocks. According to legend, Creek Indians "cured" their victims' scalps around the Towaliga—hence the name, which means "roasted scalp."

Two hiking trails offer views of the falls, the river, and adjacent woodlands and past ruins of old mills from the 1800s. You can wade into the river, but be extremely careful of the slick, mossy rocks. Also in the 1,050-acre park, you'll find a 650-acre lake for fishing and boating, a swimming pool, and 142 tent and trailer sites, with water and electrical hookups. There is a $5 per visit parking fee. Contact Park Superintendent: Route 5, 76 High Falls Park Dr., Jackson; (478) 993-3053, (800) 864-PARK; gastateparks.org/HighFalls. Open 7 a.m. to 10 p.m. For reservations call (800) 864-PARK. It's 1.8 miles east of I-75 exit 198/ High Falls Road.

Tiny *Porterdale* on GA 81 just south of I-20 often gets overlooked but if you enjoy old mill towns, you can't beat this one. First settled along some cascading shoals of the Yellow River in the 1830s, it is home to the oldest intact cotton mill village in the southeast. Tours of this time capsule of a town can be arranged through (678) 931-8052 or visit porterdalehistorytour.com.

The little Walton County town of *Social Circle* (socialcirclega.gov/welcome) about 8 miles west of Hard Labor Creek on GA 11, is a delightful place to stroll and browse. The 19th-century storefronts have been brightly repainted and are home to coffee shops, cafés, and antiques shops. The town allegedly got its name when a stranger happened onto a cluster of idling locals and found them so friendly he proclaimed, "Why, this is sure some social circle." Still social, the town hosts a Friendship Festival each year at the beginning of October.

The *Blue Willow Inn Restaurant* (294 N. Cherokee Rd., Social Circle; 770-464-2131; bluewillowinn.com) is like a nostalgic Sunday dinner at Grandma's. The dining room of the 1890s Victorian house is filled with a bountiful buffet that includes fried chicken, pork chops, chicken and dumplings, baked ham, an array of vegetables (including state-of-the-art fried green tomatoes), congealed salads, cake, and fruit cobbler—all at astonishingly modest prices. After your feast, sit on front porch rockers, walk in Billie Van Dyke's gardens, and stroll down Social Circle's Main Street. Open Mon through Fri from 11 a.m. to 2:30 p.m. and 4:30 to 8 p.m.; Sat from 11 a.m. to 2:30 p.m. and 4:30 to 8 p.m.; Sun from 11 a.m. to 7 p.m. Adjacent to the inn is the *Blue Willow Gift Shop.*

Lake Oconee, a mammoth Georgia Power Company impound of the Oconee River, is a major destination for outdoor recreation. The 19,000-acre lake, with a 375-mile shoreline, has numerous marinas, campsites, picnicking areas, and swimming beaches. The Georgia Power Company office at the lake

(800-886-LAKE; visitlakeoconee.com) can supply further information about recreational facilities. The lake is easily accessible from I-20.

The ***Ritz-Carlton Lodge at Reynolds Plantation*** (1 Oconee Lake Trl., Greensboro; 800-241-3333, 706-467-0600; reynoldslakeoconee.com) brings high luxury to Lake Oconee's shores. The Adirondacks-style lodge's 251 guest rooms and suites have all the deluxe bells and whistles. Guests enjoy fine wining and dining; water sports, tennis, 4 superb golf courses; and pampering in the wellness center. Expensive.

The Ritz-Carlton and other upscale developments around the lake have been a boon to nearby Greensboro. Antiques shops around the courthouse square attract browsers and buyers, who can also visit a couple of historic curiosities. The ***Old Rock Gaol***, a fortress-like jail built in 1807 and in use until 1895, bears a grim resemblance to Paris's notorious Bastille, on which it was allegedly modeled. Granite walls 2 feet thick, with small barred windows and a rooftop gallows, warned citizens to stick to the straight and narrow. Or else. It can be toured by appointment with the Greene County Chamber of Commerce, 111 N. Main St., Greensboro; (706) 453-7592, (866) 341-4466, (800) 886-5253; greeneccoc.org. After visiting the Gaol, stroll through the ***Greensboro Antique Market*** (101 Main St.; 706-453-9100) and enjoy lunch or dinner at ***The Yesterday Cafe*** (114 N. Main St.; 706-453-0800; theyesterdaycafe.com).

The Iron Horse, visible in a pasture on GA 15 at the Oconee River Bridge, was originally a public sculpture placed on the University of Georgia campus in 1954. But after students looked the gift horse in the mouth, then shamefully vandalized it, the 2,000-pound scrap-iron sculpture was relocated in a cornfield where he safely grazes in sight but out of harm's way. The matter of where the horse ultimately belongs remains in dispute.

Antebellum Trail

Milledgeville was Georgia's capital city from early after the American Revolution until after the War Between the States. Laid out in 1803–1804 on a precise grid of broad streets and public squares, it was the only American city other than Washington, DC, specifically planned as a capital. In its own way, it was to post-Revolutionary Georgia what Brasilia was to mid-20th-century Brazil: a magnet intended to lure settlers away from the comforts of the Atlantic coast.

Statesmen and public officials eased the burdens of the wilderness by building palatial Greek Revival mansions filled with the finest American and European furnishings, books, and art. Halcyon days ended in the fall of 1864, when General William T. Sherman's Union army, marching from Atlanta to Savannah, captured the city.

According to which legend you choose to believe, Milledgeville was spared Sherman's torch because (a) he was met at the outskirts by fellow brothers of the local Masonic lodge, who pleaded for leniency; (b) he didn't want to burn a town he'd chosen as temporary headquarters; or (c) he had a local lady friend and did not wish to break her heart.

The real reason was that Milledgeville had no military significance. Union troops burned the military arsenal and stoked molasses down the pipes of the Episcopal church, which was used as a horse stable. When the "March to the Sea" resumed, the Governor's Mansion and everything of nonmilitary importance was left unharmed. The Reconstruction government moved the capital to Atlanta, an action ratified by the state's voters in 1868.

The Old State Capitol and Old Governor's Mansion are the most tangible landmarks of Milledgeville's tenure as Georgia's capital city from 1804 to 1868. When Union troops occupied the city in 1864, they held a mock session of the state legislature in the Gothic-style capitol and "revoked" the Ordinance of Secession that took Georgia out of the Union in 1861. Fully restored, the imposing, fortress-like building at 201 E. Greene St., Milledgeville (478-453-1803; visitmilledgeville.org) is now a classroom building for Georgia Military College. Cadets lead tours Mon through Fri, 10 a.m. to 4 p.m.; Sat noon to 4 p.m. that include a historical museum and the antebellum House Chamber. Adults $6, students $5.

The **Old Governor's Mansion** (120 S. Clark St., Milledgeville; 478-445-4545; gcsu.edu/mansion), completed in 1839 in Palladian Greek Revival style, underwent a $10 million restoration, completed in 2005, that returned it to its 1850s grandeur. The Marquis de Lafayette danced the minuet in the mansion's ballroom during his 1825 farewell to America tour. One of Georgia's most beautiful public buildings, the rose-hued mansion features four Ionic columns and a wealth of antiques, art, and unique architectural features. Open Tues through Sat from 10 a.m. to 4 p.m.; Sun 2 to 4 p.m. Adults $10, seniors $7, students $2.

American literature fans should also visit the **Flannery O'Connor Room** (478-445-4047; libguides.gcsu.edu) in the library of Georgia College and State University. The late author wrote her two novels (*The Violent Bear It Away* and *Wise Blood*) and short story collections while living here. She died in 1964 and is buried in Memory Hill Cemetery. The Flannery O'Connor Room at her alma mater displays first editions, manuscripts, gifts from admirers, memorabilia, and drawings she did as a hobby. It's in the Georgia College and Instructional Technology Center, Georgia College, Milledgeville. Tours are self-guided but guided tours are available by appointment. Open Mon through Sat 10 a.m. to 4 p.m. Donations are accepted.

O'Connor's fans shouldn't miss **Andalusia,** the author's 544-acre farm on US 441, 4 miles northwest of Milledgeville (2628 N. Columbia St.), where she wrote many of her stories. A self-guided tour includes the gently rolling farmland that inspired so much of her fiction, the main house, barns, equipment and milk-processing sheds, horse stable, and 3 tenant houses. On your tour, you'll probably encounter some of the "residents": white-tailed deer, wild turkeys, red-tailed hawks, beavers, raccoons, opossums, birds, reptiles, and amphibians. In the main house, rooms open to the public include O'Connor's bedroom, the dining room, and the kitchen. Guests are invited to view the video production of O'Connor's story, *The Displaced Person*, which was filmed on location at Andalusia in 1976. Andalusia is open for tours Tues through Sat from 10 a.m. to 4 p.m.; Sun 2 to 4 p.m. Admission is free, but there is a

TOP ANNUAL EVENTS

MARCH

Macon Cherry Blossom Festival
Macon
(800) 768-3401
cherryblossom.com

APRIL

Masters Golf Tournament
Augusta
(800) 726-4067
masters.com

Washington-Wilkes Tour of Homes
Washington
(706) 678-2013
wwtourofhomes.com

MAY

Madison's Spring Tour of Homes
Madison
(706) 342-4743
visitmadisonga.com

SEPTEMBER

Ocmulgee Indian Celebration
Ocmulgee National Monument, Macon
(478) 752-8257

OCTOBER

Blind Willie McTell Blues Festival
Thomson
Blindwillie.com
(706) 597-1000

Green Tomato Festival
Juliette
(478) 992-8886

Oliver Hardy Festival
Harlem
harlemga.org
(706) 556-0401

NOVEMBER

Christmas in Milledgeville
Milledgeville
(800) 653-1804

DECEMBER

Christmas at Callaway Plantation
Washington
historicwashingtonga.com
(706) 678-7060

suggestion of a $10 donation. For information, call (478) 454-4029 or visit gcsu .edu/adalusia.

The best way to enjoy the town's heritage is on a 2-hour motorized **Milledgeville Trolley Tour,** which covers the major landmarks and includes a visit to the Governor's Mansion. Guides weave a wealth of humor and anecdotes into their historical narrative. Tours leave the Milledgeville Convention and Visitors Bureau (200 W. Hancock St., Milledgeville), Tues and Fri at 10 a.m. and Sat at 2 p.m. Adults are $18; children 6 to 12, $10. The tourism office (478-452-4687; visitmilledgeville.org) also has free maps and information for self-guided walking tours. It's directly across the street from the handsome **Baldwin County Courthouse.**

Milledgeville is a "high-spirited" town. If you'd like to hear about some of its specters, join the **Haunted Trolley Tour**. Tickets are $15 for adults, $10 for children.

The **Lockerly Arboretum** is like a secret garden in the heart of Milledgeville (1534 Irwinton Rd.; 428-452-2112; lockerly.org) that surrounds the antebellum mansion Rose Hall. Built in 1851 for $5,500, the stunning home has 4 interior chimneys and gives you a real sense of mid-1800s living. The gardens feature native plants, a collection of camellias, nature trails, as well as a conifer garden. No charge to visit the gardens but the house is $3 for adults and $1 for children. Open Mon through Fri 8:30 a.m. to 4:30 p.m.

When you've worked up an appetite, try **Ms. Stella's** (960 N. Wilkinson St.; 478-453-7311) where ravenous students and other townsfolk satisfy their craving for perfectly prepared fried chicken, fish, sweet potato casserole, turnip and collard greens, squash soufflé, pecan pie, and other Southern comfort food. Named for the owner's grandmother, the staff treat you like family. Lunch and dinner daily. Inexpensive. Also downtown, you'll find sushi bars, Chinese buffets, Mexican, Italian, and barbecue restaurants.

After Milledgeville's history lesson, you'll probably be ready for some quiet relaxation. **Lake Sinclair,** a 15,330-acre, 420-mile shoreline impoundment of the Oconee River, has plenty of stretching room. Marinas, fishing docks, and campgrounds are off US 441 north of Milledgeville.

While Milledgeville's literary lioness was Flannery O'Connor, **Eatonton**, about 15 miles north on US 441, was the birthplace in 1848 of Joel Chandler Harris, who turned the slave legends he heard as a youngster on a Putnam County plantation into the *Uncle Remus: Tales*.

The **Uncle Remus Museum** (214 Oak St.; 706-485-6856; uncleremus museum.org), on US 441, Eatonton, south of the town of 4,800, has Harris's personal mementos and illustrations of the tales of the devilish Br'er Rabbit, sly-but-perpetually-outwitted Br'er Fox, dumb ole Br'er Bear, and, of course, the Tar Baby. Also in the log cabin, which was created from 3 original slave cabins, you'll see first editions, a diorama of an antebellum plantation, and other historical artifacts. The museum is open Mon through Sat from 10 a.m. to 4 p.m. and Sun 1 p.m. to 4 p.m. Adults are $5; children, $3.

Eatonton also is the home of Alice Walker, Pulitzer Prize–winning author of *The Color Purple*. With the **Alice Walker Driving Tour** brochure from the Putnam County Chamber of Commerce office (105 S. Washington Ave., Eatonton; 706-485-7701; eatonton.com), see the church she attended, her parents' graves, the house where she grew up, and other landmarks of her life.

As you drive past the Putnam County Courthouse in the center of Eatonton, look for the little likeness of Br'er Rabbit on the lawn facing US 441. Many well-kept antebellum homes are on the shady streets leading off the courthouse square. Putnam County is also the center of Georgia's dairy industry, so you'll spot several contented herds as you drive out of town.

Rock Eagle, 4 miles north of Eatonton, is a relic of Indian civilizations that flourished here more than 6,000 years ago. A creamy white quartz effigy— about 10 feet high, 103 feet from its head to its tail, 32 feet from wingtip to wingtip—the great bird seems poised for flight. Archaeologists believe Rock Eagle was a focus for Indian tribal rituals. The best views are from an observation tower. It's located in a 4-H Club Center, 350 Rock Eagle Rd., Eatonton, off US 441. Call (706) 484-2899 or visit rockeagle4h.org for more information.

Morgan County, between Augusta and Atlanta, claims **Madison** (I-20 exit 114/US 441), one of Georgia's prettiest antebellum towns. It's consistently listed by *Southern Living* as one of "The Best Places to Live." Strolling along the tree-shaded streets and picturesque town square, admiring Madison's treasury of glorious antebellum architecture, we should say "thank you" to a United States senator who put himself between the town and General William T. Sherman's torch. In late 1864, Atlanta in ruins 60 miles away and the cruel "March to the Sea" in full stride, Sherman's Union army approached Madison's outskirts. They were met by former senator Joshua Hill, a foe of secession who'd been acquainted with Sherman in Washington. He peacefully surrendered the town, which was miraculously spared war's ravages.

Your first stop should be the **Madison–Morgan County Chamber of Commerce Welcome Center** (115 E. Jefferson St., Madison; 706-342-4454; visit madisonga.com). In this former 1880s fire station on the courthouse square, you can load up on walking-tour maps and brochures and get any information you may need on festivals, bed-and-breakfasts, and restaurants. Stop next at the **Madison–Morgan County Cultural Center** (434 S. Main St., Madison; 706-342-4743; mmcc-arts.org). The Romanesque-style redbrick schoolhouse, circa 1895, is now the hub for regional arts, theater performances, and the source of walking-tour maps of the fetching little town of 3,000. The former schoolrooms now show pottery, weaving, paintings by Georgia artists and traveling exhibitions, 19th-century furniture, farm implements, clothing, and Civil War artifacts. You can also see a log cabin from the early 1800s and an 1890s schoolroom, complete with pot-bellied stove and hickory switch. The center's August theater festival features everything from Shakespeare to Tennessee Williams. The center is open Tues through Sat from 10 a.m. to 4:30 p.m.; Sun from 2 to 5 p.m. Admission is $5 for adults, $4 for seniors, $3 for students; 6 and under free.

With a self-guided tour map, walk through the **Madison National Historic District** and admire more than three dozen gorgeous Greek Revival, neoclassical, Victorian, Federal, and Romanesque homes, many of them graced by gardens and stately trees. A number of these old beauties are open to the public during Madison's May and December festivals.

The **Morgan County African-American Museum** (156 Academy St., Madison; 706-342-9191; mcaam.org) documents the contributions blacks have made to the area's cultural and social life. Located in the 1895 Horace Moore House, the museum has rooms with period furnishings, a reference library, paintings, books, and exhibits. Open Tues through Fri from 10 a.m. to 4 p.m.; Sat noon until 4 p.m. Admission is $5 for adults, $3 for children.

You can take a guided tour of **Heritage Hall** (277 S. Main St., Madison; 706-342-9627; friendsofheritagehall.org), a white-columned 1830s Greek Revival showplace near the courthouse square. Look for romantic messages etched on the windows, and be mindful of a mysterious presence that sometimes evidences itself in an upstairs bedroom. Open Mon through Sat from 11 a.m. to 4 p.m. and Sun 1:30 to 4:30 p.m. Adults are $10; students, $7.

Madison's town square is one of Georgia's most delightful, and the **Morgan County Courthouse** one of the grandest in Georgia's 159 counties. A number of antiques and handicraft stores will draw your attention as you stroll around the square.

Several of Madison's loveliest homes welcome bed-and-breakfast guests: **Brady Inn** (250 N. 2nd St.; 706-342-4400; bradyinn.com); **Southern Cross Guest Ranch B&B** (1670 Bethany Church Rd.; 706-342-8027 or 800-342-8027; southcross.com); **The Farmhouse Inn** (1051 Meadow Ln.; 706-342-7933; thefarmhouseinn.com); and **Kirby House** (877 South Main St.; 706-342-8777; kirbyhouse.us).

The **Steffen Thomas Museum and Archives** (4200 Bethany Rd., Buckhead; 706-342-7557; steffenthomas.org), near the rural Morgan County community of Buckhead, houses hundreds of oil and watercolor paintings, mosaics, and sculptures by late German-born expressionist artist Steffen Thomas, who did most of his work in Atlanta. Like many artists, Thomas was his own model: *The Goat of Mentelle* is the self-portrait sculpture of the artist as a billy goat. (He lived on Mentelle Street in Atlanta.) The museum is open Tues through Sat 11 a.m. to 4 p.m. Adults $10; seniors and students $8; children under 6 free.

Hard Labor Creek State Park (1400 Knox Chapel Rd.; 706 557-3006; georgiagolf.com/the-creek), 12 miles west of Madison, near the small community of Rutledge, is a nice place to relax for a day, or several days. The recreational possibilities include a very good 18-hole golf course and a lake for swimming, boating, and fishing. Plenty of picnic tables are spread among the pines, and there's a playground for the youngsters. If you're planning to play the 6,682-yard, par-72 course, bring your own clubs. You may rent an electric cart in the clubhouse, which has showers and a snack bar. The park's 50 campsites have water, electricity, restrooms, and showers; 20 2-bedroom cottages are completely furnished, including towels, sheets, and kitchen utensils. There is a $5 per visit parking fee. The park office is open daily from 8 a.m. to 5 p.m. Contact Superintendent: 5 Hard Labor Creek Rd., Rutledge; (706) 557-3001. For reservations call (800) 864-PARK or log on to gastateparks.org/HardLaborCreek.

Work your way to the heart of the park at night and enjoy the **Hard Labor Creek Observatory** (2010 Fairplay Rd.; 404-413-6033; astro.gsu.edu/hlco). There are three powerful telescopes to explore the night sky. Check website for hours.

With a population of 780, **Rutledge** (I-20 exit 105, rutledgega.us) lives up to its motto of "Small but Special." You'll pass through on the way to Hard Labor Creek. A cadre of artists and craftspeople from as far away as New England have found their way here, bringing life to this off-the-beaten-path town. **Rutledge Hardware** (114 Fairplay St.; 706-557-1770) has been in continuous operation since the late 1800s and changed only marginally the past half century. Paul Jones fills orders for galvanized tubs, cast-iron cookware, tools, seed, farm implements, and chamber pots "like my great-grandpa used." Its shelves are filled with gifts and collectibles, bath products, and lotions. When it's time for a break, many shoppers enjoy ice cream, colorful shaved ices, sandwiches, and salads at **The Caboose** (102 E. Main St.; 706-557-9021), a revamped 1910 railroad car. The entire delightful town is now on the National Register of Historic Places. Around the corner, **Markets on Main** (119 E. Main St.; 706-818-0608) sells handmade quilts, handcrafted furniture, original artwork, pottery, and antiques.

For breakfast and lunch locals and visitors take tables and booths at **Yesterday's Cafe** (122 Fairplay St.; 706-557-9337; yesterdayscaferutledge.net). Kris Bray's delicious repertoire includes Southern breakfast, highlighted by blueberry and buttermilk pancakes, grits, and country ham. At lunchtime the menu

Star Gazing

If you are fascinated by the night sky and all of those little lights up there called stars and planets, then make a plan to head to the **Hard Labor Creek Observatory** (2010 Fairplay Rd.; 404-413-6033; astro.gsu.edu/HLCO/openhouse.html). Operated by Georgia State University, it's located in the heart of Hard Labor Creek State Park in Rutledge, a good 50 miles from the downtown Atlanta campus.

Once a month, astronomers from GSU's Department of Physics welcome stargazers to the observatory to peer through each of their three powerful telescopes. You'll be able to gaze at objects as close as the moon and as far away as the edge of our visible universe. It's exhilarating to climb the dome as it opens up to the heavens above. Because the location is so remote, there's no light pollution and the stars seem so close you could touch them.

If the weather is bad, or it's simply too cloudy, the scientists are prepared to still give a tour of the buildings and telescopes and give a slideshow. No reservations are needed but it's good to call ahead. Call or check the website for the days of the open house and any special events.

features burgers, sandwiches, soups, and the cafe's signature dish, buttermilk pie. Open for breakfast and lunch Thurs through Sat. Inexpensive to moderate.

A. H. Stephens State Historic Park, on GA 22, Crawfordville, outside the small town of Crawfordville, includes the home and gravesite of Alexander Hamilton Stephens, governor of Georgia and vice president of the Confederacy. *Liberty Hall,* the 2-story frame house Stephens built around 1830, is filled with his furnishings, personal effects, and the wheelchairs to which he was bound much of his life.

The adjoining *Confederate Museum* (706-456-2602, 800-864-PARK; gastateparks.org/AHStephens) is highlighted by a bronze statue of Stephens by Gutzon Borglum, sculptor of the US presidents on Mount Rushmore, South Dakota. This fine collection of memorabilia also includes dioramas of soldiers in the heat of battle and the quiet of the campfire; rifles and shot; field gear; battle flags; and touching personal belongings—Bibles, prayer books, and bloodstained photos of wives and sweethearts.

As in all wars, Civil War soldiers used sharp-edged humor to help blunt the insidious enemies of fear and homesickness. "In this army," a Confederate foot soldier wrote, "one hole in the seat of the breeches indicates a captain, two holes is for a lieutenant, and the seat of the pants all out is for us privates." Liberty Hall and the Confederate Museum are open Mon and Wed through Sat from 9 a.m. to 5 p.m.; Sun from 2 to 5:30 p.m. Closed Tues. Admission is $4 for adults, $2.75 for children 5 to 18; free for children under 5.

After your history lesson, relax at the park's recreation area. Located 0.25 mile from Liberty Hall, you'll find a swimming pool, 2 fishing lakes, picnic shelters, 4 cottages, and 22 tent and trailer sites, with water and electrical hookups, showers, and restrooms. The museum and park are 2 miles from I-20 exit 148, Crawfordville. There is a $5 per visit parking fee. On a more modern note, scenes from the 2002 Reese Witherspoon film *Sweet Home Alabama* were filmed in Crawfordville.

Incorporated in 1780, the picture-book little town of **Washington** (cityof washington.gov) was the first American community named in honor of the father of our country. Skirted by General William T. Sherman's rampaging "March to the Sea" and treated kindly by progress and time, the town of about 4,000 is today like a living Williamsburg. More than 30 Greek Revival homes, churches, and public buildings predate 1850. Most of them are still well-maintained residences. Three antebellum landmarks are open to visitors year-round.

The **Robert Toombs House State Historic Site** (216 E. Robert Toombs Ave., Washington; 706-678-2226; gastateparks.org/RobertToombsHouse) was the home of Georgia's "Unreconstructed Rebel," US senator, and Confederate secretary of state. At odds with the Confederacy—he was resentful of Jefferson Davis's presidency—as well as the Union, he fled to the Caribbean and Europe

Where, Oh Where, Can Jim Williams Be?

The quiet, final resting place for the protagonist of the best-selling book *Midnight in the Garden of Good and Evil* is surprising given the flamboyant lifestyle of the fastidious Savannah antiques dealer. For the uninitiated, Jim Williams withstood three mistrials for the 1981 murder of his gay lover before dying of a heart attack following being acquitted in the fourth. I happened to be living across the street from Williams but was lucky enough to be out of town the night of "the incident." The book by John Berendt chronicled the eccentric people he met when he covered the story—people I somehow avoided during my time in Savannah.

Williams was from the Wilkinson County town of Gordon and now lies outside of town, in a vast garden of stone a few yards from the prim, white frame Ramah Primitive Baptist Church. His black granite marker, inscribed james arthur williams, dec. 11, 1930, jan. 14, 1990, is well kept and weedless. The bucolic country churchyard is 200 miles from his old compadres, many of whom are still reaping the benefits of fame from the book. No doubt he'd love to get his manicured hands on whoever keeps putting pots of plastic flowers on his stone. But in case he's tempted to break out and have another fling at his glamorous old life, his mama is right there to rein him in. If you'd like to drop by, he's on the left side of the cemetery, on GA 57 at GA 18, between Macon and Irwinton.

after the war. Returning in 1880, he scorned political pardon. "I am not loyal to the government of the United States," he declared, "and do not wish to be suspected of loyalty." The guided tours of his Greek Revival house include a documentary film, anecdotes, historical exhibits, and several rooms with period furnishings. Open Tues through Sat from 9 a.m. to 5 p.m. Admission is $7 for adults, $5 for children 5 to 12; free for children under 4.

The **Washington Historical Museum** (308 E. Robert Toombs Ave., Washington; 706-678-2105; historicwashingtonga.com) houses an outstanding collection of Civil War artifacts, including Jefferson Davis's camp chest (given to him by English sympathizers), weapons, uniforms, signed documents, photographs, and furnishings. The main floor of the circa 1835–1836 2-story frame house is furnished as a typical 19th-century double parlor, dining room, and bedroom. The ground floor has been restored as a period kitchen. The grounds are noted for beautiful landscaping and one of Georgia's largest camellia gardens. Hours are Tues through Sat from 10 a.m. to 5 p.m. The $12 admission also gives you access to visiting Callaway Plantation.

Callaway Plantation (2160 Lexington Rd., Washington; historyofwilkes .org) is a living heritage museum rich in lessons about Southern antebellum life. Three restored homes and the adjoining farm are like a walk back in time. The redbrick, white-columned manor house was the heart of a 3,000-acre cotton plantation. Rooms are furnished with period antiques and many unique architectural features. The outbuildings include a hewn log cabin, circa 1785, with early domestic and agricultural tools and primitive furniture and a smokehouse, barn, pigeon house, and cemetery. Surrounding fields are planted with cotton, corn, cane, and vegetables, just as they were in the mid-19th century. The plantation has been owned by the same family since the late 18th century. Call (706) 678-7060 for tours.

The **Mary Willis Library** (204 E. Liberty St., Washington; 706-678-7736) is an architectural gem, with a place in history and a mystery in its foyer. Georgia's first free public library, the redbrick high-Victorian landmark with its stately round tower was founded in 1888 by Dr. Francis T. Willis in honor of his daughter, Mary, whose likeness is the centerpiece of a priceless Tiffany Studios stained-glass window. The mystery revolves around an old iron trunk in the foyer. Did it once hold part of a shipment of "Lost Confederate Gold" that still attracts fortune hunters to Wilkes County? It's keeping a tight lid on the secret. Mary Willis is part of a regional library system called the **Bartram Trail** (btri.net) and partners with the Taliaferro County Library and the Thomson-McDuffie County Library.

Washington also figured in the Revolutionary War. A marker at **Kettle Creek Battleground** (299 War Hill Rd.; 706-678-2013), 8 miles south of town on GA 44, Washington, commemorates the patriots' 1779 rout of the British and the Redcoats' subsequent withdrawal from this area of Georgia. Picnic tables are at the site so enjoy a lunch atop "War Hill."

When hunger overwhelms your hunt through history, head for **Cade's Home Cooking** (9 East Sq.; 706-678-5586) for—as the name says—home cooking. Lunch buffet includes all the Southern staples like fried chicken, pork chops, mac n' cheese and a plethora of greens. Inexpensive to moderate.

Many of Washington's most magnificent homes are open during the early April **Washington-Wilkes Tour of Homes.** Contact Washington-Wilkes Chamber of Commerce at 26 West Sq., Washington; (706) 678-2013; washington wilkes.org.

Stop by the Thomson–McDuffie County Tourism Bureau in the restored train depot at 149 Main St., Thomson (706-567-1000; visitthomsonga.com) for information on some of Georgia's best off-the-beaten-path secrets. You'll discover places like the **Old Rock House** (1455 Old Rock House Rd.), a 1785 fieldstone farmhouse that was an old trading post and is one the oldest structures in Georgia; **Alexandria** (435 Shadowmoor Dr.), a stately Virginia-influenced brick plantation house and boxwood gardens built by revolutionary war patriot Thomas Carr from 1805; and the site of November's **Belle Meade Fox Hunt** (3532 Wrightsboro Rd.; bellemeadehounds.com). A number of gracious antebellum homes line Thomson's tree-shaded streets.

On US 78, you'll also find traces of **Wrightsboro** (4736 Wrightsboro Rd.), a 1767 settlement of Quakers. Royal Governor James Wright had granted 12,000 acres of formerly Creek land to the religious group and they immediately built mills and began farming the area, eventually getting more than 43,00 acres. The Civil War took a toll on the community and it dwindled until the final service was held at the church in 1966. Built in 1810, the church, the cemetery, a cabin, and old general store are maintained by the Wrightsboro Foundation.

The **Old Market House** is a souvenir of the period from 1796 to 1805 when little Louisville ("Lewis-ville") was Georgia's first capital. Built in the 1790s in the heart of town, the Market's weathered timbers are held together by 1-inch-diameter wooden pegs. The Market's bell was cast in France in 1722 and was on its way to a New Orleans convent when it was hijacked by pirates and somehow ended up in Louisville. Louisville's tenure as state capital was immortalized by the Great Yazoo Land Fraud of 1795, which cost Georgia the territory that later became the states of Alabama and Mississippi. Contact the Jefferson County Chamber of Commerce at 302 E. Broad St., Louisville; (478) 625-8134; jeffersoncounty.org.

Masters Golf & Big Water

Augusta, a metro area of 600,000, traces its heritage to 1736, when General James Edward Oglethorpe, founder of the Georgia Crown colony, laid it out as the state's second city, after Savannah. Fought for during the Revolutionary War and skirted by General William T. Sherman's "March to the Sea," Augusta has mild winters and a genteel Old Southern lifestyle that caught the attention of post–Civil War Northern aristocrats, who found the right formula for golf—a pastime that symbolizes this city to people around the world.

For many years Augusta almost forgot that the Savannah River ran by its doorstep. All that has changed since **Riverwalk Augusta** has become the center of downtown activity. The main entrance to Riverwalk is at Eighth and Reynolds Streets, a block off Broad Street. The top of the old river levee has been turned into an inviting brick esplanade with seating clusters overlooking the river, historical displays, and playground and picnic areas. Major hotels, shops, and dining are along the Riverwalk. Stop first at the **Augusta & Company Visitor Center** (1010 Broad St.; 706-724-4067; visitaugusta.com) for information and historic exhibits on Augusta's once-lucrative trade in "white gold." It's open Mon through Sat 10 a.m. to 5 p.m.; Sun from 1 to 5 p.m. Self-guided walking and driving tours as well as group tours are available at the welcome center.

The **Augusta Museum of History** (560 Reynolds St.; 706-722-8454; augustamuseum.org) lays out the city's past in a 48,000-square-foot home at Sixth and Reynolds Streets. The 23 permanent galleries are filled with Revolutionary and Civil War weapons and uniforms, Native American culture, natural history (including a major dinosaur exhibit), space exploration, communications, vintage photographs, and a tribute to the city's and Georgia's founder, General James Edward Oglethorpe. Savannah River marine life inhabits a small aquarium. Train buffs shouldn't miss "Old No. 302," the Georgia Railroad's last steam engine. Contemporary times are represented by exhibits on the 1960s Civil Rights Movement and stage costumes worn by the late James Brown, Augusta's flamboyant "Godfather of Soul." The museum is at 560 Reynolds St., Augusta. Open Thurs through Sat from 10 a.m. to 5 p.m.; Sun from 1 to 5 p.m. Adults are $5, seniors $5, children 6 to 18 $5.

The **Jessye Norman Amphitheater** (9th Street Plz.; 706-821-2300) down by the water honors the late opera singer, who was an Augusta native. It stays busy as the scene of festivals and outdoor concerts. She's also honored through the **Jessye Norman School of the Arts** (739 Green St.; 706-828-7786; jessye normanschool.org), a free, comprehensive after-school art program, serving mostly disadvantaged youth.

AUTHOR'S FAVORITES

Antebellum Madison	Hay House
Antebellum Milledgeville	Hard Labor Creek Observatory
Antebellum Washington	Indian Springs State Park
Augusta Canal boat rides	Laurel and Hardy Museum
The buffet tables at the Blue Willow Inn Restaurant	Old Governor's Mansion
	Riverwalk Augusta
Cherry Blossom Festival	Whistle Stop Cafe

Morris Museum of Art is at Riverfront Center (1 10th St., Augusta; 706-724-7501; themorris.org). Two centuries of Southern art are represented in this museum designed like a private home. The permanent collection includes works by Augusta native Jasper Johns and mixed media artist Robert Rauschenberg. Special exhibits are held throughout the year. Open Tues through Sat from 10 a.m. to 5 p.m.; Sun from noon to 5 p.m. Admission is $5 for adults, $3 for students and senior citizens.

As long as you are downtown, whip out your phone and take the *James Brown Journey Sidewalk Vinyl Tour.* The free audio tour highlights 12 locations significant to Brown's life and career including his childhood home on Twiggs Street and the Bell Auditorium where he performed numerous times. Each site has a special street medallion. You can get a map of the walking tour at the Augusta & Co. Experience Center or access it online along with the audio tour at visitaugutusa.com/soul-starts-here.

Woodrow Wilson's Boyhood Home (419 E. 7th St., Augusta; 706-722-9828; wilsonboyhoodhome.org) has been beautifully restored to his time here as a young child with his family. In 1858, when the future 28th president was 1 year old, his father became pastor of Augusta's First Presbyterian Church. The family lived 13 years in the church-owned manse in downtown Augusta. Wilson's earliest memory was hearing of Abraham Lincoln's 1861 election. In 1865 he saw Federal troops escorting captive Confederate President Jefferson Davis through the streets. In 1871 he met Robert E. Lee, a guest of the city. He scratched his name, "Tom" (his first name was Thomas)—which is still visible—on a parlor window and left scuff marks from his shoes on the dining room table, one of 13 church-owned pieces in the house when the Wilsons lived there. The only item that belonged to the Wilsons and that is still in the house is a butter dish, part of a silver service given to the family their first Christmas in Augusta. In 1991 Historic Augusta, Inc., purchased the house from owners who'd used it as a flower shop and beauty shop. Following a $2 million restoration, the 2-story redbrick house is open for guided tours Tues through Sat, 10 a.m. to 4 p.m. Adults $5, seniors $4, students $3.

New York has its Erie Canal; Georgia has the *Augusta Canal National Heritage Area.* Built in 1845 to harness the waterpower of the Savannah River, it's the nation's only industrial canal still used for its original purposes. The Heritage Area offers history, recreation, and unique experiences at its Interpretive Center and boat tours on 8.5 miles of waterway and towpath. Located inside Enterprise Mill, a colossal 19th-century redbrick textile mill once powered by the harnessed waters of the Savannah River, the Interpretive Center's film and exhibits explain the canal's construction by African-American, Irish, Chinese, and Italian laborers and also the mechanics and physics of turning water into industrial power. Large windows reveal the working 1920s-era electrical turbines that are once again generating hydroelectric power. Artifacts and audiotape interviews with former mill workers enhance the experience that's culminated with hour-long tours in shallow-draft, 19th-century, Petersburg-style canal boats. The Interpretive Center (Enterprise Mill, 1450 Greene St., Augusta; 706-823-0440; augustacanal.com) is open Mon through Sat 10 a.m. to 6 p.m.; Sun 1 to 6 p.m. Boat tours last an hour and cost $14, which also allows you into the Discovery Center. Tickets to the Interpretive Center and boat tour can be purchased separately or in combination: $6 interpretive center, $13.75 for the combo. During the summer, there are also 3-hour sunset cruises for $25, music cruises for $25, and Moonlight Music Cruises on Fridays for $25.

If you want to see more of the canal, head over to the *Savannah Rapids Park* up the road in Martinez (3300 Evans-to-Locks Rd.; 706-868-3373; savannahrapids.com). Located at the headgate of the canal, the park is 33 acres of great trails, in general, but you can visit the canal's spillway. If you are feeling romantic, you and your sweetie may want to add a lock of love to the already festooned guard rails. Open daily. Free.

Ezekiel Harris House (1840 Broad St., Augusta; 706-724-0436) is Augusta's second-oldest structure. In 1797, the prominent tobacco merchant Harris came to the area from South Carolina with plans to build a town to rival Augusta as a tobacco market. On a hill overlooking Augusta, the house is an outstanding example of post-Revolutionary architecture. The gambrel roof and vaulted hallway are reminiscent of New England. Tiered piazzas are supported by artistically beveled wooden posts. Rooms are furnished with period antiques. It's open Sat from 10 a.m. to 5 p.m. Adults are $2; students, $1.

Meadow Garden (1320 Independence Dr.; 706-724-4174; historicmeadow garden.org) was the home of George Walton, one of Georgia's signers of the Declaration of Independence. Built around 1791, it's the city's oldest documented structure and one of the oldest house museums in the US. Meadow Garden has been restored and refurnished by the Georgia Society, Daughters of the American Revolution. Hours are Tues through Sat from 10 a.m. to 4 p.m. Admission is $5 for adults, $4 for seniors and military, $1 for children.

Gertrude Herbert Institute of Art (506 Telfair St., Augusta; 706-722-5495; ghia.org) is an architecturally unique early 19th-century residence that showcases regional and Southeastern contemporary art. Built in 1818 by Augusta Mayor Nicholas Ware, the elliptical 3-story staircase, Adam-style mantels, and other rich ornamentation earned it the name "Ware's Folly." Hours are Tues through Fri from 10 a.m. to 5 p.m.; Sat from 10 a.m. to 2 p.m. Admission is $2 for adults, $3.50 for seniors, $3 for students, $1 for children.

The *Lucy Craft Laney Museum of Black History* (1116 Phillips St., Augusta; 706-724-3576; lucycraftlaneymuseum.com) honors the beloved late educator, born in slavery, who established Augusta's first black secondary schools and a nurses' training school. Her former home has exhibits and photos on her remarkable life and many contributions to African-American culture. Open Tues through Fri 9 a.m. to 5 p.m.; Sat 10 a.m. to 4 p.m.; Sun by request. Adults $5, seniors $3, children $2.

Until the 1960s, Broad Street, America's second widest main street after New Orleans's Canal Street, was downtown Augusta's hub. When suburban malls suffocated its retail trade, Broad nearly died of neglect. Happily, it's been revitalized as the *Artists Row* (artistsrow.wordpress.com). More than a dozen art galleries, antiques and gift shops, and fun little restaurants have taken over historical mercantile stores. Have lunch or dinner at *Nacho Mama's* (976 Broad St.; 706-724-0501; nachomamasaugusta.com) for killer burritos, tacos, and margaritas. Or stop at *Luigi's* (590 Broad St.; 706-722-4056; luigisinc.com)

That Green Jacket

Those green jackets with the Augusta National emblem on the pocket that are awarded to winners of the Masters were originally created not for the winners, but for the club members to wear during the tournament. In 1937, when the contest began, members wanted to be identified so that guests and spectators would know who they were and could ask them any questions about the course or the contest. They decided a green jacket would help them stand out. When Sam Snead won the Masters in 1949, he was presented his own jacket and the tradition stuck.

which has seen Broad Street through good and bad times since 1946. Spin your favorite Bing Crosby, Andrews Sisters, and Glenn Miller platters on your personal booth jukebox while you tuck into good old Italian-American spaghetti and meatballs, lasagna, and ravioli.

Kids and adults who love wild things will have a wonderful time exploring **Phinizy Swamp Nature Park** and the **Phinizy Center for Water Sciences** (1858 Lock-and-Dam Rd., Augusta; 706-828-2109; phinizycenter.org). The park's 1,100 acres of uncorrupted wetlands, swamps, nature trails, boardwalks, and observation decks put you in sight of herons, egrets, red-shouldered hawks, otters, alligators, amphibians, and other free-ranging creatures. The Center offers hands-on educational opportunities to help understand wetlands and water systems. Open daily. Free.

For golfers around the globe, Augusta is Christmas, the World Series, the rainbow's end. In late March and early April, fortunate faithful congregate along the dogwood- and azalea-rimmed fairways of storied **Augusta National Golf Club** to hail the game's elite as they pursue the Green Jacket, symbolic of the **Masters Golf Tournament** championship. Unless you know a player or a club member, tickets to the championship rounds will be impossible to find. But don't despair. You can see all the greats up close—even take their pictures—during the practice rounds preceding the tournament. The bad news is the **Masters Practice Rounds** have become so popular that tickets must now be purchased in advance through a lottery. To receive an application form, go to tickets.masters.com.

Bass anglers and those seeking more off-the-beaten-path relaxation should look into a minivacation at **Mistletoe State Park.** About 35 miles north of Augusta, on 76,000-acre Clarks Hill Reservoir, this very tranquil park reputedly commands some of America's finest bass fishing waters. You may also swim and boat in the lake, hike 5 miles of woodland trails, and ride rental bikes around the 1,920 acres. Ten 2-bedroom furnished cottages and 96 camping sites with water, electricity, showers, and restrooms are available. There is a $5 per visit parking fee. Contact Park Superintendent at 3723 Mistletoe Rd., Appling; (706) 541-0321. For camping and cottage reservations, call (800) 864-PARK or go to gastateparks.org/Mistletoe.

Elijah Clark State Park, north of Mistletoe, is another wooded retreat on the western shores of Clarks Hill Lake. Twenty furnished cottages and 175 tent and trailer sites are a few steps from the water. You'll also find marinas, docks, boat ramps, a swimming beach, nature trails, and plenty of picnic areas. The park was named for Revolutionary War hero Elijah Clark. A colonial museum displays relics from the period. The park is 7 miles east of Lincolnton at 2959

McCormick Hwy. Phone (706) 359-3458 for information. For reservations, call (800) 864-PARK or log on to gastateparks.org/ElijahClark.

Burke County, between Augusta and Savannah, hails itself as "The Bird Dog Capital of the World." You can test its veracity with an organized bird and game hunt at the 5,000-acre *Boll Weevil Plantation* (4264 Thompson Bridge Rd., Waynesboro; 706-554-6227). Contact the Burke County Chamber of Commerce at 828 Liberty St., Waynesboro; (706) 554-5451.

Places to Stay in Middle Georgia

AUGUSTA

Olde Towne Inn
349 Telfair St.
(706) 833-9463
or (706) 831-2823
oldetowninnaugusta.com
Moderate
Five guest rooms with private baths; Fox's Den pub downstairs offers live acoustic music

Partridge Inn
2110 Walton Way
(706) 737-8888
partridgeinn.com
Moderate to expensive
Hilton property with 155 executive, studio, and deluxe suites; Southern buffet breakfast included

Queen Anne Inn
406 Greene St.
(706) 723-0045
queenanneinnaugusta.com
Moderate
3-story Victorian inn; spa packages available

GREENSBORO

Goodwin Manor
301 S. Main St.
(706) 453-6218
goodwinmanor.com
Moderate
Five spacious guest rooms in a 100-year-old home; full breakfast and evening reception included

JULIETTE

The Jarrell 1920 House
715 Jarrell Plantation Rd.
(888) 574-5434
(478) 986-3972
jarrellhouse.com
Inexpensive to moderate
1850s-style plantation house; 2 large guest rooms with private baths; full breakfast included

MACON

1842 Inn
353 College St.
(478) 741-1842
(877) 452-6599
1842inn.com
Expensive
See p. 122 for details

Burke Mansion
1085 Georgia Ave.
(478) 238-1731
Burkemansion.com
Moderate to expensive
Boutique B&B offers 4 suites and a private cottage; breakfast and evening reception included

WASHINGTON

Fitzpatrick Hotel
16 W. Public Sq.
(706) 678-5900
thefitzpatrickhotel.com
Inexpensive to moderate
Seventeen guest rooms in a restored 1898 hotel; continental breakfast included

Holly Ridge Country Inn
2221 Sandtown Rd.
(706) 401-7651
Moderate to expensive
95-acre plantation; 8 guest rooms across 2 historical homes with porches, parlors, and sunrooms

HELPFUL WEBSITES

Augusta Convention & Visitors Bureau
visitaugusta.com

Macon Convention & Visitors Bureau
maconga.org

Madison-Morgan County Chamber of
Commerce
visitmadisonga.com

Milledgeville Visitors Center
visitmilledgeville.org

Washington–Wilkes Chamber of
Commerce
washingtonwilkes.org

Liberty Inn
108 W. Liberty St.
(706) 401-7651
Built in 1790 and fully
restored; 5 guest rooms

**Southern Elegance Bed
and Breakfast**
115 W. Robert Toombs
Ave.
(877) 678-4775
southernelegancebandb
.com
Inexpensive to moderate
Elegant B&B; breakfast and
gourmet dinners available

Places to Eat in Middle Georgia

AUGUSTA

French Market Grille
425 Highland Ave.
(706) 737-4865
thefrenchmarketgrille.com
Moderate to expensive
Cajun, Southern

Frog Hollow Tavern
1282 Broad St.
(706) 364-6906
froghollowtavern.com
Moderate to expensive
New American

Luigi's
590 Broad St.
(706) 724-0501
luigisinc.com
Inexpensive
Italian, American

GREENSBORO

The Yesterday Cafe
114 N. Main St.
(706) 453-0800
theyesterdaycafe.com
Inexpensive to moderate
American

MACON

Natalia's
2720 Riverside Dr.
(912) 741-1380
natalias.net
Moderate to expensive
Italian

Tic Toc Room
408 Martin Luther King Jr.
Blvd.
(478) 744-0123
tictocroom-macon.com
Moderate to expensive
New Southern, Italian, and
American

MADISON

Town 220
220 W. Washington St.
(706) 752-1445
Moderate
French, fine dining

Coastal Georgia

Historic Savannah

Founded in 1733, **Savannah** is one of America's truly special cities. Not long after founding father General James Edward Oglethorpe came ashore on Yamacraw Bluff and dispersed his 144 settlers, he set about planning Savannah in a style befitting the capital of a Crown colony named for King George II. He hunkered down in his damask tent on the bluffs and with military precision laid out a grid of straight, broad streets, braided at 2-block intervals by spacious public squares. Initially, the 24 squares were mustering places for troops and convenient locales for citizens to draw water and exchange news.

In 1793 Eli Whitney, a visiting New Englander given to tinkering with gadgets, devised a mechanized way to separate cotton seeds from the fluffy white bolls. His cotton gin revolutionized Southern planting. On the tragic downside, it also perpetuated the waning practice of slavery and indirectly led to the Civil War. Soon, real gold earned from "white gold" enabled planters, merchants, and shipbuilders to embellish Oglethorpe's squares with English Regency, Georgian, Federal, and Gothic Revival showplaces, filled with fine furniture and

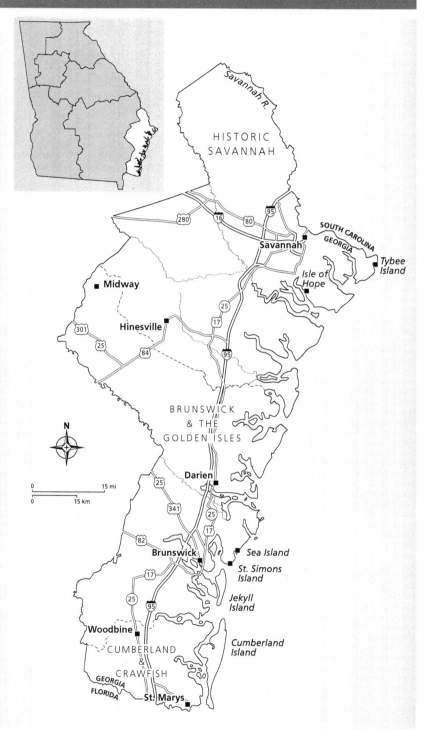

Historic Accommodations

More than 3 dozen historic bed-and-breakfast inns surround you with the aura of Old Savannah. For information and reservations, call (912) 238-2453 or go to visitsavannah.com/bed-breakfasts.

art objects shipped from Europe. As "front yards" for the affluent, the squares were dressed up with trees, flowering plants, benches, fountains, and memorials to Revolutionary heroes and other notables.

In the 1950s, much of the city's heritage teetered on the brink of extinction. Scores of venerable landmarks, even a couple of Oglethorpe's squares, were crunched in the jaws of progress before the Historic Savannah Foundation rode in like the cavalry and saved the day. To date, more than 1,500 historic structures have been restored in the 2.2-square-mile *Savannah National Historic District,* the nation's largest.

Before you leave home, phone the Savannah Convention & Visitors Bureau (912-644-6400 or 877-SAVANNAH) for advance information. When you arrive, stop first at the Savannah Welcome Center (101 E. Bay St., Savannah; savannah .com). You'll find everything you need: free brochures, tour and restaurant information, lodging reservations, and an orientation film. There are also restrooms, water fountains, and attendants ready to load you up with information. The center is located on Bay Street which is on a bluff above *River Street,* a wide brick pedestrian esplanade also known as Riverfront Plaza. It's a great place to start your visit. An elevator at Bay and Bull Streets next to the Hyatt Regency Savannah Hotel will take you down to River Street. As a major plank in the restoration movement, the antebellum brick cotton warehouses were refashioned as seafood restaurants, taverns, touristy shops, and art galleries. On the west end, a massive new entertainment, hotel, and shopping complex called the *Plant Riverside District* now occupies an early 1900s Power Plant. You now have an entire mile along the Savannah River you can browse, have a drink or a bite, or simply sit on a bench and watch the cargo ships cruising to the Georgia Ports Authority docks and heavy industries upriver and the open Atlantic 20 miles downriver.

Then take the hotel elevator or climb up the cobblestoned steps to Bay Street and you're ready for your walk on Savannah's most beautiful street. Few cities are fortunate to be blessed by a thoroughfare as charming as the 10 blocks of *Bull Street* from Savannah's gold-domed City Hall to the green bower of Forsyth Park. Five of Oglethorpe's most picturesque squares are set

A Prophecy Fulfilled

Savannah is full of ghosts and tales of ghosts. Jack Richards, an artist fascinated by the subject, leads true believers and the openly skeptical on *"Ghost Talk, Ghost Walk"* tours of the historic district (ghosttalkghostwalk.com). He relates tales of apparitions at the Pirates House and Olde Pink House restaurants, cemeteries, and private homes. One of his favorites is a romantic story about the mother of Girl Scouts founder Juliette Gordon Low. In the 1890s, when workers were digging the foundation in Wright Square for the monument to William Washington Gordon, founder of the Georgia Railroad and grandfather to Juliette Gordon Low, they inadvertently dug up the remains of Tomochichi, the Indian chief who had befriended General James Edward Oglethorpe. They reported the discovery to Eleanor Kinsey Gordon, Gordon's daughter-inlaw and Juliette Gordon Low's mother.

Embarrassed by the incident, she ordered the big granite stone now on Tomochichi's grave in Wright Square. Although she asked for a bill several times, the Stone Mountain Granite Company never sent one.

After a decade of repeated requests, she finally got a bill for a dollar, "Due on Judgment Day." She sent a check for a dollar, with a curt note: "I'll be much too busy on Judgment Day to pay my debts."

On the day she died, her prophecy apparently came true. She called her deceased husband's name, as if she were seeing an apparition. He was known as "The Old Captain," his rank in the Confederate Army. Minutes later, as her daughterin-law, Margaret, rested in the downstairs parlor, a man in a Confederate officer's uniform walked down the stairs and out the front door. He was followed by Margaret's husband, who announced Mrs. Gordon's death. He hadn't seen the mysterious officer. When they walked outside, the family servant was crying. He said, "I just saw the Old Captain and he said, 'I'm taking Miss Eleanor for her afternoon ride.'" Just as she predicted, Mrs. Gordon was too busy on Judgment Day to worry about her debts.

like gems on this glorious avenue named for a British colonial officer. It divides the historic district into east and west halves. Before you leave, you'll be drawn back time and again to this wonderful, old-worldly street. Revolutionary hero General Nathanael Greene is buried under the granite shaft in Johnson Square. Wright Square honors the founder of the Central of Georgia Railroad, William Washington Gordon.

At Bull Street and Oglethorpe Avenue, Girl Scouts and students of American history should pause at the ***Juliette Gordon Low Girl Scout National Center*** (142 Bull St., Savannah; 912-233-4501; juliettegordonlowbirthplace.org). Designed by noted early 19th-century English architect William Jay, the dignified English Regency mansion was the 1860 birthplace of "Daisy" Low, granddaughter of William Washington Gordon and founder of the Girl Scouts of America. Her paintings and sculpture, personal effects, and GSA mementos are in the high-ceiling rooms. Because of its popularity, the museum tours often sell out and you are encouraged to book online. It's open Mon through Sat from 10 a.m. to 5 p.m.; gift shop open 10 a.m. to 4 p.m. There are several tour options, ranging from general tours for $15 to a 3 1/2 hour "Girl Scout Experience" for $26. Discounts are offered for Girl Scouts, senior citizens, students, and active military.

A bronze statue of General Oglethorpe, by Daniel Chester French (who sculpted the seated statue at Washington's Lincoln Memorial), looks south from its pedestal in *Chippewa Square,* daring the Spanish in Florida to move against his city. Sergeant William Jasper, killed in the 1779 British siege of the city, brandishes the flag atop the monument in the center of Madison Square.

The tree-shaded benches are usually filled with earnest-looking young people who've drifted over from the *Savannah College of Art and Design.* Chartered in 1979, with 71 students and 4 faculty, SCAD has grown from the redbrick, late-1800s Guards Armory on the square's east side into an internationally known institution with campuses not only in Savannah, but also Atlanta; Hong Kong, China; and Lacoste, France. The Savannah campus features 12,200 students and 1,900 faculty and staff. SCAD has restored more than 70 buildings in the historic district, and all those students infuse the area with electrifying energy.

When Savannah peacefully surrendered to the Union army in December 1864, General William T. Sherman lodged in the Gothic Revival *Green Meldrim House* (14 W. Macon St.; 912-232-2151; stjohnssav.org), now St. John's

Savannah's First Big Scandal

The founder of Methodism had Savannah tongues wagging some 250 years before Jim Williams shot Danny Hansford in the scandal immortalized in *Midnight in the Garden of Good and Evil.* According to John Duncan, book dealer and raconteur extraordinaire, the parson's tale went something like this:

"*John Wesley* came to Savannah in the 1730s to minister to the Indians, but he became pastor of Christ Anglican Church. His undoing was falling in love with the original Hard-Hearted Hannah, Vamp of Savannah. It was one of those May-December romances—he was 36, Sophia Hopkey was 18. They'd walk hand-in-hand in the moonlight, and read poetry together, but when he asked her to marry him, she dropped him like a hot potato and married another man. After the marriage, when Sophia and her new husband came to services at Christ Church, Wesley refused to give his ex–lady friend communion. Sophia's in-laws sued Wesley for defamation of character. He was indicted, but never came to trial. It was Savannah's first big public scandal, of which we've had many ever since."

parish house, on Madison Square's west side. From the house, he sent a telegram to his commander in chief: "Dear Sir, President Lincoln: I beg to present you as a Christmas gift, the city of Savannah with 150 heavy guns and also about 25,000 bales of cotton." You're welcome to walk in and admire magnificent Gothic wood carvings, plasterwork, and spacious rooms. Open Tues, Thurs, and Fri from 10 a.m. to 4 p.m.; Sat 10 a.m. to 1 p.m. Admission is a "suggested donation" of $5 each. Bear in mind that because it is connected to the church, the house may be closed because of church functions.

If you're starting to flag a bit, pep up with a cappuccino or latte at **Gallery Espresso**'s indoor or sidewalk tables (6 E. Liberty St.; 912-233-5348; gallery espresso.com), across from the DeSoto Hilton Hotel. You can also tuck into shepherd's pie and a pint of something from the bar at **Six Pence Pub,** an authentic bit of Olde England at 245 Bull St. (912-233-3151; sixpencepub.com).

Patriotic Savannahians named **Monterey Square** for an American victory in the 1840s Mexican War. The monument in the center of the square salutes Count Casimir Pulaski, a Polish nobleman who gave his all for the American cause during the 1779 British siege. **Temple Mickve Israel** (20 E. Gordon St.; 912-233-1547; mickveisrael.org), on the east side, is Georgia's oldest Jewish congregation. Spanish and German Jews, who landed five months after Oglethorpe, brought Torahs and other sacred objects and documents that are now part of a collection you're welcome to see. Just knock on the side door Mon through Fri from 10 a.m. to 3:30 p.m. There's a $7 charge for the tour. The Judaica & Gift Shop is open 10 a.m. to 4 p.m.

COASTAL GEORGIA'S TOP HITS

Christ Church

Cumberland Island National Seashore

Fort Frederica National Monument

Fort Jackson/Oatland Island Education Center

Fort King George State Historic Site

Hofwyl—Broadfield Plantation State Historic Site

Jekyll Island Historic District

Midnight in the Garden of Good and Evil tours

Midway Church

Mighty Eighth Air Force Museum

St. Simons Lighthouse

Sapelo Island Tours

Savannah National Historic District

Skidaway Island State Park

Tybee Lighthouse and Museum

Woodbine Crawfish Festival

Wormsloe State Historic Site

Savannah's most famous house is directly across the square. Some tour guides used to tell visitors that the **Mercer Williams House Museum** (429 Bull St.; 912-236-6352 or 877-430-6352; mercerhouse.com) was songwriter Johnny Mercer's boyhood home. Mercer's grandfather built it after the Civil War, but the family never lived in the stately redbrick Italianate mansion. Antiques dealer, social arbiter, and arts patron Jim Williams lived there until he shot his companion to death in 1981 and became fodder for John Berendt's international best-selling nonfiction book *Midnight in the Garden of Good and Evil*, loosely made into a 1997 movie (see page 149). The house is open for tours of about 30 to 35 minutes Mon through Sat 10:30 a.m. to 4:10 p.m.; Sun noon to 4 p.m. Purchase tickets, $12.50 for adults, $8 for students, at Mercer House Gift Shop, behind the main house. Jim Williams's sister, Dorothy Kingery, lives full-time in the house.

Another 2 blocks and you're in **Forsyth Park.** The centerpiece of the 20-acre sanctuary is an ornate, wrought-iron fountain that looks a bit like a 3-tiered wedding cake decorated with swans and water-spouting tritons.

Squares east and west of Bull Street are blessed with landmarks in a variety of styles. **Isaiah Davenport House** (324 E. State St., Savannah; 912-236-8097; davenporthousemuseum.org), on Columbia Square, played a pivotal role in the restoration crusade. Built between 1815 and 1820 and considered one of America's most perfect Georgian mansions, the redbrick house was threatened with demolition in the 1950s to make space for a funeral home parking lot. The Historic Savannah Foundation came to the rescue and went on to help save hundreds of other imperiled structures. The restored Davenport House gleams with Chippendale and Sheraton furnishings, woodwork, and plaster crown moldings. It's open Mon through Sat from 10 a.m. to 4 p.m.; Sun from 1 to 4 p.m. Admission is $9 for adults, $5 ages 6 to 18. As for the funeral home, it's now Kehoe House, one of the city's grandest historic inns.

The **Owens-Thomas House, Telfair Academy of Arts & Sciences,** and the **Jepson Center for the Arts** are part of the same cultural family, with the same hours, fees, and website (telfair.org). Open Mon from noon to 5 p.m.; Tues through Sat 10 a.m. to 5 p.m.; Sun 1 to 5 p.m. Admission for the 3-site combination is: adults, $20; seniors and AAA, $18; students 13 to 15, $15; children 6 to 12, $5; ages 5 and under are free. Family membership is $80, so it could be worth it.

The Jepson Center for the Arts is a dramatically contemporary expansion of the Telfair Museum in downtown Savannah. With 64,000 square feet in 2 buildings that are connected by a glass bridge over a historic lane, the glistening white Portuguese stone–clad Jepson, with floor-to-ceiling windows and abundant natural light, includes 2 galleries for traveling exhibits; dedicated galleries

Dashing Through the Spanish Moss

Born in Boston, **James Lord Pierpont** wrote the popular Christmas song "Jingle Bells" in Savannah in 1857. A distant kin of financial baron J. P. Morgan, Pierpont arrived in Savannah in 1852 and played the organ at the Unitarian church, where his brother was pastor. He married the daughter of Savannah's Civil War mayor and, with visions of New England's snowy landscapes dancing in his head, gave the world the tune that's been played ad infinitum ever since. A historical marker in downtown Savannah's Troup Square commemorates his contribution to the holiday repertoire.

for African-American art, Southern art, and photography and works on paper; a 2-level hands-on "experience" gallery for young people; 2 outdoor sculpture terraces; and an auditorium and cafe.

The $24.5 million Jepson was dedicated in 2006 as the first major expansion of the 120-year-old Telfair, designed in 1819 by renowned architect William Jay, whose other Savannah landmarks include the Owens-Thomas House. The Regency-style building was originally the home of the Telfairs, a distinguished Savannah family, and became the South's oldest public art museum in 1875. The stately rooms and a ballroom where the Marquis de Lafayette danced minuets during his 1825 visit to Savannah house collections of American and European paintings, sculpture, and decorative arts. You can also view the original *Bird Girl* statue, featured on the book cover of *Midnight in the Garden of Good and Evil*. Originally located at Bonaventure Cemetery, the statue was moved here for its own protection after thousands of *Midnight* fans started flocking to see it. The Telfair and Jepson are at 121 Barnard St., Savannah. Call (912) 232-1177.

The Marquis de Lafayette slept at the Owens-Thomas House on Oglethorpe Square (124 Abercorn St., Savannah; 912-790-8889), during his 1825 farewell-to-America tour. He addressed the populace from the wrought-iron side balcony. William Jay's elegant Regency-style urban villa is filled with art, antiques, and intriguing architectural details and is now operated by the Telfair.

The **Beach Institute African American Cultural Center** (503 E. Harris St.; 912 335-8868; beachinstitute.org) was the first official school for African-Americans in Savannah. Founded in 1865, it is now a museum for African-American and Gullah-Geechee heritage. It is also a genealogical research center. Open Tues through Sat 12 p.m. to 5 p.m. Tickets are $10 with military ID; students and children $7. The ticket also gives entrance to the nearby **King-Tisdell Cottage/Black History Museum.** This 1890s Victorian cottage (514 E. Huntington St., Savannah; 912-234-8000) displays documents, furniture, and artifacts of Low Country black heritage. The King-Tisdell Cottage Foundation also operates the Negro Heritage Trail Tour, which includes landmarks of black history going back to the first slaves. Also open Tues through Sat noon to 5 p.m.

Ships of the Sea Maritime Museum (41 Martin Luther King Jr. Blvd., Savannah; 912-232-1511; shipsofthesea.org) has an extensive collection of sailing ship models, ships in bottles, scrimshaw art, maritime paintings, ornamental figureheads, and other nautical artifacts, all located in the spacious galleries in the 1819 Scarbrough House (built by shipping merchant William Scarbrough). Open Tues through Sun from 10 a.m to 5 p.m. Adults, $9; students and senior citizens, $7.

For a good sense of Savannah's rich history, swing by the *Savannah History Museum* (303 Martin Luther King Jr. Blvd.; 912-651-6825; chcgeorgia .com/shm) which takes you back to even pre–Revolutionary War Savannah. Located at the Tricentennial Park, which includes the former 1860s Central of Georgia Railway depot, the museum offers displays, multimedia presentations, a steam locomotive, and homage to famous citizens like songwriter Johnny Mercer ("Moon River," "Two of a Kind," and countless other standards). You can also see the movie prop bus stop bench where Tom Hanks told his tale in the Oscar-winning film *Forrest Gump*. Outside the museum, take one of the many guided orientation tours in an open-air tram or air-conditioned van or minibus. The museum is open Mon through Fri from 8:30 a.m. to 5 p.m.; Sat and Sun from 9 a.m. to 5 p.m. Adults $9; children 2–12 $5. Tickets are valid for three days.

The role Savannahians played in the 1960s Civil Rights Movement is portrayed with memorabilia, photos, documents, and displays at the *Ralph Mark Gilbert Civil Rights Museum* (460 Martin Luther King Jr. Blvd., Savannah; 912-777-6099; rmgilbertcivilrightsmuseum.com). Gilbert was among Savannah's civil rights leaders in the 1960s but this museum pays homage to the entire movement while highlighting the local efforts. It's open Mon through Sat from 9 a.m. to 5 p.m. Admission is $10 for adults, $8 senior citizens, and $6 for students.

City Market, once-neglected blocks of brick warehouses on West Congress, West St. Julian, and Barnard Streets, 2 blocks from River Street, is now one of the city's most popular places to stroll, shop, and dine. You can browse about two dozen artists' studios and enjoy casual dining and nighttime entertainment in a growing number of venues. Several have outdoor tables. Horse-drawn carriage tours begin and end at the market.

Some of the city's most intriguing sights are outside the historic district. The *Mighty Eighth Air Force Museum* (175 Bourne Ave., Pooler; 912-748-8888; mightyeighth.org) pays tribute to the juggernaut that was born in Savannah in January 1942. Although its headquarters soon moved to England for the duration of the war, Savannah has always had an affectionate place in its heart for "The Mighty Eighth," which won the WWII air war over Europe. Hundreds of high-tech exhibits, artifacts, films, and dioramas take you on a time trip through harrowing years. *The Darkest Hour,* a documentary film, recounts the Battle of Britain, the Japanese attack on Pearl Harbor, the Holocaust, and other atrocities. Through a doorway, displays trace the US entry into the conflict; the buildup of men, women, and war machines; and the Eighth Air Force's birth. Through another door, you're on a 1943 English airfield. In a small hut, you sit in on a briefing session for crews about to take off on a bombing raid over Germany. Leaving the hut, you're in front of a 2-story control tower, similar to hundreds that dotted the English countryside during the war. Original 16 mm color combat film and the sounds of flak, antiaircraft guns, and German fighter planes re-create the terrors Allied crews experienced.

A following exhibit shows the tide of war turning in favor of the Allies, the coming of D-Day, V-E Day, and the atomic bombs on Japan that brought the Pacific War to a close. The combat gallery features a "Flying Fortress" B-17, acquired from the National Air and Space Museum. The ground includes a garden as well as a replica of a British pub where you can enjoy lunch. Open daily from 9 a.m. to 5 p.m. Admission is $10 for adults, $9 for seniors and AAA or AARP members, $5 ages 6 to 12; free for children under 6.

Old Fort Jackson (on US 80/Islands Expressway, Savannah; 912-232-3945, chsgeorgia.org/OFJ) was constructed on the Savannah River between 1808 and 1879. It is the oldest standing brick fort in Georgia. All shipping bound for Savannah's port had to pass by the fort's heavy guns. A tidal moat still guards the stout brick walls. Artifacts include cannons, small arms, machinery, and tools demonstrated at annual events. In summer, uniformed soldiers conduct cannon firings and military drills. Open Wed through Sun from 9 a.m. to 5 p.m. General admission is $6, children 6 and under free.

Oatland Island Wildlife Center (711 Sandtown Rd., Savannah; 912-395-1212; oatlandisland.org) is a fascinating nature experience for all ages. Operated by the Chatham County Board of Education, the center is a focus of nature education programs and special events. You can walk a nature trail and see an astonishing variety of wildlife secured in natural habitats, including gators, wolves, bobcats, bears, panthers, deer, bald eagles, egrets, and heron. Open daily from 10 a.m. to 5 p.m. Admission is $5 for adults; $3 ages 3 to 17 and 65 and over. Free for age 3 and under.

Coastal Georgia Botanical Gardens at the Historic Bamboo Farm (2 Canebrake Rd., Savannah; 912-921-5460; coastalbg.uga.edu) exhibits what's purportedly the world's largest living collection of bamboo varieties. It began in 1890, when Mrs. H. B. Miller planted three bamboo canes in her farm garden.

By 1915, Mrs. Miller's trio covered more than an acre of the Miller farm with tall, sturdy stalks that towered 30 to 70 feet high, with a girth of several inches. By and by, the farm was sold to the US Department of Agriculture as an experiment station, with bamboo types and other plants brought from around the world to test their compatibility with coastal Georgia soil and climate. Experiments were made to develop paper from bamboo. During WWII, goldenrod and dog fennel were tested as substitutes for rubber trees. During the Vietnam War, bamboo did its patriotic duty as material for mock villages to train soldiers at Fort Benning, Georgia. When the USDA closed the station in 1978, the University of Georgia took it over as a research and education center. UGA added palms, black walnut, crape myrtle, Chinese elm, and fruit and nut trees. The expansive gardens include camellia trails, rose gardens, a crape myrtle alley, and an orchid greenhouse. A pavilion built by Friends of the Coastal Gardens holds weddings, family reunions, gardening classes, and conferences. Open Thurs through Sun, 10 a.m. to 4 p.m. Admission is $5 for adults; children $3.

Fort Pulaski National Monument (1 Cokesbury Island, Savannah; 912-786-5787; nps.gov/fopu), off US 80, a half hour east of downtown Savannah, guards the Savannah River's entrance from the Atlantic. The star-shaped fortress took 18 years to construct. A young West Point engineering grad named Robert E. Lee lent his talents—but it surrendered to Union forces on April 11, 1862, following a devastating attack by new cannon rifles. Following the Union occupation of the fort, it was used as a launching point for many former slaves seeking to make their way on the Underground Railroad. Historical exhibits, weapons, and uniforms are displayed. Open daily from 9 a.m. to 5 p.m. Extended summer hours. Admission $7; free for children under 15.

There's not one iota of chic or glamour anywhere on **Tybee Island.** In truth, it's the antithesis of rich and trendy Hilton Head Island, just across the water in South Carolina. Therein lies the charm of this comfortable old shoe of a beach and summer home retreat 20 miles east of downtown Savannah. Many Savannah families spend the torrid summers in cottages near the beach, where the mild Atlantic surf laps 3 miles of hard-packed sand. Stop first at the Tybee Visitor Center, 802 1st Street, Tybee Island, as you enter the island. For info call (912) 786-5444 or visit visittybee.com.

In warm weather, you'll probably want to make a beeline for the Tybee beaches. The most popular stretch for swimming and sunbathing is the commercial area around Butler Avenue and 16th Street—a quirky time warp straight out of Coney Island, circa 1940. Here's where you'll find ice cream and fudge shops, hot dog stands, beer joints, old department stores, convenience stores, chair and beach umbrella vendors, motels, condos, and public restrooms. The **Tybee Island Pier & Pavilion,** jutting far out into the water, is a fine place to cast your fishing line. It was modeled after the old 1891 Tybrisa Pier which stood there for three quarters of a century. A legendary stop on the Big Band tour, young swains and their belles used to dance to the Dorseys and Benny Goodman before fire destroyed it in 1967. Nostalgia for having such a gathering place simply screamed for a new pier and pavilion and the new structure was dedicated in 1996.

Don't be disappointed that the Atlantic on the Georgia coast isn't Caribbean blue-green. The grayish-green surf isn't polluted—rivers like the Altamaha flowing down from Georgia's interior leave a silt bottom, rather than a sand bottom that would reflect the sunlight and create more translucent colors.

Tybee Lighthouse and Museum (30 Meddin Dr., Tybee Island; 912-786-5801; tybeelighthouse.org) are must-see landmarks. The lighthouse is Georgia's oldest and tallest. You can climb 178 spiraling steps to the 154-foot top of Tybee Light, which first guided ships in between the river and ocean in 1773. Partially destroyed by Confederate raiders during the Union occupation, it was rebuilt after the war. An extensive restoration was completed in 1998. Tybee Island Museum is across from the lighthouse, inside Fort Screven, a Spanish-American War coastal artillery battery. Inside the fort's old bunkers are uniforms, weapons, and displays that reflect the fort's active service through World War II. The museum and lighthouse are open daily except Tues from 9 a.m. to 5:30 p.m. Adults $10, ages 62 and over and ages 6 to 17 $8.

Skidaway Island, south of downtown, also has a trove of off-the-beaten-path adventures. ***Skidaway Island State Park*** (52 Diamond Causeway, Savannah; 912-598-2300; gastateparks.org/SkidawayIsland) is a 490-acre preserve that's relaxed and quiet even in busy seasons. The nature trails through the maritime forest and salt marsh include an elevated boardwalk and an observation tower where you can observe an array of birds and wildlife. The 87 tent and trailer camping sites have electrical and water connections, showers, and restrooms. Amenities include a swimming pool, picnic shelters, and a playground. No fishing areas or beaches are inside the park, but they are plentiful nearby. There's a $5 per visit parking fee. Open daily 8 a.m. to 8 p.m. For camping reservations, call (800) 864-PARK or visit gastateparks.org.

The ***UGA Marine Education Center and Aquarium*** (30 Ocean Science Circle, Skidaway Island; 912-598-2496; marex.uga.edu/aquarium), operated by the University of Georgia, is small but unique. There are 16 tanks with an array of coastal marine life, including moray eels, barracuda, catfish, pigfish, monkfish, and 50 or so others. Located on the Skidaway River, there are also hiking trails and picnic tables where you can have lunch or a snack. Open Tues through Fri 9 a.m. to 4 p.m.; Sat from 10 a.m. to 5 p.m. Register ahead through their website for a visit. Admission: $25 for up to 5 visitors in a group and $50 for 6 to 10 people.

At ***Wormsloe State Historic Site*** (7601 Skidaway Rd., Savannah; 912-353-3023, 800-864-PARK; gastateparks.org/Wormsloe) a stunning 1.5-mile avenue of live oaks leads to the ruins of the colonial estate built by Noble Jones, one of the contingent of settlers who arrived with General Oglethorpe in 1733. A physician and carpenter in Surrey, Jones was one of the first Georgians to fully realize the American dream. He became a constable, soldier, surveyor, rum agent, and member of the Royal Council. Between 1739 and 1745, he built his fortified tabby home on the Isle of Hope. Tabby was a popular building material made by pouring equal parts of water, lime, sand, and oyster shells into wooden molds. When the substance hardened, the wooden molds were removed and the next layer was poured. It was designed to last forever, but alas it didn't. You can see a model of it in the visitor center, along with artifacts found on the estate and an audiovisual show about the Georgia colony's early years.

Walk a nature trail to the Jones family grave site and the ruins of Noble Jones's great house. Wormsloe hosts a lot of history related programs and events throughout the year featuring costumed interpreters so check their schedule. Particularly popular is Georgia Week in February. Open Mon through Fri 8 a.m. to 8 p.m.; Sat and Sun from 9 a.m. to 5 p.m. Adults $10, seniors $9, and children $4.50.

The ***Isle of Hope*** is a photogenic place for a drive or walk. The scenic Historic District includes homes dating to the early 1800s. Go to the end of LaRoche Avenue (off Skidaway Road, southeast of downtown Savannah) and follow Bluff Drive along the Wilmington River. Many lovely homes or

Beards in Trees

The gray Spanish moss you see draped across branches of oak trees along the Georgia coast (and beyond) have no real connection to Spain except through legend. Native Americans called the plant "tree hair." One legend has it that when the Spaniards arrived with their long beards, the Natives were fascinated. French explorers as an insult to their rivals started called the gray flowing plant Spanish Beard, which evolved to its present name.

Yet another legend says an early settler and his Spanish fiancée were attacked by a Cherokee warrior who was less than pleased they were taking his land. He cut off her hair and flung it into a tree, where it shriveled and turned gray before hopping from tree to tree.

"cottages" and a Roman Catholic church are set off by towering live oaks and banks of azaleas. The historic Sandfly neighborhood at the island's heart has a host of quaint shops and restaurants to enjoy and help you spend your day.

If you really want off-the-beaten-path, how about heading straight into the salt marshes? *Savannah Canoe and Kayak* (414 Bonaventure Rd.; 912-341-9502; savannahcanoeandkayak.com) offers guided tours by kayak or canoe to Little Tybee Island, the Skidaway Narrows, and through swamps and marshlands for an up-close look at the region's ecosystem.

Fort McAllister State Historic Park (3984 Fort McAllister Rd., Richmond Hill) in Bryan County, 25 miles south of Savannah, has some of the South's best preserved earthwork fortifications. Built on bluffs above the south bank of the Great Ogeechee River, the earthworks withstood seven Union land and sea assaults before finally surrendering in December 1864. It was the last major obstacle on General William T. Sherman's "March to the Sea" and led to Savannah's peaceful surrender a few days later. The earthworks and heavy guns have been restored to their wartime appearance. The museum and visitor center has Civil War weapons and other artifacts.

Fort McAllister's recreation area has 7 cottages; 65 tent and trailer camping sites with electricity, water, restrooms, showers, picnic tables, and grills; 5 miles of hiking trails; and boat ramps and docks. Open daily, 7 a.m. to 10 p.m. Adult admission $9, children $5. There's a $5 per visit parking fee. Drive GA 144 for 10 miles east of I-95. For reservations, call (912) 727-2339 or (800) 864-PARK for reservations or go to gastateparks.org/FortMcAllister.

As you drive US 17 between Savannah and Brunswick, *Midway Church* looms out of the gnarled arms of a live oak grove, like a New England meeting house that's lost its way. The white clapboard church, with its gabled roof and square belfry, traces its heritage to Massachusetts Puritans, who established the Midway Society in 1754. The church dates from 1792. Illustrious parishioners have included two signers of the Declaration of Independence and Theodore Roosevelt's great-grandfather. The fathers of Oliver Wendell Holmes and Samuel F. B. Morse have each served as pastor.

Pick up the big iron church key at the neighboring *Midway Museum* (491 N. Coastal Hwy., Midway; 912-884-5837; themidwaymuseum.org). The sanctuary's unadorned interior has straight-back pews and a slave gallery. The churchyard across the highway is the resting place of the church's founders and Revolutionary heroes. Midway Museum has colonial furnishings, documents, and exhibits. Open Tues through Sat from 10 a.m. to 4 p.m. Adults, $10; seniors and military, $8; children 12 and under, $5.

The Midway area also has two other historic sites (historicmidway.com). A biracial community effort led the restoration of *Seabrook Village* (660 Trade

Hill Rd., Midway; 912-884-7008; seabrookvillagefoundation.org), a post–Civil War African-American community that thrived until the 1930s. Descendants of original former slave settlers lead tours of the one-room schoolhouse, homes, and outbuildings and give demonstrations of activities like grinding corn or washing clothes with a scrub board. Open Tues through Fri, 10 a.m. to 4 p.m. Group rates are available.

At the 67-acre *Fort Morris State Historic Site* (2559 Galley Ln., Midway; 912-884-5999 or 800-864-PARK; gastateparks.org/FortMorris), a film and museum tell the story of Sunbury, a pre-Revolutionary port that rivaled Savannah and died after the British captured it in 1778. A cemetery is the only physical remains of the town. A marked trail goes around the earthworks of Fort Morris, which failed to protect the town from invasion. A nature trail with excellent bird-watching goes through the woodlands and along the marshes. Open daily 9 a.m. to 5 p.m., and 9:30 a.m. on Sun. Adult admission $4.50, children $3; $5 parking fee.

McIntosh County, between Savannah and Brunswick, was the site of a British fort that predated Georgia's founding as a colony in 1733. Marshy bays and coastal islands are home to national marine and wildlife refuges and fleets of fishing boats and shrimping trawlers.

Stop first at the Darien and McIntosh County Visitor Center (1111 Magnolia Bluff Way, Darien; 912-437-4837; visitdarien.com) for general information. The *Fort King George State Historic Site* (a mile off US 17, Darien; 912-437-4770, 800-864-PARK; gastateparks.org/FortKingGeorge) marks an earthwork and palisaded log fortress South Carolinians built in 1721 to fend off hostile advances by the Spanish in Florida. It is the oldest English fort remaining on Georgia's coast. Most of the fort was destroyed by fire in 1726. A state visitor center and museum has displays, artifacts, and a film about the fort and early

Staying Planted

The Savannah Airport was built on old farmland and when it needed to expand in the 1980s, the only direction to go included the old Dotson family cemetery. Descendants weren't happy about disturbing those who were supposed to be enjoying eternal rest. Eventually, about 100 graves were moved, but they dug in when it came to relocating the couple who originally toiled the land. Family matriarch and patriarch Richard and Catherine Dotson died in 1884 and 1877 and remain where they were planted. Look closely at the end of runway 10 as you take off and you will see concrete slabs marking their final resting places. Relatives Daniel Hueston and John Dotson's headstones are in the brush nearby.

Georgia life. Open Tues through Sun from 9 a.m. to 5 p.m. Admission is $7.50 for adults, $4.50 for children 6 to 12.

On the way to the fort, you can stop and photograph Darien's shrimp fleet and **St. Cyprian's Episcopal Church** (301 Fort King George Dr.; 912-437-4562; standrewsstcyprians.org), McIntosh County's first black house of worship (1870).

Christ's Memory Chapel, purportedly "America's Smallest Church," was built in 1949 by McIntosh County grocery store owner Agnes Harper, who apparently thought travelers on US 17 needed divine guidance as they traveled the coastal highway between the northeastern United States and Florida. The 10-by-15-foot wooden chapel, with a steeple and imported stained-glass windows, seats 13, just large enough, it's said, to accommodate Christ and his 12 Apostles. It's open to the public daily. Donations are appreciated. Just switch off the lights when you leave. Take I-95 to the US 17/South Newport exit. The chapel is right beside the highway.

Unlike in neighboring states, most of Georgia's barrier islands have remained undeveloped. **Sapelo Island** is the state's fourth largest barrier island. It is accessible only by private boat or the state-run ferry. Because access is limited, you may want to make prior arrangements. The ferry leaves from the Sapelo Island visitor center/museum at the little fishing community of Meridian. On the 30-minute voyage, you'll skirt wavering stands of cord grass and scores of small islets and hammocks.

You can explore on your own or take advantage of tours offered by the Georgia Department of Natural Resources or some enterprising island natives who offer their own personalized trips. Touring the 10-mile-long, 16,000-acre island on a bus or tram, you'll see marine, bird, and animal life in the Sapelo Island National Estuarine Research Reserve (SINERR), the University of Georgia Marine Institute, and the R. J. Reynolds State Wildlife Refuge. You'll also pause at the exterior of the mansion North Carolina tobacco baron Reynolds got when he purchased the island from Hudson Motors executive Howard Coffin during the Great Depression. Naturalists will show you how to seine a flounder, explain some of the mysteries of the marshes, and point out deer, wild turkey, and many species of waterfowl that call the island home. You'll have time to walk the beaches and collect shells. Sapelo Island's historic lighthouse has been restored. About 1 percent of the island is owned by Hog Hammock, a black community of slave descendants who operate a small store with sandwiches, cold drinks, and insect repellent.

DNR tours are conducted year-round Tues through Fri 7:30 a.m. to 5:30 p.m.; Sat 8 a.m. to 5:30 p.m.; Sun 1:30 to 5 p.m. Tickets are $15 for adults, $10 for those 6 to 18; free for children under 6. Sapelo Island Visitors Center is at 1

TOP ANNUAL EVENTS

MARCH

Jekyll Island Arts Festival
Goodyear Cottage
(912) 635-3920
jekyllartists.com/festivals

St. Patrick's Celebration
downtown Savannah
(912) 233-4804
savannahsaintpatricksday.com

Savannah Music Festival
Savannah
(912) 234-3378
savannahmusicfestival.org

Savannah Tour of Homes & Gardens
Savannah
(912) 234-8054
savannahtourofhomes.org

APRIL

Great Golden Easter Egg Hunt
Jekyll Island Historic District
(912) 635-4036
jekyllisland.com

N.O.G.S. Tour of Hidden Gardens
downtown Savannah
gardenclubofsavannah.org

OCTOBER

Sapelo Island Cultural Festival
Sapelo Island
(912) 223-6515
sapeloislandbirdhouses.com

NOVEMBER

Kingsland Catfish Festival
(912) 729-2848
kingslandcatfishfestival.org/

DECEMBER

Christmas in Savannah
Savannah
(800) 444-2427

Historic St. Marys Christmas Tour
St. Marys
(912) 882-4000
visitstmarys.com

Landing Rd., Meridian (912-437-3224; toursapelo.com). *Sapelo Island Tours* (912-506-6463; toursapelo.com) also utilize the ferry, but are run by some island residents who will travel on the ferry with you. They even offer housing if you care to stay overnight.

Hofwyl-Broadfield Plantation State Historic Site (5556 US 17, Brunswick; 912-264-7333 or 800-864-PARK; gastateparks.org) is the last vestige of the rice culture that once flourished along the Altamaha River. Developed by South Carolinian William Brailsford in 1806–1807, the plantation grew to 7,300 acres, largely on the backs of 350 black slaves who labored in hellish conditions of heat and disease. A path takes you by the tabby ruins of the rice mill and along the top of the rice field dikes to the antebellum plantation house, furnished as it was in the early 1970s, when it was willed to the state by the last owner. Open Wed through Sat from 9 a.m. to 5 p.m. Adults, $8; children, $5.

Brunswick & the Golden Isles

"The Golden Isles" are a necklace of lush, subtropical barrier islands snaking languidly along Georgia's 120-mile Atlantic coast. Several of the principal islands are part of Glynn County. Even the most developed islands—St. Simons and Jekyll—are low-key, laid-back, and lightly commercialized compared to other resort islands on the Eastern Seaboard.

Blessed with long stretches of hard-packed beaches, marshes, inlets, rivers, and Spanish moss–veiled live oak trees, the islands are inviting places to get off-the-beaten-path and commune in solitude with unsullied nature.

Brunswick, the Glynn County seat and a center of Georgia's shrimping and fishing industry (population 16,000), is the gateway to St. Simons, Jekyll, Sea Island, and Little St. Simons Island. Chartered in 1771, Brunswick was named for King George II's German ancestral home. Like Savannah, it was laid out on a precise grid of broad, straight streets and public squares named for English places and nobility. Albany, Amherst, Dartmouth, Egmont, George, Gloucester, London, and Newcastle Streets, and Halifax, Hanover, and Hillsborough Squares kept their names after the Revolution. They're in the Old Town National Historic District. Queen Anne, Neo-Gothic, Italianate, Mansard, and Jacobean homes are enhanced by towering live oaks and banks of azaleas, camellias, and dogwoods. Several are charming bed-and-breakfast inns. See "Places to Stay in Coastal Georgia."

Get advance information from the **Brunswick–Golden Isles Convention & Visitors Bureau** (4 Glynn Ave., Brunswick; 912-265-0620, 800-933-2627; goldenisles.com). When you get here, pick up maps and information at the Brunswick–Golden Isles Visitors Center at US 17 and the F. J. Torras/St. Simons Island Causeway. Open daily except holidays from 9 a.m. to 5 p.m. Or visit the Brunswick I-95 Visitors Center, north of the city on I-95.

In downtown Brunswick, the turreted Queen Anne–style City Hall was built in 1883. Around the corner, the Glynn County Courthouse, at Reynolds and G Streets, is a good place to rest a spell. The classical, cupolaed building sits in a botanical garden of moss-draped oaks, Chinese pistachio, magnolia, and swamp trees and flowering shrubbery.

Get off-the-beaten-path and walk the **Earth Day Nature Trail,** a self-guided tour that takes you on wooden boardwalks over a wading-bird habitat. A true hidden gem, you'll also see an osprey/eagle nesting platform and wildlife observation decks. The wavering salt marshes, where your favorite seafood begins its life cycle, was immortalized in Sidney Lanier's 1878 poem "The Marshes of Glynn," which goes in part: ". . . Sinuous southward and sinuous northward the shimmering band of the sand beach fastens the fringe of the marsh to the folds of the land." Lanier was inspired by the same view you'll see from **Marshes of Glynn Overlook Park**. The trail starts at the DNR Coastal Resource Division Headquarters, 1 Conservation Way. Call (912) 264-7218 for information.

If you'd like to go deep-sea fishing or just get out on the open water for a spell, many charter boats are at the Brunswick docks at the end of Gloucester Street. Get information at the Brunswick–Golden Isles Convention & Visitors Bureau.

Jekyll Island

Jekyll Island is connected to Brunswick by a 6-mile causeway and the high-span Sidney Lanier Bridge that allows boats to go under while you head unimpeded for your holiday. You can fish from the remains of the mothballed, nearly 70-year-old adjacent bridge. Stop first at the Jekyll Island Guest Information Center (901 Downing Musgrove Causeway, Jekyll Island; 912-635-9704 or 877-4-JEKYLL; jekyllisland.com). Open daily from 9 a.m. to 5 p.m. On the island, the Jekyll Island Museum Visitors Center (100 Stable Dr.; 912-635-4036, 877-4-JEKYLL; jekyllisland.com) has exhibits on the island's "Millionaires' Era" and carriage tours and Sea Turtle Walks.

Between 1886 and 1942, Jekyll was the winter home of many of America's richest and most famous families. From the Gilded Age until early in World War II, Astors, Pulitzers, Vanderbilts, Morgans, Rockefellers, Cranes, Goodyears, and other aristocrats lived in secluded luxury on their remote Georgia island. Shortly after Pearl Harbor, they boarded up their elegant "cottages" and left the island for the last time.

After the war, the state of Georgia paid $675,000 for the island and turned it into a state park. Although the purchase price now seems a pittance, Governor M. E. Thompson, who championed it, was widely lambasted for what political enemies labeled "Thompson's Folly."

According to the legislation creating the state park, only 35 percent of the island can be developed. That's a blessing for vacationers, who can hike and bike and bird-watch in a wilderness as pristine as when it was created and enjoy amenities the old plutocrats could never have imagined. One side of the island is skirted by nearly 10 miles of hard-packed Atlantic beaches, washed by a usually mild surf perfect for young children and waders and the family dog. A rock wall intended to stop erosion prevents your Fidos from racing off the beach into woods where they're hard to find. Free showers, restrooms, and changing rooms are at regular intervals along the beachfront. Even on the busiest holiday weekends, there's plenty of room to get away from everybody else. The island's mainland side is washed by the Intracoastal Waterway and

130 Years of History

The grand *Jekyll Island Club Hotel* (371 Riverview Dr.; 855-787-3857) was originally built as a hunting retreat in 1886 where the likes of the Rockefellers, the Vanderbilts, and the Astors would come and play away. Since the entire island was purchased by the State of Georgia in 1947, the hotel has gone through several major incarnations. It was fully restored to its splendor in 1987 and today is again considered an exclusive retreat, only now available to the public. The year 2016 was celebrated as not just its 130th anniversary, but the 30th anniversary of the Jekyll Club being open to the public. Guests can dine in the once-exclusive dining room or take part in up to 50 different island activities ranging from golf to horseback riding.

scenic salt marshes. Deer, raccoon, armadillo, wild turkey, and many species of waterfowl roam the marshes, live oak, and pine forests.

Tours of the *Jekyll Island Historic District* start at the Visitors Center. You can see a video presentation about Jekyll's colorful history, and guided tram tours take you inside several of the millionaires' restored cottages. Indian Mound Cottage, Standard Oil director William Rockefeller's shingled Cape Cod–style cottage, has been furnished as it was when the family began wintering here in 1917. You'll probably wonder why there's no kitchen in most of the houses. The Club House, now the Jekyll Island Club Hotel, was the social center, where members gathered for meals, cards, and other activities. Other stops on the tour include Mistletoe Cottage, a Dutch Colonial Revival with a collection of sculpture by noted artist Russell Fiore, a longtime Jekyll resident. Cypress-shingled Faith Chapel is illuminated by Louis Comfort Tiffany and D. Maitland Armstrong stained-glass windows. Jekyll's recreational riches include 63 holes of golf that wind through marshes and woodlands, indoor and outdoor tennis, a fishing pier, marinas, a water slide park and wave pool, rental bikes, picnic grounds, and hiking trails.

Former shop buildings and servants' quarters now house an array of unique shops. Nature's Cottage, built in 1916 for the island's engineer, has hand-carved wooden ducks, bears, birds, and other wildlife. The Servants Dining Hall, from 1900, now sells beautiful sterling silver jewelry and Native American crafts. The Island Design Store, in the 1905 butlers' and valets' dormitory, specializes in casual clothes and decorative arts. For a rainy day at the beach, check out the new, used, and rare books at Jekyll Books and Antiques in the 1890s Furness cottage.

Jekyll hosts more than 100 monitored sea turtle nests, so it's only natural that the *Georgia Sea Turtle Center* (214 Stable Rd.; 912-635-4444;

georgiaseaturtlecenter.org) is available to monitor the turtles and assist in care of turtles throughout the year. Located in the former 1903 power plant, the facility has a museum-style learning center, a state-of-the-art rehabilitation center, and a veterinary clinic. Guided turtle walks are conducted nightly from May through Aug. The center is open daily year-round 9 a.m. until 5 p.m. Adults are $7, seniors $6, and children ages 4 to 12 are $5. Walks are $10 for members and $20 for nonmembers.

To truly explore Jekyll, the Visitor Center also has an Island Treasure hunt year-round (jekyllisland.com/signatureevents/island-treasures). Throughout the year, volunteers called beach buddies hide about 250 plastic globes around the island. If you find one, you can return it to the visitor center and be rewarded with a hand-blown glass globe, commissioned by Jekyll Island.

St. Simons & Sea Islands

The F. J. Torras Causeway takes you to St. Simons Island. The most developed of the four Glynn County "Golden Isles" has seen a big increase in hotels, condos, restaurants, and shopping areas in recent years, but that hasn't dimmed the natural glories of the Manhattan-size island's salt marshes, beaches, and live oak forests wrapped in Spanish moss. You can swim and sunbathe on long strands of beach—all Georgia beaches are public domain—fish, kayak the salt marshes, ride horseback, play golf and tennis, and visit historic sites dating back to the early 18th century.

Fort Frederica National Monument (Frederica Rd., St. Simons Island), at the island's northern end, includes remnants of a tabby fortress the British built in the 1730s as a bulwark against Spanish invaders from Florida. Leading up to the fort are foundations of homes and shops once occupied by 1,500 troops and civilians. The fort was never tested. The Spanish attacked in 1742, and their defeat at the nearby Battle of Bloody Marsh kept England firmly in control of Georgia's coast. Stop first at the National Park Service Visitors Center (6515 Frederic Rd.; 912-638-3639; nps.gov/fofr) for a film and historical displays. Bring insect repellent, and don't step on the fire ant mounds! Those interested in learning about archeology can inquire about the fort's Archaeology Summer Camp held in the park which teaches research, excavation, and lab work. Open daily from 9 a.m. to 5 p.m. Admission is free.

Christ Church, a Gothic wooden sanctuary on the road to Fort Frederica, is the island's most beloved (and most photographed) landmark. The site of services John and Charles Wesley conducted for Frederica's garrison, the original church was built in 1820. Desecrated by Union soldiers, it was rebuilt in 1884 by the Reverend Anson Phelps Dodge, whose life was chronicled by late St. Simons novelist Eugenia Price in *Beloved Invader*. The church is framed by

Ghostly Light

If you stand outside the walls of Christ Church burying ground late at night, you might see a light flickering through the darkness. Legend says a young woman with a terrible fear of the dark was buried there. To ease her spirit, her husband brought a lighted candle to the grave site every night, and long after his own death, the candle still burns.

an arbor of live oaks, dogwoods, and azaleas. The interior is illuminated by stained-glass windows. The church is at 6329 Frederica Rd., St. Simons Island (912-638-8683; ccfssi.org). Open daily, donations are appreciated. Episcopal services are conducted every Sunday.

St. Simons Lighthouse (912-638-4666; coastalgeorgiahistory.org/visit/st-simons-lighthouse) at the island's southern end, has been a landmark since 1872. The present 104-foot brick sentinel—still maintained as an operational beacon by the US Coast Guard—stands on the site of an 1810 lighthouse that was destroyed by retreating Confederate troops in 1861. The old lightkeeper's cottage houses the *St. Simons Lighthouse Museum,* with collections of colonial furniture, shipbuilding tools, and changing exhibits of coastal art. The second floor gives you a sense of how the lighthouse keeper and his family would have lived during the turn of the century in 1900. Open Mon through Sat from 10 a.m. to 5 p.m.; Sun from 1:30 to 5 p.m. The last climb is at 4:30 p.m. Admission for adults is $12; ages 6 to 11 $5; under 6 free.

Neptune Park Fun Zone (550 Beachview Dr.), around the lighthouse, is a place to plunge, putt, and play. There is a waterpark pool open during summer months. Year-round, visitors can enjoy seaside picnic tables, a playground, and steps down to the beach. You can fish from the beach or take a cooler and lawn chair onto the Municipal Pier and angle for flounder and whiting, even pull up a startled hammerhead shark or barracuda. No license is required for saltwater fishing. The pier, lighthouse, and Neptune Park are in The Pier Village, around Mallery Street, the island's original commercial area, where you'll find restaurants, shops, and lodgings. You can even rent a pole at *St. Simons Bait and Tackle* (121 Mallery St.) and try your luck fishing.

Massengale Park (1350 Ocean Blvd.), between the King & Prince Hotel and the Coast Guard Station, offers a shaded area, playground, and easy public access to the beach. The best part is if you are spending the day at the beach, there are bathrooms and showers where you can rinse off.

To learn some of the lesser known historical facts of coastal Georgia, check out the *Historic Coast Guard Station* on St. Simons's East Beach.

Decommissioned in 1995, the station now serves as the **World War II Home Front Museum** (4201 1st St.; 912-634-7098), inviting visitors to learn about the important role Georgia played in WWII. Discover the perils of German U-boats off the Georgia coast in the early days of the war and the ship building efforts in nearby Brunswick. The museum is open Mon through Sat from 10 a.m. to 5 p.m.; Sun noon to 5 p.m. Adults $12; $6 ages 6 to 12.

For information about any sites of activities on the island, contact Golden Islands Visitors Center at 529 Beachview Dr., St. Simons Island; (800) 933-2627; goldenisles.com. The website includes information about all the Golden Isles.

By the time you've made the 20-minute launch crossing from "big" St. Simons to **Little St. Simons Island,** the world's problems will have vanished in the sunlight of another glorious Low Country morning. A fortunate set of circumstances has left the privately-held island—7 miles long by 2 to 3 miles wide—very nearly as nature created it.

Through the 1800s, the 10,000 acres were the domain of one rice planter family. In 1903, a pencil company bought the island, but when the red cedars proved too wind-gnarled for writing instruments, it became an off-the-beaten-path retreat, now open to the public.

Dedicated to the island's conservation, your congenial hosts at **The Lodge** on Little St. Simons Island will put you up in rustic but comfortable, air-conditioned guest rooms and cottages that accommodate up to 32. At mealtime, sit at a communal table and enjoy regional fare, with many vegetables coming from their own organic garden. Things to do are bountiful: sunbathing, swimming in a pool or in 7 miles of wild beaches, boating, canoeing, crabbing, bird-watching, fishing, and walking through forests inhabited by deer, raccoon, armadillos, pelicans, red-tailed hawks, great blue heron, egret, and more than

AUTHOR'S FAVORITES

Bonaventure Cemetery	Midway Church
Breakfast and lunch at Mrs. Wilkes Dining Room	Sapelo Island
	Savannah National Historic District
Cumberland Island National Seashore	St. Simons Island
Isle of Hope	Telfair Art Museum
Jekyll Island	World War II Home Front Museum
Little St. Simons Island	Wormsloe State Historic Site

200 other species of birds. Gators cruise like ironclad vessels in marshes and rivers. All meals and activities are included in expensive double occupancy daily rates. Phone (912) 638-7472 or (888) 733-5774 or visit littlestsimonsisland .com. Write 1000 Hampton River Club Marina Dr., St. Simons Island, 31522.

Neighboring **Sea Island** is another rare coastal gem. Accessible through a gated causeway, only homeowners and guests at the exclusive Cloister Resort are allowed on the island (seaisland.com). Since 1928, the private five-star resort has been known for its private beaches, championship golf and tennis, hunting, fishing, and, of course, relaxing at its world renowned spa.

Cumberland & Crawfish

Cumberland Island National Seashore is an intricate web of nature's rarest, most wondrous gifts. Maintained by the National Park Service, the island—18 miles long and 1 to 2 miles wide—preserves astonishing treasures of marshes and dunes, pristine beaches, live oak forests, lakes, ponds, estuaries, and inlets. "Natives" include great blue heron, wood storks, egrets, and dozens of other bird species, many rarely seen beyond these shores; giant sea turtles, which plod over the beaches to regenerate their endangered kind; fiddler, hermit, and ghost crabs; shrimp, oysters, and flounder; deer, armadillo, mink, wild horses, and wild boar; playful otters; and gators that cruise the waterways like men o' war.

Mankind's 4,000-year habitation began with ancient Timucuan Indians, followed by 16th-century Spanish missionaries, 18th-century British troops, and pre–Civil War indigo and cotton planters. Thomas Carnegie, of the Pittsburgh Carnegies, bought the entire island in the 1880s. His family's splendid estates were mostly abandoned when the Gilded Age gave way to the Roaring Twenties, and high society discovered more fashionable wintering places. With only a few intrusions, the island has passed into public trust largely as it was created.

Truly off-the-beaten-path, unless you own your own boat, the only way to enjoy Cumberland's glories is via a 45-minute ride on the **Cumberland Queen** from St. Marys. With a capacity of 150, the Queen departs St. Marys daily from Mar 1 to Nov 30 at 9 a.m. and 11:45 a.m., arriving at Cumberland at 9:45 a.m. and 12:30 p.m., respectively. The rest of the year, it operates at the same times daily except Tues and Wed. One-way fares are $15 for adults, $14 for those 65 and older, $10 for children 12 and under. If you are bringing your bike, that's another $10. You must check in 30 minutes beforehand or they will cancel your reservations. When you arrive on the island, the National Park Service will collect a $10 per person user fee which can be purchased ahead of time online but remember to bring your confirmation with you. For information and

Nuclear Submarine Base Creates Population Explosion

Since its establishment in 1979, the Kings Bay Nuclear Submarine Base—home port for 8 Trident missile nuclear subs—has mushroomed St. Marys's population from 2,000 to nearly 9,000. A flood of fast-food outlets, video rental stores, and chain stores has grown up on the outskirts, but the historic old town on the St. Marys River is as quaint and unchanged as ever.

reservations, phone (912) 882-4336 or (877) 860-6787 or go to nps.gov/cuis. The NPS visitor center on the St. Marys waterfront is open daily from 8 a.m. to 4:30 p.m. Bear in mind that sailing times are as precise as Swiss trains. If you miss the last ferry from the island, you'll have to hire a boat from St. Marys or Florida's Fernandina Beach.

Campers have a choice of developed and primitive campgrounds available for a small cost, which varies according to the site you choose. *Sea Camp*, 5 minutes' walk from the ferry dock, has bathrooms and showers ($4 per person per day, plus $4 one-time day-use fee); primitive campsites, a 3.5- to 10-mile hike from the dock, have trench latrines and cold water spigots ($2 per person per day, plus $4 one-time day-use fee). If you're a day-tripper, you can walk several nature trails, or swim and sun and view the remains of Dungeness, the Carnegies' fabulous estate destroyed by fire in the 1950s. Park Service rangers lead history and nature walks. There's absolutely nothing at all for sale on the island, so remember to bring food, cold drinks, insect repellent, and sunscreen.

The *Greyfield Inn* (4 N. Second St. #300, Fernandina Beach, FL; 904-261-6408, 866-401-8581; greyfieldinn.com) is Cumberland's only hotel-type accommodation. The late John F. Kennedy, Jr., and his wife, Carolyn, had their wedding reception in the Carnegie family's old Georgian-style mansion after taking their vows at the island's African-American chapel. Staying overnight is a one-of-a-kind experience. Guests sleep in 17 air-conditioned rooms with four-poster beds, bathe in claw-footed tubs, and relax amid family portraits and mementos. All meals, boat transportation from Fernandina Beach, Florida, and walks with naturalists are included in the expensive rates.

Historic and quaint St. Marys is a great place to spend the day strolling. In fact, there's a self-guided Historic Walking Tour that takes you down tree-lined streets, to the St. Marys Peace Garden and along the St. Marys River. The oldest home in town dates to 1801 and has the dubious honor of being where Aaron Burr hid out after his ill-fated duel with Alexander Hamilton. Contact

Aaron Burr Slept Here

After being indicted for murder for killing popular Founding Father Alexander Hamilton in an 1804 pistol duel, US Vice President Aaron Burr fled south, first to Cumberland Island, where he was unwelcome, then to the home of his Princeton law school classmate, Major Archibald Clark, in St. Marys. Mistress Clark reportedly didn't cotton to an accused murderer under her roof, so Burr, who was never tried for Hamilton's death, returned to Washington and resumed his duties as Thomas Jefferson's veep. A bronze plaque on the front of the Clark-Bessant House on Osborne Street (St. Marys's oldest house, 1801) notes Burr's visit and that of Gen. Winfield Scott, who R&R-ed on returning from Indian wars in Florida. The house's current occupants are descendants of Archibald Clark.

the St. Marys Tourism Council at 400 Osborne St., St. Marys; (912) 882-4000; visitstmarys.com.

St. Marys Submarine Museum (102 St. Marys St.; 912-882-2782; stmarys submuseum.com) will tell you everything you ever wanted to know about submarines, with special emphasis on the nuke fish at nearby Kings Bay Submarine Base. You can also see diving equipment, research documents, uniforms, and a re-created sub interior. Looks pretty cozy, eh? Imagine spending several months in these quarters without seeing the surface of the seas you're cruising under. Open Tues through Sat from 10 a.m. to 5 p.m.; Sun from 12 to 5 p.m. Admission is $5, $4 for military and seniors, $3 children 6 to 18.

The **Cumberland Island National Seashore Museum** (113 St. Marys St.; 912-882-4336; nps.gov/cuis) in downtown St. Marys tells the story of the War of 1812's "forgotten invasion." In the early morning hours of January 13, 1815,

The Downside of Spanish Moss

Spanish moss, which isn't a moss at all, but an air plant loosely related to pineapple, hangs in wispy picturesque veils from live oak trees in the southern and coastal parts of the state. It's lovely to look at, but the very devil to touch. Chiggers (aka redbugs) are voracious little pests that make their home in Spanish moss. They enjoy nothing better than feasting on a fresh, tasty smorgasbord of anybody unwary enough to think the moss would be picturesque in a home garden or stuffed in a pillow. Chiggers attack en masse and make you itch and scratch until you think you'll lose your sanity. Modern medications like Benadryl can relieve the torture, but many Southerners prefer old-fashioned remedies like Epsom salt baths, nail polish, and Chapstick. It's best to avoid the scenario altogether no matter how tempting it may be to take some home.

5 days after Andy Jackson's backwoodsmen and Jean Lafitte's French pirates bested the British at New Orleans, effectively ending the war, 600 British sailors landed at Point Peter, a fort guarding St. Marys. They overwhelmed the 130 American defenders in what was the war's belated last battle. Nearly two centuries later, musket balls, uniform buttons, pottery shards, cooking utensils, and other artifacts recovered at Point Peter are on display at the National Seashore Museum. The museum also exhibits artifacts and photos of Cumberland Island's human history, from ancient Timucuan Indians, through the Gilded Era of the Carnegies and the island's acquisition as a national seashore in 1972. The museum is on Osborne Street, a few steps from St. Marys's waterfront. Open daily from 1 to 4 p.m. On Saturdays, it opens at 10 a.m. Free admission.

The **Woodbine Crawfish Festival** takes over the tiny Camden County seat the last weekend of April. The chance to see beauty queens, marching bands, parades, and arts and crafts, and put away mountains of delicious crustaceans—fried, gumbo'd, étoufféed, jambalaya'd, and boiled in savory Cajun herbs—lures crowds from all over the Georgia coast, even down into Florida. Phone (912) 576-3211 or visit woodbinecrawfish.com for information.

Places to Stay in Coastal Georgia

BRUNSWICK

Brunswick Manor
825 Egmont St.
(912) 265-6889
brunswickmanor.com
Moderate
1886 Romanesque mansion with 4 suites and a separate cottage; full breakfast and high tea included

McKinnon House
1001 Egmont St.
(912) 261-9100
(866) 261-9100
mckinnonhousebandb.com
Inexpensive to moderate
Restored Queen Anne mansion with three guest rooms; full breakfast and afternoon refreshments

JEKYLL ISLAND

The Beachview Club
721 N. Beachview Dr.
(912) 205-5826
beachviewclubjekyll.com
Moderate
Oceanfront resort with 38 rooms, on-site restaurant; pool

Jekyll Island Club Hotel
371 Riverview Dr.
(912) 635-2600
(844) 201-6871
jekyllclub.com
Expensive
134 guest rooms and suites with first-class comforts

Villas by the Sea Resort
175 N. Beachview Dr.
(912) 635-2521
(800) 841-6262
villasbythesearesort.com
Moderate to expensive
160 1- to 3-bedroom villas with fully equipped kitchens; full conference center

SAVANNAH

Bed & Breakfast Inn
117 W. Gordon St.
(912) 238-0518
savannahbnb.com
Moderate
Pair of 1835 Federal-style townhouses have 15 guest rooms, a garden suite, and 2 cottages; full Southern breakfast included

The Brice
601 E. Bay St.
(912) 238-1200
(877) 468-1200
bricehotel.com
Moderate
121-room hotel in former Coca-Cola bottling plant; full restaurant and bar; pool and gardens

Foley House
14 W. Hull St.
(912) 232-6622
(800) 647-3708
foleyinn.com
Expensive
1896 Victorian townhouse has 19 guest rooms; continental breakfast, afternoon tea, and cordials included

The Gastonian
220 E. Gaston St.
(912) 232-2869
(800) 322-6603
gastonian.com
Expensive
Pair of 1869 townhouses offer 17 guest rooms; gourmet breakfast included

Mansion on Forsyth Park
700 Drayton St.
(912) 238-5198
mansiononforsythpark.com
Moderate
1890s redbrick mansion with 125 guest rooms; on-site restaurant, cooking school, lounges, pool, and spa

The President's Quarters
225 E. President St.
(912) 233-1600
presidentsquarters.com
Moderate to expensive
Boutique hotel in twin-towered 1855 mansions offers 16 spacious suites; breakfast included

ST. MARYS

Crooked River State Park
6222 Charlie Smith Sr. Hwy.
(800) 864-PARK or (912) 882-5256
gastateparks.org/crookedriver
Inexpensive
Campsites and 11 cottages, pool, fishing areas, and playgrounds

Goodbread House Bed and Breakfast
209 Osborne St.
(912) 882-7490
goodbreadhouse.com
Inexpensive to moderate
1870s Victorian B&B offers 6 guest rooms with private baths; full breakfast included; wine social in afternoon

Riverview Hotel
105 Osborne St.
(912) 882-3242
riverviewhotelstmarys.com
Inexpensive to moderate
Historic riverfront inn; on-site restaurant and bar

Spencer House Inn
200 Osborne St.
(912) 882-1872
(888) 840-1872
spencerhouseinn.com
Inexpensive
1872 National Register House features 14 rooms with private baths; full breakfast included

ST. SIMONS ISLAND

Epworth by the Sea
100 Arthur Moore Dr.
(912) 638-8688
epworthbythesea.org
Inexpensive
223 modern motel rooms and 12 family apartments; Methodist conference center, spiritual retreat, and vacation center; no alcohol or unmarried couples allowed

The Grey Owl Inn
1602 Denmere Rd.
(912) 434-6292
(800) 870-3736
greyowlinn.com
Moderate
B&B with 5 full suites; cook-to-order breakfast and high tea, followed by wine and cheese included

**King & Prince Beach
& Golf Resort**
201 Arnold Rd.
(912) 638-3631
(800) 342-0212
kingandprince.com
Expensive
Deluxe, full-service resort
offers guest rooms and
suites, oceanfront cabanas,
and 2- and 3-bedroom
villas; indoor pool, spa,
restaurants and bars, tennis
courts, and golf privileges at
nearby courses

**St. Simons Inn
by the Lighthouse**
609 Beachview Dr.
(912) 638-1101
stsimonsinn.com
Moderate
Thirty-four modern guest
rooms; pool; continental
breakfast included

Village Inn and Pub
500 Mallory St.
(912) 634-6056
(888) 635-6111
villageinnandpub.com
Moderate
Restored 1930s beach
cottage with 28 rooms;
breakfast included; in-room
massages available

TYBEE ISLAND

**Lighthouse Inn Bed
& Breakfast**
16 Meddin Dr.
(912) 786-0901
(866) 786-0901
tybeebb.com
Expensive
1910 beach house offers
3 guest rooms with private
entrances; full breakfast
included

Tybee Island Inn
24 Van Horne St.
(912) 786-9255
(866) 892-4667
tybeeislandinn.com
Moderate
Restored 1902 B&B with 7
rooms, each with its own
bath

Places to Eat in Coastal Georgia

BRUNSWICK

Indigo Coastal Shanty
1402 Reynolds St.
(912) 265-207
indigocoastalshanty.com
Inexpensive
Seafood

Jinright's Seafood House
2815 Glynn Ave.
(912) 265-1590
jinrightsseafoodhouse.com
Inexpensive to moderate
Southern, seafood

JEKYLL ISLAND

The Grand Dining Room
Jekyll Island Club Resort
371 Riverview Dr.
(912) 635-5155
Expensive
Fine dining

Tortuga Jack's
201 N. Beachview Dr.
(912) 342-2600
Tortugajacks.com
Moderate
Baja-style Mexican

Zachry's Riverhouse
Jekyll Harbor Marina
1 Harbor Rd.
(912) 319-2174
zachrys-riverhouse
.business.site
Moderate
Seafood and cocktails

SAVANNAH

Alligator Soul
114 Barnard St.
(912) 232-7899
alligatorsoul.com
Moderate
Southern, soul food; dinner
only

Belford's
315 W. St. Julian St.
(912) 233-2626
belfordssavannah.com
Moderate to expensive
Seafood and steaks

Garibaldi Cafe
315 W. Congress St.
(912) 232-7118
garibaldisavannah.com
Moderate to expensive
Seafood, pasta, and steaks

Goose Feathers Café
39 Barnard St.
(912) 233-4683
goosefeatherscafe.com
Inexpensive
Sandwiches, soups, and
salads

The Lady and Sons
102 W. Congress St.
(912) 233-2600
ladyandsons.com
Moderate to expensive
Southern

Lulu's Chocolate Bar
42 Martin Luther King Jr.
Blvd.
(866) 462-8681
luluschocolatebar.com
Inexpensive to moderate
Dessert and cocktails

**Mrs. Wilkes
Dining Room**
107 W. Jones St.
(912) 232-5997
mrswilkes.com
Inexpensive
Southern, served
family-style

The Olde Pink House
Reynolds Square,
23 Abercorn St.
(912) 232-4286
theoldepinkhouserestaurant
.com
Expensive
Fine dining, Southern

Six Pence Pub
245 Bull St.
(912) 233-3151
sixpencepub.com
Inexpensive to moderate
British pub fare

ST. MARYS

Riverside Cafe
106 W. Saint Marys
(912) 882-3466
riversidecafesaintmarys
.com
Inexpensive
American and
Mediterranean

ST. SIMONS ISLAND

Barbara Jean's
214 Mallery St.
(912) 634-6500
barbarajeans.com
Inexpensive to moderate
Southern and Seafood

Bennie's Red Barn
5514 Frederica Rd.
(912) 638-2844
benniesredbarn.com
Moderate to expensive
Seafood and steaks

Crab Daddy Seafood Grill
Ocean Boulevard
(912) 634-1120
crabdaddyseafoodgrill.com
Moderate to expensive
Seafood

Del Sur Artisan East
321 Mallery St.
(912) 638-1223
delsursaintsimons.com
Moderate to expensive
Argentinian and Italian

Sandcastle Café
117 Mallery St.
(912) 638-8883
sandcastlessi.com
Inexpensive to moderate
American

SUNBURY

Sunbury Crab Company
541 Brigantine-Dunmore
Rd.
(912) 884-8640
sunburycrabco.com
Inexpensive
Seafood

TYBEE ISLAND

AJ's Dockside
1315 Chatham Ave.
(912) 786-5434
ajsdocksidetybee.com
Inexpensive
Seafood

The Crab Shack
40A Estill Hammock Rd.
(912) 786-9857
thecrabshack.com
Inexpensive
Seafood

Fannie's on the Beach
1613 Strand Ave.
(912) 786-6109
fanniesonthebeach.com
Inexpensive
Seafood

Marlin Monroes
404 Butler St.
(912) 786-4745
marlinmonroessurfsidegrill
.com
Moderate
Seafood

North Beach Grill
41A Meddin Dr.
(912) 786-4442
northbeachbarandgrill.net
Inexpensive to moderate
Southern, Caribbean

Spanky's Beachside
1605 Strand Ave.
(912) 786-5520
spankysbeachside.com
Inexpensive
Seafood

Northeast Georgia

Depending on which direction you've pointed your hiking boots, the 2,015-mile *Appalachian Trail* either begins or ends with 79 miles of northeastern Georgia mountainland. Many AT veterans acclaim the Georgia section as the most beautiful in all the 14 states between here and Mount Katahdin, Maine.

The AT's southern terminus is atop 3,782-foot *Springer Mountain,* in Dawson County, 75 miles northeast of Atlanta. An 8-mile approach trail begins at Amicalola Falls State Park. There hikers can camp out, get their gear together, and have their packs weighed by park rangers.

From Springer Mountain the AT's Section I is a 22.3-mile easy-to-strenuous hike to GA 60 at Woody Gap. Section II, 10.7 miles from Woody Gap to Neels Gap, has just one long uphill stretch and is popular with one-day and weekend hikers. At Neels Gap, the trail crosses US 19/US 129 and goes "indoors" as it passes through a covered breezeway of the *Mountain Crossing/Walasi-Yi Center.* At this stone-and-log legacy of the 1930s Civilian Conservation Corps, hikers can get trail information and replenish supplies of dehydrated foods and camping gear, do their laundry, and enjoy a hot shower.

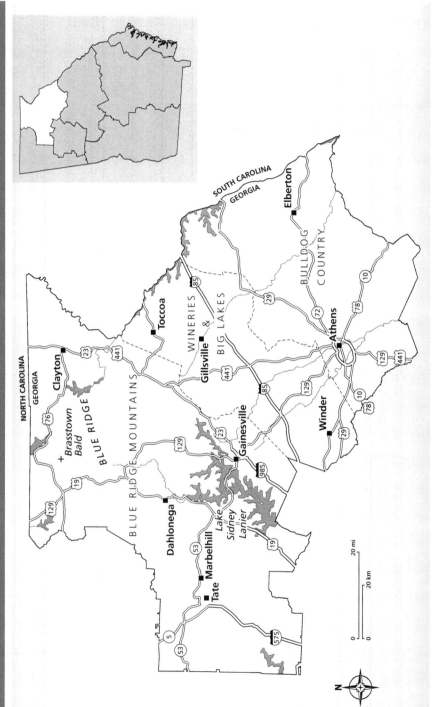

NORTHEAST GEORGIA

NORTHEAST GEORGIA'S TOP HITS

Alpine Helen	Hart State Park
Amicalola Falls State Park	Lake Chatuge
Anna Ruby Falls	Lake Lanier Islands
Appalachian Trail	Lake Rabun Hotel/Rabun Beach Recreation Area
BabyLand General Hospital	
Black Rock Mountain State Park	Lake Winfield Scott Recreation Area
Bobby Brown State Park	Mark of the Potter
Brasstown Valley Resort	Moccasin Creek State Park
Château Élan Winery & Resort	Northeast Georgia Folk Pottery Museum
Chattahoochee National Forest	Oconee Cultural Arts Foundation
Chattooga River rafting	Old Sautee Store/Stovall Covered Bridge
Crawford W. Long Museum	Richard B. Russell State Park
Dahlonega Courthouse Gold Museum	Richard B. Russell-Brasstown Scenic Highway
Elachee Nature Science Center	Tallulah Gorge State Park
Elberton Granite Museum	Travelers Rest
Georgia Guidestones	Tugaloo State Park
Fort Yargo State Park	Unicoi State Park
Foxfire Museum	University of Georgia
Georgia Mountain Fair	Victoria Bryant State Park
Georgia Mountains Museum	Vogel State Park

Motorists stop by for mountain handicrafts and short hikes on the trail. Phone (706) 745-6095 or (888) 689-4647 or log on to mountaincrossings.com. Open daily from 9 a.m. to 5 p.m.

From Walasi-Yi, Section III is a moderately difficult 5.7 miles to Tesnatee Gap on the Richard Russell Scenic Highway (GA 348). Sections IV–VI carry the trail upward and onward. At Bly Gap, near the Rabun County/Towns County border, you bid adieu to Georgia and cross into the North Carolina Great Smokies. Mount Katahdin, here we come!

Blue Ridge Mountains

In Georgia's far northeast corner, up against the North Carolina and South Carolina borders, Rabun County is the heart of the state's dramatically rugged **Blue Ridge Mountain** country. About 80 percent of the county is included in national forests and state parks. Outdoor adventures range from tranquil trout fishing in mountain streams, canoeing, swimming, off-the-beaten-path hiking, and browsing for handmade crafts at country stores to the ultimate heart-pounding adventure: **Chattooga River rafting.**

Until the early 1970s, when Jon Voight, Burt Reynolds, and the rest of the *Deliverance* movie crew let the world in on the secret, the Chattooga River was the remote domain of mountain folk along the Georgia–South Carolina border. Nowadays daredevils come from early spring through late fall to test their courage against the river's steep sluices, whirlpools, and roller-coaster rapids. To see that they accomplish their missions safely, the US Forest Service licenses professional outfitters to conduct the trips, which are made in sturdy 6-person rubber rafts and are led by guides who know every rock and rill along this tempestuous waterway.

Outfitters offer a variety of Chattooga experiences. Beginners usually test their wings on Section III, a 7-hour, 6-mile ride that sweeps them through many of the *Deliverance* landmarks. At lunchtime guides pull a small deli out of their waterproof packs and spread the feast at the foot of a waterfall.

Section III is a mere warm-up for "The Ultimate Challenge," the Chattooga's wild and woolly Section IV. Suggested only for well-seasoned white-water hands in top physical condition, this rip-snorting 7-hour cruise carries you through swiftly moving currents; steep, wooded gorges; up and over, down and around such potential perils as Seven Foot Falls, Corkscrew, and Jawbone. At day's end, the Chattooga finally turns you loose, into the peaceful waters of Tugaloo Lake.

For those who really want to get to the heart of the river, outfitters offer 2-day trips, which include overnight camping, a steak dinner, and a bountiful breakfast. Some packages offer the option of lodgings at rustic inns and cabins.

Day trips on Section III are about $105, $110 higher on weekends. For Section IV, figure on paying around $120, $150. You'll be supplied with all the necessary equipment and transportation to and from river access points. You'll also get a briefing on paddling techniques and safety rules, expert guide service, lunch, and a place to shower and change clothes at the end of your ride. Choices includes traditional rafting, canoeing, or kayaking. Half-day trips are also offered. Contact Nantahala Outdoor Center at (828) 786-4855, noc.com;

Bald Peanuts

A drive through the mountains is your chance to experience an indigenous culinary treat. You'll catch the savory aroma of boiled peanuts as you approach roadside stands and country stores, where the goobers are boiling in brine in big iron kettles. Some of the tastiest are billed as "balled," "bald," "biled," or "bolled." City slickers and other greenhorns pry open the mushy shells and pluck out the soft, salty fruit with their fingers. Real fans eat the shell and all. Like grits and chitlins, it's an acquired taste, but once a convert, you're a fan for life.

Wildwater Limited at (866) 319-9970, wildwaterrafting.com; and Southeastern Expeditions at (800) 868-7238, southeasternexpeditions.com.

If the Chattooga sparks memories of *Deliverance*, **Lake Rabun,** near the little town of Tallulah Falls, may remind you of the film *On Golden Pond*. Ringed by the soft green humps of the Blue Ridge Mountains and unpretentious summer cottages, some dating back to the 1920s and 1930s, this small, off-the-beaten-path lake is the embodiment of peace and quiet.

Built in 1922, the **Lake Rabun Hotel** is the perfect complement to the lake. The wood-and-stone lodge has 13 themed rooms and two separate cottages. The award-winning restaurant offers seasonal farm-to-table fare in a rustic lodge dining hall, or if weather permits, one of the decks among the woodlands. The Lake Rabun offers rare tranquility and hospitality that draw guests back year after year. In the evenings you can sit by the flagstone hearth, play parlor games, swap tips on local eateries and "secret" waterfalls, and store up energy for the next day's boating, fishing, and hiking. Doubles, with breakfast, are inexpensive. Contact Lake Rabun Hotel at 35 Andrea Ln., Lakemont; (706) 782-4946 or (800) 398-5134; lakerabunhotel.com.

Ask a local where to rent fishing boats and canoes and they'll send you next door to the hotel to Hall's Boat House, although the name changed long ago to **Rabun Boat House** (1897 Lake Rabun Rd.; 706-782-4981; rabun boathouse.com). **Lake Rabun Road,** which twists and turns about 15 miles between US 441 near Tallulah Falls, to GA 197, is a very scenic drive. It curves around Lake Rabun and Seed Lake, with many lovely vistas of the water and woodlands. During the summer **Rabun Beach Recreation Area** (5315 Lake Rabun Rd., Lakemont; 706-782-3320; fs.usda.gov) is a relaxing place to swim, have a picnic, and enjoy boating, hiking, and fishing. Campsites have electrical and water hookups. Hike the Angel Falls trail up from the beach and treat yourself to not one, but two cascading waterfalls. **Angel Falls** and **Panther**

Falls are both multi-tiered cascades along Joe Branch Creek, with a trail that is almost as beautiful as the falls themselves.

Local artists are showcased at the **Lakemont Gallery** on Historic Old 441 (8538 Old 441 South, Lakemont; 706-212-0440; lakemontgallery.com). Housed in the restored Lakemont Lodge building built in 1910, the gallery is open Fri and Sat. The gallery contains paintings, wood crafts, pottery, photography, furniture, and home décor and gifts.

The Rabun County Visitors Bureau and Welcome Center (232 US 441 North, Clayton; 706-782-4812; gamountains.com) can give you further tips on off-the-beaten-path outdoor adventures.

It may be difficult to imagine now, but early in the 20th century, **Tallulah Falls** was one of the South's most popular summer resorts. Honeymooners, families, and other nature-loving city folk came to admire the cataracts of the Tallulah River, which stormed through a gorge 820 feet across and more than 1,200 feet deep. All that ended in the early 1920s, when a series of hydroelectric dams diverted water from the falls but at the same time created Lake Rabun, Lake Burton, and other recreational areas.

Tallulah Gorge State Park invites hikers to explore the depths of the 1,000-foot-deep gorge. The parks department and Georgia Power Company periodically open the floodgates and allow kayakers to experience the falls' glorious power. The 2,700-acre park area has a fishing pier and picnic tables on the Tallulah River. Exhibits explain Georgia Power's conservation efforts. Fifty campsites have water and electrical hookups. Phone (800) 864-PARK for reservations. If you'd like to hike the gorge, you'll need to register, free of charge, at the Jane Hurt Yarn Interpretive Center, which has exhibits on the gorge's plant and animal life and a film on the gorge's fascinating ecology. For general information, contact Park Superintendent at 338 Jane Hurt Yarn Dr., Tallulah Falls; (706) 754-7981 or (800) 864-7275; gastateparks.org/TallulahGorge. You must have a park permit (it's free) to go to the floor of the gorge. The most strenuous hike takes you down 400 steep metal stairs to a suspension bridge swaying 80 feet above the river and rocky floor. Another 200 steps go the rest of the way down to the bottom of the gorge. Bring plenty of water and stop for breathers and views of the gorge, the river, and waterfalls. Depending on your physical fitness, going back up can seem 2 or 3 times as far. A bit of trivia: 1930s actress Tallulah Bankhead was named for the gorge by her grandparents, who vacationed at the resort in its heyday. There's a $5 parking fee.

Tallulah Overlook on the Tallulah Gorge Scenic Loop is a prime location for a free look at the gorge. A store that had stood there for more than 100 years was forced to move in 2020. Now called **The General Store at Tallulah Falls** (940 Tallulah Gorge Scenic Loop; 706-754-4318; tallulahpoint.net),

Where Wallenda Walked on Air

On July 18, 1970, 65-year-old Karl Wallenda walked across Tallulah Gorge. While 35,000 spectators held their breath, the patriarch of the Flying Wallendas trapeze family stepped onto a thin steel cable strung 700 feet across the 1,200-foot-deep gorge. Balancing a 36-foot pole, he did a pair of handstands before reaching the other side. He earned $10,000 for his 18 minutes of fame, which set a new record for cable height.

His luck and pluck ran out on March 22, 1978, when he fell to his death from a cable between two hotels in San Juan, Puerto Rico. You can read about his feat at Tallulah Point Overlook on Historic US 441 in the town of Tallulah Falls (706-754-6040; tallulahfallsgeorgia.org).

Just up the highway, the Jane Hurt Yarn Interpretive Center at Tallulah Gorge State Park has a display on Wallenda's walk, with his gold-fringed powder blue costume. In 2012, his grandson Nik Wallenda wowed the world by walking a tightrope across a bigger gorge, the one above Niagara Falls.

the store has traded the view for an old-fashioned front porch where you can enjoy an RC Cola and a Moonpie. It still offers the wide variety of old-time general store fare of vintage candies and toys, as well as hiking guides, cabin accessories, souvenirs, and locally made goodies.

When you want to take a break from exploring, stop by **Main Street Grill & Barbeque** (110 Main St.; 706-838-1445; facebook.com/MainStreetGrill Barbeque) where they serve up inexpensive 'Que and burgers for lunch and dinner daily.

If you've read the Foxfire books and magazines or would like to learn more about the vanishing Appalachian Mountain culture, plan a visit to the new **Foxfire Museum and Heritage Center** complex (98 Foxfire Ln., Clayton; 706-746-5828; foxfire.org), up a mountain road from the old museum on US 441. (If you're not familiar with the Foxfire books, they chronicle research by students who scour the mountains to preserve elements of the old, isolated mountain lifestyle.) The complex's more than 20 log structures include an authentic 1820s one-room home that raised three generations; "dog trot" cabins; a chapel; animal barns; a folk art museum; and complete gristmill, blacksmith shop, and working craft shops, where classes are held. The Zurow Wagon is the only existing wagon known to have taken Cherokees to Oklahoma on the 1830s Trail of Tears. The visitor center/gift store sells Foxfire books and handmade Appalachian crafts. You can take a self-guided tour or a guided tour with a group of 6 or more. Motor homes and other large vehicles can't negotiate the steep, winding mountain road. Call ahead and someone will come and pick you up on the highway. Open Mon through Fri 8:30 a.m. to 4:30 p.m. Self-guided tour, $10 for adults, $8 for seniors, students $8, $3 for ages 7 to 10, 6 and under free.

Beechwood Inn Bed & Breakfast (220 Beechwood Dr., Clayton; 706-782-5485; beechwoodinn.ws) is one of mountain country's best inns and dining and wining experiences. Transplanted Californians David and Gayle Darugh pride themselves on their gourmet dinners which are matched with wines from Georgia and the couple's native Napa and Sonoma. Gayle was even national president of the American Wine Society. Cooking classes and wine tastings are offered, and package plans are offered for golf, winery tours, white water rafting, and other activities. On a terraced wooded rise overlooking Clayton and the mountains, the 100-year-old former country home has eight tastefully appointed guest rooms and suites with private baths, balconies, porches, and working fireplaces as well as two cabins. Full breakfast is included in moderate to expensive rates.

Two scenic state parks in Rabun County offer a wealth of incredible scenery, outdoor activities, and overnight lodgings. ***Black Rock Mountain State Park*** was named for its sheer cliffs and dark-colored metamorphic rocks. The park is 1,700 acres of brawny beauty atop a 3,600-foot elevation of the Blue Ridge Mountains. It includes an 18-acre lake, many miles of wooded nature trails, waterfalls, 10 cabins, and 44 campsites with electrical and water hookups and kitchens. Contact Park Superintendent: Black Rock Mountain, 3085 Black Rock Mountain Pkwy., Mountain City; (706) 746-2141, (800) 864-PARK; gastate parks.org/BlackRockMountain.

The much smaller ***Moccasin Creek State Park,*** on Lake Burton, is perfect for boating and fishing. It has a boat ramp and docks, a trout hatchery, hiking trails, and 55 campsites. For reservations, phone (800) 864-PARK. Contact Park Superintendent at Moccasin Creek State Park, 3655 GA 197, Clarkesville; (706) 947-3194; gastateparks.org/MoccasinCreek.

For 12 days every August, the normally unhurried Towns County seat of ***Hiawassee*** (population 900) throbs with the energy of the ***Georgia Mountain Fair.*** Against a backdrop of Blue Ridge Mountains, forests, and blue-green Lake Chatuge, the fair takes Hiawassee and the rest of Georgia's "Little Switzerland" literally by storm.

The fairgrounds resound with the music of bluegrass fiddlers, gospel singers, clog dancers, and some of the very big names of the country music entertainment world. Scores of craftspeople show off their skills at woodworking, pottery, cornshuck and applehead dolls, painting, leatherwork, furniture and toy making, jewelry, basket weaving, needlework, quilting, and macramé.

Pioneer Village is like a walk through a mountain town of yesteryear. You can peruse the canned goods and bolt cloth in the mercantile store, see the hickory switch in the 1-room schoolhouse, visit the smokehouse, and stop in at the hand-hewn log cabin. Elsewhere on the 42-acre grounds, you can enjoy midway rides, taste just-pressed apple cider, and see a "moonshine" whiskey still up close. "Revenooers" keep a close guard against any free samples. You can even bring your RV or pitch a tent at the campgrounds located at the fairgrounds. For information contact Georgia Mountain Fair: 1311 Music Hall Rd., Hiawassee; (706) 896-4191; georgiamountainfairgrounds.com.

The fairground area is surrounded by stunning *Lake Chatuge,* a 7,500-acre Tennessee Valley Authority reservoir and a tranquil retreat for trout and bass anglers, water-skiers, swimmers, and boaters. Several marinas and public boat docks offer easy access to the lake. You'll also find picnic grounds, tennis courts, a sand beach, playgrounds, and camping sites at the 160-acre *Towns County Park* on the lakeside. In fact, if you visit the fairgrounds, you can bring your RVF or pitch a tent and just walk over for the festivities. Contact Lake Chatuge Recreation Area at (706) 896-2914; fs.usda.gov.

Hamilton Gardens is a 33-acre botanical paradise right on the lake in Hiawassee. There are 33 acres with color blooming year-round. Garden trails take you past dogwoods, azaleas, 1,500 rhododendrons, and a host of native wildflowers such as trout lilies, trillium, and shooting stars. An outdoor pavilion plays host to local musicians so you can enjoy music with a natural backdrop. Located at 96 Pavilion Road, Hiawassee; (706) 970-0011; hamiltongardens.org. It is open 8 a.m. to 8 p.m. Admission $2. No pets and no smoking.

The *Chattahoochee National Forest* blankets much of Towns County with Georgia pines and hardwoods. Sections of four national wilderness areas in the county afford you the opportunity to get well off the beaten track. During certain times of the year, the Appalachian Trail, crossing Towns County near Brasstown Bald Mountain, gets downright busy as hikers test their stamina on the 2,000-mile Maine-to-Georgia route described at the beginning of this chapter.

Brasstown Bald Mountain is Georgia's highest point at 4,784 feet. A steep, winding road off GA 180 takes you to a parking area a half mile from the top, where you'll find restrooms and a gift shop. You can hike the paved, moderately strenuous trail to the visitor center and observation platform, or take a shuttle van, $3 per person round trip. From here, on a clear day you can see four states: Georgia, Tennessee, South Carolina, and North Carolina. There's a $5 parking fee in the lot. Be sure your car is up to the task before heading up the mountain. Many a vehicle has been left overheated and steaming by the roadside. The mountaintop is closed in inclement weather.

If you are up for a hike, you can follow the 5.5-mile Arkaquah Trail from the crest of Trackrock Gap and the less strenuous 2.5-mile Jack's Trail Knob to the foot of Brasstown. Wagon Train Road meanders 6 miles to a pastoral valley that cradles the pretty town of Young Harris and the campus of Young Harris College.

On Friday nights the **Rollins Planetarium** at Young Harris College (1 College St.; 706-379-4312; yhc.edu) offers a unique look at the stars and planets through its GOTO Space Simulator Star projector. If the skies are clear, the roof opens to allow free telescope viewings.

A short drive from Brasstown Bald Mountain, the **Nottely River Campground** offers a relaxing retreat with fun for the whole family. The secluded campground offers tent and RV sites as well as 4 furnished cabins from which to choose. Fishing, swimming, hiking, and tubing are available on site. The campground is located at 3832 Gainesville Hwy., Blairsville; (706) 745-6711; notteleyrivercampground.com.

Brasstown Valley Resort (6321 US 76 East, Young Harris; 706-379-9900 and 800-201-3205; brasstownvalley.com), opened in 1995 on a scenic 503-acre Blue Ridge mountainscape, has all the upscale resort bells and whistles: 102 attractively appointed guest rooms in the 4-story main lodge and 32 adjacent cottages; 18-hole, 7,000-yard Scottish links–style golf course; and tennis, horseshoes, trout fishing, horseback riding, indoor/outdoor pool, fitness center, and full-service restaurant and lounge. It's a great place to roost for a while and an excellent base while sightseeing in the surrounding mountain lands. Lodge rooms and cottages are moderately to expensively priced.

Deer Lodge, a hideaway near the junction of GA 66 and I-75, is another heaven-sent place to park awhile and savor the glories of the mountains. In business for almost 50 years, hospitable proprietors Richard and Willene Haigler serve some of the biggest, best, and lowest-priced steaks and trout anywhere in these parts. Contact Deer Lodge: 7466 GA-17/I-75, Hiawassee; (706) 896-2181. Open for dinner Wed through Sun.

The **Richard B. Russell-Brasstown Scenic Highway,** in White and Union Counties, takes you through the heart of some of northeastern Georgia's most spectacular mountain country. Designated as GA 348, the 14-mile paved highway takes you from the outskirts of Georgia's "Alpine Village" of Helen, across the Appalachian Trail, to the state's highest mountain and a picture-perfect state park. Several parking areas and overlooks give you the chance to stop and admire the rugged beauty of the Blue Ridge Mountains. The winding, twisting drive is especially striking in mid-Oct to early Nov, when the hardwoods turn a brilliant orange, yellow, and scarlet. Keep your eye out for motorcycles. It's a favorite road for day tripping cyclists.

TOP ANNUAL EVENTS

APRIL

Bear on the Square Mountain Festival
Dahlonega
(706) 864-7817
bearonthesquare.org

Southworks Arts Festival
Watkinsville
(706) 769-4565
ocaf.com

MAY

Mountain Laurel Festival
Clarkesville
clarkesvillega.com
(706) 778-4654

JUNE

Blairsville Highland Games
Blairsville
(706) 745-2161
blairsvillescottishfestival.com

**Helen-to-Atlantic Hot Air Balloon
Race and Festival**
Helen
(706) 878-2271
helenballoon.com

SEPTEMBER

Oktoberfest
through Oct
Festhalle, Helen
(706) 878-2271
helenchamber.com/helen/oktoberfest

OCTOBER

Georgia Mountain Fall Festival
Hiawassee
georgiamountainfairgrounds.com
(706) 896-4191

Gold Rush Days
Dahlonega
dahlonegajaycees.com/gold-rush

Mule Camp Market
Gainesville
(770) 532-7714
gainesvillejaycees.org

Sorghum Festival
Blairsville
(706) 745-4745
blairsvillesorghumfestival.com

NOVEMBER

Toccoa Harvest Festival
Toccoa
(706) 282-3269
mainstreettoccoa.com/harvest-festival

Alpine Helen Winter Festival
through Jan
Helen
(706) 878-3300
winterfestartstour.org

Old Fashioned Christmas
through Dec
Dahlonega
(706) 864-3513
dahlonegachristmas.com

One of the Scenic Highway's "high points" is 3,137-foot Tesnatee Gap, where the Appalachian Trail crosses on its way between Maine and Springer Mountain, Georgia. You can get out of your car here and mingle a while with the earnest hikers. At its northwestern end the Scenic Highway intersects with GA 180. If you turn right, you can explore 4,784-foot Brasstown Bald. A steep, paved road ends at a parking area 930 feet below the summit. From here either hike to the crest of Georgia's highest peak or take a commercial van up to the view of four states.

A left turn at GA 180 will lead you to US 19 and *Vogel State Park.* Cradled in mountains, it is beside a pretty lake. Located at the base of Blood Mountain, the 233-acre park was one of the state of Georgia's first two parks when the state park system was created in 1931. Vogel is a delightful place for fishing, boating, warm weather swimming, and year-round hiking on woodland trails. The park's 103 campsites have electricity, water, hot showers, and restrooms; 34 rustic but very snug cottages, by the lake and in the adjacent woodlands, are equipped down to sheets, towels, pots, and pans. For reservations, phone (800) 864-PARK. The park also has a $5 one-time parking fee. The park office is open from 8 a.m. to 5 p.m. Contact Vogel State Park at 405 Vogel Park Rd., Blairsville; (706) 745-2628, (800) 864-PARK; gastateparks.org/Vogel.

GA 180, which joins US 19 north of Vogel Park, is a 22-mile scenic mountain route to the little community of Suches. Along the way take the time to stop at *Sosebee Cove Scenic Area* (706-745-6928; fs.usda.gov). This easy half-mile loop trail crisscrosses Wolf Creek and takes you through a second-growth forest with wildflowers, rhododendron, and a boulder field. Farther along, *Lake Winfield Scott Recreation Area* (770-747-3816; fs.usda.gov) is a favorite for mountain campers. It has a 32-acre, 36-campsite campground with showers and an 18-acre man-made fishing and swimming lake. There is a $5 parking fee for noncampers. A large furnished cabin rents for a 2-night minimum.

Habersham County claims some of northeast Georgia's most photogenic Blue Ridge Mountain country. These mountains and valleys, thousands of acres of Chattahoochee National Forest, and scores of lakes and streams offer limitless opportunities to take a hike, ride a bike, camp out, and fish, swim, and otherwise unwind.

Habersham is one of Georgia's major apple producers. Rich soil and a cool climate encouraged English and Canadian families to initiate the apple-growing arts here in the 1920s. In October, roadside stands overflow with Red Delicious, Stayman Winesaps, dark red Yates, and bright yellow-green Granny Smiths. You can buy 'em by the sackful or the carload and also purchase homemade apple jelly, apple butter, and ice-cold, freshly squeezed sweet apple cider by the glass and gallon jugful.

The Big Red Apple, in front of the old train depot in downtown *Cornelia,* is a tribute to Habersham County's apple industry, which saved the local economy that had been nearly decimated after boll weevils ruined the cotton crop. Weighing in at about 5,200 pounds, the 7-foot-tall Grande Pomme, with a 22-foot "waist," has defied winds, rains, worms, and schoolboy vandals since its dedication in 1926.

Elvis fans who've been to Graceland and think they've seen it all may think again after seeing Joni Mabe's Panoramic Encyclopedia of Everything Elvis at the **Loudermilk Boarding House Museum** (271 Foreacre St., Cornelia; 706-778-2001). An Athens artist, Mabe's 30,000-piece collection includes hundreds of photos, show posters, newspaper and magazine articles, and souvenirs in varying degrees of taste and two rarities: Mabe found the "Maybe Elvis Toe-nail" in the shag carpeting at Graceland and acquired the "Elvis Wart" from Presley's dermatologist, who removed it before the King was inducted into the army. "The Big E Celebration," honoring his August death anniversary, is the Loudermilk Museum's big day (bigefest.com). Impersonators croon his big hits and toast his memory with his favorite food, fried peanut butter and banana sandwiches. You almost have to be reminded that all of this is held in a historic home built in 1908 and on the National Register of Historic Places. Self-guided tours Fri and Sat, 10 a.m. to 4 p.m.; other times by appointment. Closed during winter months. Admission is $10.

Clarkesville, Habersham's snug little county seat, was established in 1823. It is a happy hunting ground for antiques and mountain handicrafts. The Visi-tor's Center is located in a large Victorian house called the Mauldin House at 458 Jefferson. The property includes a millinery shop and The Big Holly Log Cabin. A walking tour takes you past quaint houses and historical churches. Several shops around the courthouse square on US 441 are loaded with hand-crafted furniture, pottery, paintings, weaving, leatherwork, handmade baskets and quilts, toys, dolls, jellies, jams, and preserves.

The **Glen-Ella Springs Hotel** (1789 Bear Gap Rd., Clarkesville; 706-754-7295; glenella.com) sits on 17 pastoral acres between Clarkesville and Tallulah Falls. Owners Ed and Luci Kivett manage the 100-year-old, 16-room country inn, which is full of rustic touches and modern conveniences. In warm weather, enjoy the outdoor swimming pool and explore the 12-acre meadow or hike the creek path. All the rooms have porches with rocking chairs, antiques, and heart-pine paneling. Some have fireplaces and whirlpools. The dining room features fresh mountain trout but varies from traditional mountain fare with veal dishes, pasta, scallops, fresh fish, and other American/continental entrees. Doubles are moderately to expensively priced, including full breakfast.

North 40 Lodge (15702 GA 197 North; 706-947-1075 or 800-379-6170; north40lodge.com) is a true gem. Just a mile from Lake Burton, each of the cozy rooms has its own fireplace and kitchen. The largest has 3 bedrooms. Innkeepers Jinger and Bobby Blackburn keep the lodge open year-round so you can explore the 12-acre property in all seasons. A continental breakfast is included, but Bobby is also known for his smokehouse goods. Inexpensive.

GA 197, twisting and turning north between Clarkesville and Clayton, is considered one of north Georgia's prettiest drives. Nine miles north of Clarksville, the **Mark of the Potter** (9982 GA 197, Clarkesville; 706-947-3440; markofthepotter.com) has been a favorite stop for mountain visitors for a half a century. The weathered old white frame corn-grinding mill, by the rapids of the Soque River, sells some of the finest work of Georgia's most accomplished craftspeople. Shelves are laden with superb pottery, colorful fabrics, metal, and leatherwork.

Browsing will inevitably take you onto the porch overhanging the Soque to throw treats to the fat, pampered trout swimming in the river's pools. Mark of the Potter is open daily.

South of Clarkesville, the little town of **Demorest** (cityofdemorest.org), on US 441, is worth a visit. Founded in 1889 as a private venture by the Demorest Home, Mining & Improvement Company, it is home to the state's longest running Fourth of July festivities. A couple of antiques shops, an art museum, and a bookstore/coffee shop are on the short main street. You can also stroll through the peaceful campus of Piedmont College.

When your children pose that age-old question—"Where do babies come from?"—take them to **Cleveland** and show them. At Cleveland's 70,000-square-foot **BabyLand General Hospital** (300 N. O. K. Dr., Cleveland; 706-865-2171; cabbagepatchkids.com), some very special "babies" come from a cabbage patch.

The soft-sculpted **Cabbage Patch Kids** were created by White County's own Xavier Roberts. Uniformed "nurses" lead you through the nursery, day-care center, and delivery room. At the magic moment, a "doctor" in surgical garb plucks a newborn Kid from a patch of sculpted cabbage leaves to "oohs" and "aahs" all around. So much detail goes into this "event" that you may find yourself doing some 'splainin' to young children about what the term "Mother Cabbage is dilated" means. You can take home a cuddly Cabbage Patch Kid of your very own. Just remember, they're "babies" not "dolls"; not "bought" but "adopted." The "hospital" is open Mon through Sat from 9 a.m. to 5 p.m.; Sun from 10 a.m. to 5 p.m. Free admission.

If the sheer granite escarpments of **Mount Yonah,** off I-75 north of Cleveland, get your rock-climbing juices flowing, make plans to scale the heights with nearby commercial outfitters **Wildwood Outfitters** (26 Megan Dr., Cleveland; 706-865-4451; wildwoodoutfitters.com). They will put you in the proper climbing gear and send you up Yonah's 150- to 300-foot cliffs with experienced guides. In addition to being a popular hiking destination, Mount Yonah is also one of Georgia's best and most popular hang-gliding points.

Driving up to the rustic-looking **Old Sautee Store** (2315 GA-17, Sautee; 706-878-2281; sauteestore.com), you might imagine an old-time mercantile stocked with bolts of cloth, seeds, farm implements, and sacks of cornmeal. After greeting the big-nose Norwegian troll on the front porch, inside you'll see a small museum's worth of yesteryear merchandise. Farther along you'll be tempted by high-quality sweaters and jackets, caps, gloves, T-shirts, cheeses, jams and jellies, specialty foods, and gifts. The adjacent Old Sautee Market is a cozy deli with sandwiches, salads, coffee, cookies, and cold drinks. The store and market are open Mon through Fri 11 a.m. to 5 p.m.; Sat 11 a.m. to 5:30 p.m.; Sun 11:30 a.m. to 5 p.m.

Around the US 17/GA 255 junction you can also browse a Native American store, a furniture and home accessories store, and other businesses. The nearby **Northeast Georgia Folk Pottery Museum** (283 GA 255, Sautee-Nacoochee; 706-878-3300; snca.org/fpm/home.php) illuminates two centuries of pottery making by Georgia's mountain artists. The 3,200-square-foot exhibition hall is a centerpiece of the Sautee-Nacoochee Center, a former mountain school that houses a local history museum, art studio, gallery, and theater. Constructed of heavy timbers with soaring windows overlooking the Sautee-Nacoochee Valley's rolling countryside, the Folk Pottery Museum features farm churns, kitchenwares, and other utilitarian pottery, as well as face jugs and other decorative pieces by such acclaimed pottery makers as the Meaders, Hewell, and Ferguson families and newer generations of pottery artists. The museum is open Mon through Fri from 10 a.m. to 5 p.m.; Sat and Sun noon to 5 p.m. Admission is $5 for adults, $4 for seniors, $3 for students, and $2 for children; children under 5 are free.

Michael Crocker, who was instrumental in the museum's creation—his large pottery piece is in the lobby—is one of more than 30 artists with studios on the **Folk Potters Trail of Northeast Georgia.** For information on the trail, visit the Folk Pottery Museum's website. A half hour south at Crocker's studio (6345 W. County Line Rd., Lula; 770-869-3160) you can watch him create face and snake jugs, vases, pots, and utilitarian wares and take home the finished products. He's open Mon through Fri from 9 a.m. to 5 p.m.; Sat by appointment.

Pottery is a family affair for the Crockers, as Michael's brothers Dwayne and Melvin, and their mother Pauline, all create museum-quality work. Michael even has pieces in the Smithsonian. **Dwayne Crocker's studio** is 10 minutes away in Gillsville (6717 Diamond Hill Rd.; 678 316-3146; crockerfolkpottery.com).

With a population of only 250, Gillsville seems to be a full-on pottery town with artisans whose families have been throwing clay since the early 1900s. Potters here pride themselves on their unique face and snake vases. Drive down Highway 52 and you'll also find **Hewell's Pottery,** known also for its terracotta and bent hickory furniture (6035 GA-52; 770-869-3469; hewellspottery.com);

Craven Pottery, known for terracotta and statuary (6616 GA-52; 770-869-3675; cravenpottery.com); and the seventh-generation potters of *Ferguson Family Pottery* (6468 GA-52).

You can spread a picnic by the *Stovall Covered Bridge,* in a small park by Chickamauga Creek on GA 255, between Helen and Batesville. Only 33 feet long, it's the shortest covered bridge anywhere in Georgia and legend has it—it's haunted. If you dare to go at night, you may hear horse-drawn carriages crossing or babies crying.

The *Stovall House* (1526 GA 255 North, Sautee; 706-229-4434; stovall house.com) is one of the nicest country inns anywhere in the state. Built in 1837, the handsome 2-story frame house is in the heart of the scenic Sautee-Nacoochee Valley. Five guest rooms are decorated with country antiques and all the modern comforts. The dining room features Southern and continental cooking and is one of the best anywhere in the mountains. For pure, sweet relaxation, settle yourself into a porch swing and listen to the absolute peace of this lovely countryside. Moderate rates; all rooms with private bath and breakfast.

GA 255 intersects with US 17, which cuts a most picturesque path through the Sautee-Nacoochee Valley as it meanders westerly toward Helen. You may want to stop for a picture—or attend Sunday services—at *Crescent Hill Baptist Church,* on a wooded hillock near the intersection of US 17 and GA 75 (hrga.org/crescent-hill-baptist). The pretty Carpenter Gothic church with its green roof and shutters was built in the 1870s by Captain James Nichols, the same well-off gentleman who built the grand Victorian house and gazebo atop the Indian mound at US 17 and GA 75. Now known as the *Hardman Farm* (gastateparks.org/HardmanFarm), you can tour the grand Italianate house and the dairy barn.

Going north on combined US 17/GA 75, stop off at *Nora Mill Granary & Store* (706-878-3275; noramill.com). Founded in 1876 on the banks of the Chattahoochee River, the mill's current owners still grind corn into meal and grits in the tried-and-true old-fashioned way. You can watch it being ground and take home a sackful. It's open daily. Free.

Habersham Winery, across GA 75 from Nora Mill, is one of Georgia's oldest and largest wine producers. In their attractive red-roofed wineshop (7025 S. Maine St.; 706-878-9463; habershamwinery.com), you can free-sample their many varieties, which have won 150 national and international awards. Shop for your favorite gourmet foods and wine accessories in the gift shop. It's in Nacoochee Village, a half mile south of Alpine Helen (nacoocheevillage.com). This fun group of shops allow you to browse for antiques, fishing, and boating gear, as well as enjoy lunch and dinner at the Nacoochee Grill.

Don't try to pinch yourself awake as you drive by the WILKOMMEN signs of **Alpine Helen** (helenga.org). You haven't wandered onto a Disney film set. In an effort to boost tourism back in 1969, this then-humble mountain logging hamlet underwent a wholesale transformation into a make-believe Alpine village. Nowadays, the red-tile roofs, flower boxes, biergartens, and stuccofronted shops selling cuckoo clocks, Christmas ornaments, Tyrolean hats, and loden coats put the once-quiet village very much on the well-beaten path. Outlet stores, with all the usual suspects, are amassed on the south end of town.

Like it or disdain it, Helen's worth at least a short stroll and a browse. The many inns and "hofs" around town are good bases for more off-the-beaten-path adventures, such as the Appalachian Trail, Richard B. Russell-Brasstown Scenic Highway, white-water rafting, and Chattahoochee National Forest. In trout season, you can don your waders and cast in the Chattahoochee River, which rises near here and wends its bonny way through the middle of town.

More Blue Ridge than Bavarian, **Betty's Country Store** (18 Yonah St., Helen; 706-878-2943; bettysinhelen.com) on the north end of town, has grown into a full-blown supermarket. The modern store with some rustic ambience is loaded with jams and jellies, fresh vegetables, gourds, cookbooks, canned goods, cheeses, fresh meat and fish, gourmet coffee, apple cider, and other goods. The quality is unsurpassed, and the family-owned business makes sure it stays that way.

Hofer's of Helen (8758 N. Main St.; 706-878-8200; hofers.com) fits tongue-in-groove with Helen's Bavarian motif. Walk in the door and you'll be intoxicated by the aromas of fresh-baked breads, cakes, cookies, and strudels. In the cozy dining room, treat yourselves to Belgian waffles with maple syrup and whipped cream, Alpine French toast, and a variety of bountiful omelets; the lunch menu includes bratwurst and sauerkraut, German-style meat loaf, smoked pork chops, and grilled and deli sandwiches. Breakfast and lunch daily.

At **Troll Tavern** (8590 Main St., Helen; 706-878-3181; trolltavern.com) sit on an outdoor terrace by the Chattahoochee River and watch the tubers float gently through Helen. The menu includes bratwurst, smoked pork chops, chicken, fish, deli sandwiches, Mexican and Italian food, German beer, and wine. Lunch and dinner are served daily.

If you've never made it to Munich for Oktoberfest, **Helen** has a scaled-down replica. In mid-September through October, the town's Festhalle pavilion resounds to oompah bands and thousands of folk-dancing feet. After a lager or two, you'll be out on the floor flapping your arms to the hypnotic beat of "The Chicken Dance." In late October and early November, the mountain hardwoods change their colors as brilliantly as those in New England, making this an especially worthwhile time to visit. It's also prime season for freshly pressed apple cider and boiled peanuts. Simmered in brine in huge iron kettles, the goobers are warm, salty, sticky, and a special mountain delicacy that not everyone goes for, but that should at least be experienced. Contact the Helen Chamber of Commerce at 1074 Edelweisee Strasse, Helen; (706) 878-1908; helenga.org.

Unicoi State Park, just north of Helen, is a treat that everyone can enjoy. With 1,050 acres of highlands and woodlands, threaded by streams, lakes, and waterfalls, there's plenty of off-the-beaten-path solitude. Swimming, canoeing, ziplining, and fishing focus on a picture-postcard 53-acre lake. You can take solitary walks on 12 miles of trails and take part in nature walks led by park naturalists. The handicraft shop in the *Unicoi Lodge* (unicoilodge.com) sells an array of beautiful items. Craftspeople share the secrets of pottery, quilting, dulcimer and furniture making, and other mountain arts. Also in the lodge, you'll find the cafeteria-style dining room which serves excellent breakfast, lunch, and dinner at extremely low prices.

The park's other accommodations include 82 camping sites, with water, electricity, nearby showers, and restrooms; and 30 2- and 3-bedroom, completely furnished cottages. For reservations, call (800) 864-7275. Contact Park Superintendent: 1788 GA 356, Helen; (706) 878-2201, (800) 864-PARK; unicoistatepark.org.

The double cascading *Anna Ruby Falls* are the awesome showpiece of a 1,600-acre Chattahoochee National Forest recreation area that neighbors Unicoi. You actually get there by going through Unicoi. From the parking area follow a moderately strenuous half-mile trail through the woodlands bordering a swift-flowing stream. An observation platform sits at the base of Anna Ruby's two cascades, which drop dramatically 153- and 50-feet over the edge of Tray Mountain. Back at the parking area, restore your energy with a picnic by the water's edge. A handsome visitor center has an excellent gift shop and general store. Sit on the porch and toss treats to some of creation's fattest trout. A Trail for the Blind identifies trees and plants in Braille. There is a $5 per car parking fee.

The *Lodge at Smithgall Woods* (61 Tsalaki Trail, Helen; 706-878-3087 or 800-864-7275; smithgallwoods.com), west of Helen, is a peaceful counterpoint to the hyper Alpine village. In 1994 north Georgia publisher Charles Smithgall made his pristine 5,600 acres of woodlands and streams a gift-purchase to the state. Although it's administered by the state park system, the similarities to other parks are few. Virtually no car traffic is allowed. All visitors must sign in at the Visitor's Center and shuttle in. Mountain bikers can use 12 miles of improved roads. On the Martin's Mine Historic Trail, hikers can stop at the site

> ## "Thar's gold . . ."
>
> "Thar's gold in them there hills," was purportedly first shouted in 1849 by civic-minded M.F. Stephenson of the Dahlonega Mint, who was trying to discourage miners from abandoning the northeast Georgia hills for the newer and richer gold fields of California.

of an 1893 gold mine, with a 125-foot-deep shaft and a 900-foot-long tunnel. Guests have full access to 4 miles of Dukes Creek catch-and-release trout fishing, rated in the top 100 in the country by Trout Unlimited. In order to give everybody casting room, only 15 anglers are allowed on the creek at the same time. The $5 parking pass is the only charge.

Overnight guests stay in 6 deluxe cottages, including Charles Smithgall's former Montana lodgepole pine retreat. Nudged alongside Dukes Creek's rushing waters, some cottages have porches and others have hot tubs. The staff prepares 3 full meals daily, with wine. Rainbow and brown trout, fresh from the creek, are the kitchen's tour de force. Naturalists lead waterfall and wildflower hikes. Double occupancy rates include all meals and activities. Open daily, it's located at I-75-Alt, 3 miles west of Helen, and just south of the Richard B. Russell Scenic Highway (GA 348).

The Nacoochee Valley gets its name from a Native American version of *Romeo and Juliet*. According to legend, Cherokee Princess Nacoochee fell in love with a warrior from an enemy tribe. Her father captured the suitor and had him executed. In her grief, Nacoochee leaped to her death from Mount Yonah on the western end of the valley. Some say her tearful laments can still be heard on moonlit nights.

In 1828, a trapper named Benjamin Parks allegedly stubbed his toe on a rock in **Dahlonega** and shouted the Georgia version of "Eureka!" as he gazed at a vein of gold that soon sent prospectors streaming into these hills. Dahlonega is from the Cherokee Indian word "tahlonega," meaning "golden," and until the Civil War, the substance flowed into a major US Mint right here. Although it's no longer a major industry, enough gold is still mined here to periodically re-leaf the dome of Georgia's state capitol building and intrigue visitors who pan for it at reconstructed camps. The Dahlonega-Lumpkin County Visitors Center (13 S. Park St., Dahlonega; 706-864-3711 or 800-231-5543; dahlonega.org) on the square has restrooms and information on anything you could possibly be interested in.

True to its heritage, the ***Dahlonega Courthouse Gold Museum State Historic Site*** (1 Public Sq., Dahlonega; 706-864-2257 or 800-864-PARK;

gastateparks.org/DahlonegaGoldMuseum) in the center of the little town of 6,000, chronicles the gold rush and the numerous mines that flourished in these parts. A 28-minute film upstairs in the old courtroom is especially worthwhile. Operated by the Georgia Department of Natural Resources, the Gold Museum is open Tues through Sat from 9 a.m. to 5 p.m.; Sun 10 a.m. to 5 p.m. Admission is $8.50 for adults, $8 for seniors, and $6 children 6 to 18; free for children 5 and under.

Buildings around the square have a rustic frontier look. Shops purvey gold-panning equipment, ice cream, fudge, mountain handicrafts, gold jewelry, and antiques. Many people make the 70-mile drive north from Atlanta just to feast at the famous **Smith House** (84 S. Chestatee St., Dahlonega; 706-867-7000 or 800-852-9577; smithhouse.com), serving up deliciousness since 1899. The Smith House puts out huge family-style spreads with fried chicken, chicken and dumplings, beef stew, shrimp, numerous vegetables, biscuits, relishes, and dessert for a moderate price. They also serve breakfast and have a cafeteria line for those not up to the full board. It's open daily except Mon. If you're planning to spend the night, you can stay close to the chow line in the Smith House Inn's 16 guest rooms, all with private baths as well as a separate carriage house. Inexpensive to moderate.

The **Dahlonega Square Hotel and Villas** (135 N. Chestatee St.; 706-426-5276; dahlonegasquarevilla.com) offers a perfect place to stay in the heart of town. The hotel itself is in a modernized 1880s clapboard style home. Enjoy wine tastings in the spacious parlor. It has 12 rooms and a suite. The hotel maintains separate villas if you are looking for more space.

Gold Rush Days, the third weekend of October, celebrates the gilded heritage with arts and crafts, clog dancing, and lots of bluegrass fiddling and singing. You can pan for gold and gemstones year-round at **Crisson's Gold Mine** (2736 Morrison Moore Pkwy., Dahlonega; 706-864-6363; crissongoldmine .com). You'll feel some of old Benjamin Parks's excitement and might even whoop out "Eureka!" when you spot a few grains gleaming amid the mud in your pan.

You can also take a guided walk 200 feet underground through the tunnels of the old **Consolidated Mine** (706-864-8473; consolidatedgoldmine.com). In the early 1900s it was the largest and richest gold mine in the eastern United States. It went mysteriously bankrupt in 1906, and much of the old equipment is still in place. Open daily 10 a.m. to 5 p.m. Adults $18, ages 3 to 12 $12, and that includes free gold panning. Located off GA 60, 3.7 miles south of Dahlonega. Dahlonega is a popular gateway to the northeastern Georgia mountain vacation areas. From here, US 19 snakes north toward Vogel State Park, while other roads aim toward Helen, Cleveland, and Amicalola State Park.

If off-roading it your thing, then **Iron Mountain Resort** (116 Iron Mountain Pkwy.; 706-216-7275; ironmountainresort.com) is the place for you. Located just off Hwy. 9 on the way to Amicalola, Iron Mountain has more than 150 miles of off-road trails on 4,300 acres of rolling land that are GPS mapped. You can bring your own vehicle or rent ATCVs or UTVs for the day and roam to your heart's content. There is also camping available. Open Fri through Mon.

If you've been paying attention as you drive around, you've noticed there's a whole lot of rock in northern Georgia. But it's not just rock. In a lot of places, it's marble—really fine, high quality marble. In fact, the two little towns of **Tate** and **Marblehill** are located in what is known as **Marble Valley** and have over a century of marble quarrying history. Drive along Highway 53 which connects the two and you will see quarry after quarry. Tiny Tate has a historic district listed on the National Register of Historic Places. The stunning Etowah pink marble **Tate House** (61 Georgia Marble Rd.; 770 735-3122; tatehouse.com) was built by the Colonel Samuel Tate, son of the founder of the Georgia Marble Company, Stephen Tate. It's open for special events and weddings. The **Tate School** is the only marble elementary school in the US.

Marble from the Georgia Marble Company (founded 1884) was used in the Lincoln Memorial. You can learn all about it at the **Marble Museum** in neighboring Nelson (1985 Kennesaw St., Nelson; 770-735-2211). Each October, the annual **Marble Festival** (georgiamarblefestival.com) features tours of the quarries.

Amicalola Falls State Park and the **Appalachian Trail approach trail** are a scenic half-hour drive from Jasper, in neighboring Dawson County. The 400-acre park, centered on a majestic 729-foot waterfall, has hiking trails above and below the falls, picnic areas, fishing, campsites—with electricity, water, hot showers, and restrooms—and 14 furnished cottages with fireplaces. The rustic-contemporary mountaintop **Amicalola Falls Lodge** has 56 guest rooms with spectacular views and all the modern comforts. For reservations phone (800) 864-PARK or visit gastateparks.org/AmicololaFalls. Contact the park at 418 Amicalola Falls Lodge Rd., Dawsonville; (706) 344-1500. The Appalachian Trail is described at the beginning of this chapter.

As its name suggests, the secluded **Len Foote Hike Inn** (706-265-4703 or 800-581-8032; hike-inn.com), operated by Georgia State Parks, is accessible only by a moderately strenuous 5-mile hike through woodlands and hilly terrain that begins at Amicalola Falls State Park. Twenty rooms with bunk beds open onto a wraparound porch. A common room looks east into a spectacular sunrise. The sustainably built inn furnishes bed linens and towels, rib-sticking family-style meals, trail lunches, and snacks. Rooms have no electrical outlets,

TVs, or phones. In fact, if they see you talking on your phone, you may be asked to put it away. It's all about unplugging here. Inexpensive.

The mountain may not have come to Muhammad, as the old saying goes, but in 1957, an inland sea came to northeastern Georgia's Hall County. The US Army Corps of Engineers closed the Buford Dam on the Chattahoochee River and created Lake Sidney Lanier (known to most as Lake Lanier). Nowadays about 25,000 of the lake's 38,000 acres and some 380 miles of its green and hilly 550-mile shoreline cover former Hall County farmlands and forests.

Lake Lanier Islands were developed by the state on wooded hilltops that bobbed above the water after the dam was closed. Now, there are not one, but two water sports themed resorts which help offer just about any activity imaginable from miniature golf and championship golf to horseback riding and all kinds of rental boats, such as houseboats, pontoon boats, sport boats, ski boats, sailboats, fishing boats, and paddleboats. *The Legacy Lodge at Lanier* includes a world class spa to help you pamper yourself.

The islands' 300 lakeside campsites are equipped with water, electricity, and some sewer hookups. Campers also have their own fishing pier, outdoor pavilion, and boat launch ramp. For reservations, phone (770) 932-7200 or (800) 840-5253 or go to lanierislands.com.

Song writer Jimmy Buffet recently put his touch on the resort by creating *Margaritaville at Lanier Islands Beach and Waterpark*. The complex is divided into a Family Fun Park, which is more laid back; Paradise Beach that includes a massive wave pool, heart-thumping waterslides, a lazy river, foam parties, and a zip line; or the Land Shark Beach Cove for beach chilling and food and drink. Admission is $47.99 for adults and $33.99 for children 42 inches and under; children 2 and under are free. There are also day passes for use of the beach. Open daily 10 a.m. to 8 p.m. For information, contact Lake Lanier Islands at 7650 Lake Lanier Pkwy., Lake Lanier Islands; (470) 323-3440; margaritavilleresorts.com/margaritaville-at-lanier-islands.

Gainesville, the Hall County seat (population about 43,200; Hall County, 205,000), is a popular gateway to northeastern Georgia vacationlands. The local Hispanics who work in the city's poultry industry have fostered a number of Latino cafes, stores, a Spanish-language radio station, and other amenities. Before heading for the hills, enjoy a leisurely stroll through the *Green Street Historical District.* The wide, tree-lined thoroughfare, also designated as US 129, holds a wealth of late 19th- and early 20th-century Victorian and neoclassical Revival residences. Learn more from Gainesville-Hall County Convention and Visitors Bureau at 230 E.E. Butler Pkwy., Gainesville; (770) 532-6206; ghcc .com.

The Scent of Lavender

Nothing is more relaxing than the scent of lavender and the largest lavender farm in Georgia is just outside Dahlonega. You could almost follow your nose to find it! Over 3,000 lavender plants grace the garden area at *Red Oak Lavender Farm & Shop* (28822 Red Oak Flats Rd.; 706-974-8230; redoaklavender.com). You can pick your own in season, take lavender growing classes, or stroll through their gift shop.

Also in the Green Street Historical District, the *Quinlan Visual Arts Center* (514 Green St. Northeast, Gainesville; 770-536-2575; quinlanartscenter.org) shows the works of state, regional, and national artists. The Quinlan presents more than half a dozen special exhibits annually, showcasing realism, folk art, abstracts, landscapes, still life, portraits, photography, and other forms. Classes are offered in several fields. It's open Mon through Fri from 9 a.m. to 5 p.m.; Sat 10 a.m. to 4 p.m. No charge for admission, but there is a suggested donation of $10.

Gainesvillians don't have to go to Atlanta for live theater. The *Gainesville Theatre Alliance* (3820 Mundy Mill Rd., Oakwood; 770-718-3624; gainesville theatrealliance.org) produces four annual plays at Brenau University and Gainesville State College from Feb through Nov. They include fully staged comedy, drama, children's plays, and musicals.

The *Northeast Georgia History Center* (322 Academy St., Gainesville; 770-297-5900; negahc.org) features a permanent exhibit that details the history and culture of Northeast Georgia. One of the most popular exhibits is the "Ed Dodd Room," dedicated to the Gainesville native son who created the "Mark Trail" comic strip adventurer. You'll also see excellent displays on Native Americans, black history, textiles, Gainesville's vital poultry industry, spinning, weaving, pioneer life, and the April 1936 tornado that devastated downtown Gainesville and killed more than 200 people. Open Wed through Sun 10 a.m. to 4 p.m. Admission is $6 for adults, $5 for seniors and students, $3 for children.

Elachee Nature Science Center (2125 Elachee Dr., Gainesville; 770-535-1976; elachee.org) is a great place to get lost in the woods for a while and learn something about the world around us. Located on the heavily wooded, 1,500-acre Chicopee Woods Nature Preserve, Elachee's many fascinating experiences include please-touch fish, amphibians, reptiles, and a 300-gallon trout tank. The interactive computer and contemporary music–enhanced "If Everyone Lived Like Me" exhibit looks at the effects of our lifestyles on our environment. The Chicopee Woods Nature Preserve includes 13 miles of nature trails and

Chicopee Lake, where you can take a close look at animal and plant habitats. Check their schedule for special activities like "Raptor Fest." Open Mon through Sat from 10 a.m. to 5 p.m. Admission is $5 for adults, $3 for children ages 2 to 12.

The *Interactive Neighborhood for Kids* (I.N.K.) (999 Chestnut St., Gainesville; 770-536-1900; inkfun.org) is a wonderful place for small fry and big fry to climb on a 1927 LaFrance fire truck and a pretend train, make pottery, look at X-rays in the Radiology Department, delve into a book in the library, and spend a day doing a lot of other fun, educational things. It's open Mon through Sat from 10 a.m. to 5 p.m.; Sun 1 to 5 p.m. Admission is $9, free for ages 2 and under.

If you enjoy unusual monuments, bring your camera to *Poultry Park,* where a rooster atop a 25-foot granite obelisk hails Gainesville's distinction as "Poultry Capital of the World." Some 2.6 million broilers leave here every week for kitchens around the world. It can be found at the intersection of Jesse Jewel Parkway and Academy Street.

A Big Rabbit commemorates a time when the small community of Rabbittown on the north side of Gainesville owed its livelihood to the commercial farming of bunnies. In 1993 residents of the "Hoppin' Little Place" chipped in for the 20-foot stone rabbit that waves a hospitable "Howdy" in front of the *Rabbittown Cafe* (2415 Old Cornelia Hwy.; 770-287-3695), which serves first-rate Southern breakfast, lunch, and dinner daily. Open 5:30 a.m. until 10 p.m. daily except Sun when they close at 2 p.m. The *Rabbittown Celebration,* Saturday the week before Easter, starts with breakfast at the cafe, followed by an Easter parade, Easter egg hunt, gospel singing, and clog dancing.

An off-the-beaten-path side trip and step back in time is a visit to *Maysville.* Going west on the Hwy. 92/Maysville Rd. exit on I-85 north of Gainesville, you'll find yourself charmed by this well-preserved little community. The 192 buildings in the downtown Historic District helped it get listed on the National Register of Historic Places. The oldest building dates to 1869. Once a thriving town, the economy collapsed with the stock market in 1929, leaving the town like a time capsule.

Jaemor Farm Market (5340 I-985/GA 365, Alto; 770-869-3999; jaemor farms.com) is the one-stop place for Georgia apples, peaches, pumpkins, sweet potatoes, green vegetables, melons, jams and jellies, folk art, furniture, flowers, seeds, bedding plants, gifts, and souvenirs. It's open daily year-round but in the fall has a huge corn maze to delight and confound.

Wineries & Big Lakes

Created by US Army Corps of Engineers impoundments of the Savannah River, **Lake Hartwell** is a vast inland sea whose 55,000 acres offer limitless off-the-beaten-path opportunities for fishing, boating, swimming, and nature hikes. You can headquarter at 2 state parks on the lake and play another park's 9-hole golf course. While meandering the green, hilly back roads of Hart, Stephens, and Franklin Counties, you can rest awhile at an 18th-century stagecoach inn and reminisce with old-timers who still remember baseball's "Georgia Peach," Ty Cobb.

Hart State Park (330 Hart Park Rd., Hartwell; 706-376-8756 or 800-864-PARK; gastateparks.org/Hart) spreads 417 acres along the lakeshore. Set up housekeeping in 61 camping sites, with utility hookups, adjacent restrooms, and showers, and in furnished cottages. Enjoy swimming, boating, waterskiing, hiking, and fishing for largemouth bass, bream, black crappie, walleye, pike, and rainbow trout.

Tugaloo State Park, on a wooded peninsula jutting into Lake Hartwell (1763 Tugaloo State Park Rd., Lavonia; 706-356-4362, 800-864-PARK; gastate park.org/Tugaloo) is a prime fishing tournament location because of another mother lode of bass and other fish fry favorites. Non-fisherfolk can play tennis and miniature golf, swim, and water-ski from a sand beach, and hike and bike on trails threading through the woodlands. Lodgings include 20 furnished cottages, 6 yurts, and 113 tent and camper sites.

After driving all day, are you tantalized by thoughts of a round of golf, a swim, maybe some late-afternoon fishing? **Victoria Bryant State Park** (1105 Bryant Park Rd., Royston; 706-245-6270, 800-864-PARK; gastateparks.org/VictoriaBryant) may be the answer to your search. The park's 5,421-yard, 18-hole course is hardly a monster, but clusters of Georgia pines, hills, and plenty of water hazards will keep you on your toes. Rental clubs and pull carts are available at the clubhouse, which also has showers, changing rooms, and a snack bar.

Nongolfers can enjoy the swimming pool and angle for bass, bream, and catfish in stocked ponds. The park's 35 camping sites have utility hookups, with access to restrooms and showers.

The **Ty Cobb Museum** (461 Cook St., Royston; 706-245-1825; tycobb museum.org), in his hometown of Royston (population 2,500), honors baseball legend Tyrus Raymond "Ty" Cobb. From the early 1900s to the 1920s, the "Georgia Peach" was one of Major League Baseball's most exceptional players. While he led the Detroit Tigers to American League and World Series championships, his fierce competitiveness earned him a lifetime batting average of

.367, the highest in baseball history. He won a record 12 batting titles, hit safely 4,191 times, scored a major-league-record 2,245 runs, and stole 892 bases.

He may have been ruthless on the field, but Cobb was a humanitarian. He helped fund the Cobb Memorial Hospital in Royston, dedicated to his parents, and the Cobb Health Care System, with facilities in three northeast Georgia counties. The museum, in the *Joe A. Adams Professional Building,* exhibits vintage photos, artwork, uniforms, and equipment, and a film with rare action footage and interviews. Open Mon through Fri from 9 a.m. to 4 p.m.; Sat 10 a.m. to 4 p.m. Adults $7, seniors $5, students $4, ages 5 and under and military free.

In the 1830s and 1840s—more than a century before Ty Cobb headed to the majors—travelers enduring the bone-jarring stagecoach trip through the northern Georgia wilderness took solace in the thought that by and by they'd reach **Travelers Rest** (4229 Riverdale Rd., Toccoa; 706-886-2256, 800-864-PARK; gastateparks.org/TravelersRest).

The sturdy, 14-room plank structure was built in 1833 as the plantation home of wealthy planter Devereaux Jarrett. As more and more travelers streamed through the region, the enterprising Jarrett turned his home into a 19th-century B&B. South Carolina statesman John C. Calhoun was a guest, and Joseph E. Brown, Georgia's Civil War governor, spent his honeymoon here.

Now a state historic site maintained by the Georgia Department of Natural Resources, the 14 rooms are furnished with four-poster beds, rocking chairs, vanities, marble-topped tables, goose feather mattresses, spinning wheels, china, cutlery, glassware, and memorabilia of Travelers Rest's days as a post office. The grounds are shaded by a huge white oak tree, believed to be well into its third century, and several century-old crape myrtle trees. Open Sat and Sun from 9 a.m. to 5 p.m. Admission is $5 for adults; $3 for children 6 to 18; $1 for children under 6.

Approaching the Winder/Chestnut Mountain exit (126) on I-85, 30 miles north of Metro Atlanta's I-285 Perimeter Highway, what appears to be a 16th-century French castle, surrounded by vineyards, rises from the piney landscape. It's no mirage. *Château Élan Winery & Resort* (100 Rue Charlemagne, Braselton; 678-425-0900; chateauelan.com) was established in 1982 as Georgia's first major winery since the end of Prohibition. Inside the Château's "castle," you're welcome to stroll around a movie set French marketplace and purchase jams, mustards, wine guides, cookbooks, picnic hampers, and other gourmet foods and gifts. Before purchasing the Château's grape, take the winery tour, followed by a free tasting. In a short time, Cabernet Sauvignon, Chardonnay, Riesling, Pinot Noir, Zinfandel, and other varieties bearing the Château Élan label have won more than 300 awards in national and international

North Georgia's Wineries

Before Prohibition turned the state bone-dry, Georgia ranked sixth among the nation's wine-producing states. With Château Élan leading the way, a dozen North Georgia wineries now produce a variety of vintages. Most of them welcome visitors for tours and tastings.

Crane Creek Vineyards
916 Crane Creek Rd.
Young Harris
(706) 379-1236
cranecreekvineyards.com

Kaya Vineyards and Winery
5400 Town Creek Rd.
Dahlonega
(770) 219-2514
kayavineyards.com

Fox Vineyards and Winery
225 US 11
Social Circle
(770) 787-5402
foxvineyardswinery.com

Montaluce
946 Via Montaluce
Dahlonega
(706) 867-4060
monteluce.com

Frogtown Cellars
700 Ridge Point Dr.
Dahlonega
(706) 865-0687
frogtown.us

Stonewall Creek Vineyards
323 Standing Deer Ln.
Tiger
(706) 212-0584
stonewallcreek.com

Georgia Winery Taste Center
I-75 exit 350 6469/Battlefield Parkway
Ringgold
(706) 937-2177
georgiawines.com

Tiger Mountain Vineyard and Winery
2592 Old US 441
Tiger
(706) 782-4777
tigerwine.com

Habersham Winery
7025 South Main St.
Helen
(706) 878-9463
habershamvineyards.com

Wolf Mountain Vineyards
180 Wolf Mountain Trl.
Dahlonega
(770) 867-9862
wolfmountainvineyards.com

competitions. Southerners are partial to the sweet, fruity Summerwine, a blend of peaches and Muscadine grapes. Wines range from $10 to $250.

Ten onsite bars and restaurants include Cafe Élan with quiche, pâté, chicken breast, salads, cheeses, and other light luncheon fare. Candlelit Le Clos serves a 5-course dinner with appropriate wines (and appropriate prices). For a taste of another old country, stop in the Château's Paddy's Irish Pub. Constructed in Ireland, dismantled, and shipped to Georgia, it was reassembled by Irish craftsmen and staffed with smiling young lasses and laddies. The rough-hewn timber ceiling, beer barrel tables, slate floors, and stacked stone fireplace—and a menu that includes Irish lamb stew, Irish whiskey mousse, and Irish ales, stouts, and whiskeys—make the pub seem like a cozy corner of Eire transplanted to the Georgia hills.

The 3,100-acre resort also has 3 championship golf courses with 63 stemwinding holes, tennis, and an indoor heated pool. You can overnight in the deluxe 275-room Château Élan Inn or in furnished *Golf Villas.* The *Château Élan Spa* has diet and nutrition services, massages, mineral baths, herbal wraps, saunas, and even couples' treatments.

Fort Yargo State Park, on GA 81 at nearby Winder, takes its name from a still-standing log blockhouse that white settlers built in 1792 as protection against hostile Creeks and Cherokees. The park's big green lake is an inviting place to swim and fish and to rent paddleboats, rowboats, and canoes. You can also enjoy tennis and miniature golf, hike nature trails, and set the youngsters loose on the playground. *Will-A-Way Recreation Area,* inside the park, has facilities for persons with disabilities, including specially equipped, furnished cottages. There are also 3 furnished cottages, 6 yurts, and 52 campsites not so equipped. For reservations, call (800) 864-PARK. Contact Park Superintendent at 210 Broad St., Winder, 30680; (770) 867-3489; gastateparks.org/FortYargo.

At Christmas, many people bring their holiday mail to the post office in the nearby little community of Bethlehem for that special postmark. Bethlehem is located on GA 11, 4 miles south of Winder (bethlehem.org).

The *Crawford W. Long Museum* (28 College St., Jefferson; 706-367-5307; crawfordlong.org) in Jefferson honors the physician who first used ether for surgical anesthesia. Dr. Long, then a young Jackson County practitioner, performed the first painless surgery on March 30, 1842. The museum displays his personal papers and a diorama depicting the first operation. An 1840s doctor's office and apothecary and a general store are also part of the museum. The outdoor herb garden grows many plants commonly used in 19th-century medicine. Open Tues through Fri 10 a.m. to 5 p.m., and Sat 10 a.m. to 4 p.m. Adults $5, seniors $4, students and military $3.

Bulldog Country

Ever wonder where all the tombstones come from? The answer is **Elbert County.** "The Granite Capital of the World" is home to more than 40 quarries and 150 finishing plants, which produce hundreds of tons of blue-gray stone shipped to all 50 states and several foreign countries. The multimillion-dollar Elberton granite industry had a simple, bizarre birth in 1898, when the first finishing plant was built expressly to create a Confederate soldier for Elberton's Public Square. But when the 7-foot "Johnny Reb," on a 15-foot-tall pedestal, was unveiled, townsfolks' Rebel Yells turned to jeers and tears.

With his round face, squat legs, and a uniform that looked suspiciously Union, wiseacres said he was "a cross between a Pennsylvania Dutchman and a hippopotamus" and dubbed him "Dutchy." Resentment grew and in 1900 Dutchy was pulled from his perch, "lynched," and buried face down, a military sign of disgrace.

Fearing for his own life, the sculptor, who apparently didn't know a Reb from a Yank, fled town and never returned. But from "Dutchy's" seed, Elberton granite grew dramatically.

Forgotten for eight decades, Dutchy was exhumed from the public square in 1982, pressure washed, and in recognition of his pioneering status, given a place of honor in the **Elberton Granite Museum & Exhibit.**

Georgia Guidestones, a sort of Elbert County Stonehenge, is granite country's most curious landmark. In 1979 a mysterious stranger calling himself "R. C. Christian," commissioned the monument on a hilltop 7 miles north of Elberton. He told the president of an Elberton granite finishing company that what he called the "Georgia Guidestones" would be "for the conservation of the world and to herald a new Age of Reason." He also said his name wasn't really Christian, but he was a patriotic Christian who represented a group outside of Georgia that shared his beliefs. Only the Elberton banker who handled "Mr. Christian's" substantial deposit ever knew his true identity. The banker reportedly took the secret to his grave, and no group has ever taken responsibility.

Quarrying, cutting, and etching the stones and putting them in place took nearly a year. Fewer than 100 people came for the March 1980 dedication. A minister denounced it as a potential shrine for devil-worshippers. Perhaps to calm his fears, a self-proclaimed witch twice drew pentagrams around each stone, once to drive away negative forces, the second to invoke positive forces.

Like the 4,000-year-old original on England's Salisbury Plain, the Guidestones are arranged in a circle. The central stone, which weighs 20,957 pounds, is 16 feet, 4 inches high, 3 feet by 3 feet wide, and about 1.5 feet thick. It's surrounded by 4 upright slabs radiating from it like spokes on a wagon wheel. Each slab weighs 42,437 pounds and measures 16 feet, 4 inches high and 6.5 feet wide. A 9-foot, 8-inch capstone is across the top. Slots drilled in the center stone allow visitors to track summer and winter solstices and other celestial events.

On the 4 upright slabs, "Guides to the Age of Reason," etched in 4,000 4-inch letters, in English, Spanish, Russian, Hebrew, Hindi, Chinese, and Swahili, read like New Age Ten Commandments:

Maintain humanity under 500 million in perpetual balance with nature.

Guide reproduction wisely, improving fitness and diversity.

Unite humanity with a new living language.

Rule passion, faith, tradition, and all things with tempered reason.

Protect people and nations with fair laws and just courts.

Let all nations rule internally, resolving external disputes in a world court.

Avoid petty laws and useless officials.

Balance personal rights and social duties.

Prize truth, beauty, love, seeking harmony with the infinite.

Be not a cancer on the earth, leave room for nature.

While some who speak the living languages may find their way to this isolated monument adjoining a northeast Georgia cow pasture, only a scholar of dead languages will be able to read the admonition, "Let these be Guidestones to an Age of Reason," etched on the capstone. It's written in Egyptian hieroglyphics, Sanskrit, Babylonian cuneiform, and classical Greek.

Elberton is on US 17, 36 miles south of I-85 Lavonia exit 173. The Elberton Granite Museum and Exhibit (1 Granite Plaza, Elberton; 706-283-2551; egaon line.com) is open Mon through Sat from 2 to 5 p.m. You can see Dutchy, a model of the Guidestones, and a film and exhibits about the granite industry. Free admission. Georgia Guidestones (1031 Guidestones Rd.) is 7.2 miles north of town. Free admission. You can walk right up to it.

Two state parks on the Savannah River's big reservoirs are happy hunting grounds for bass and trout fishing. ***Bobby Brown State Park*** (2509 Bobby Brown State Park Rd., Elberton; 706-213-2046, 800-864-PARK; gastateparks.org) has boat ramps, picnic areas, a swimming pool, and 61 campsites on 70,000-acre Clarks Hill Lake. Just upriver, ***Richard B. Russell State Park*** (2650

Russell State Park Dr., Elberton; 706-213-2045, 800-864-PARK; gastateparks.org) also has campsites, cottages, a swimming beach, boat ramps, an 18-hole golf course, and fish that aim to please. Both parks have a $5 per visit parking fee.

Athens throbs with the vitality of 36,000 **University of Georgia** (UGA) students, who almost balance "The Classic City's" 127,000 townies. Founded in 1785, America's oldest chartered state university existed only on paper for 16 years before the legislature provided funds for land and academic buildings in 1800. The first classes met in 1801. That same year Athens was founded on hills above the Oconee River—hopeful of Olympian inspiration, the rude little settlement was named for Greece's hub of classical learning. Planters and literati embellished the campus and Athens's elm- and oak-lined thoroughfares with Greek Revival, Georgian, and Federal architecture. Over the ensuing decades, "town and gown" have coexisted in peace and harmony only seriously disrupted when over 97,000 Bulldog football fanatics shake the skies over Sanford Stadium with exhortations of "Go-oooo Dawgs!"

Stop first at the Historic Athens Welcome Center in the **Church-Waddel-Brumby House** (280 E. Dougherty St., Athens; 706-353-1820; visitathensga .com). The fine Federalist house was built in 1820 for Alonzo Church, who became one of UGA's early presidents. Dr. Moses Waddel, who succeeded him in the president's chair, also lived in the house, believed to be the city's oldest surviving residence. You may view the lovely rooms and pick up walking and driving tours of the Athens Historic District and information about other attractions.

As Athens and the university have grown, much of the city's antebellum heritage has been lost. Many antebellum homes have been torn down, others turned into UGA sorority and frat houses, funeral homes, commercial offices, and academic buildings. Only the **Taylor-Grady House** (634 Prince Ave., Athens; 706-549-8688; taylorgradyhouse.com) is open as a museum. It was built in 1845 by General Robert Taylor. In 1863 Major William S. Grady purchased the house and his son, Henry W. Grady, lived in it while studying journalism at UGA. Grady went on to become the nationally renowned editor of the *Atlanta Constitution* and spokesman for the post–Civil War "New South." UGA's journalism school is named for him. Open Mon through Fri 9 a.m. to 5 p.m. Tickets $3 a person.

The **State Botanical Garden of Georgia** (2450 S. Milledge Ave., Athens; 706-542-1244; botgarden.uga.edu) is a serene oasis 3 miles from UGA's high-energy campus. The 3-story glass and steel Visitors Center and Conservatory is the gateway to the 313-acre sanctuary, which UGA created in 1968 as a "living laboratory" for the study and enjoyment of plants and nature.

"Just in Case"

If you fancy Civil War oddities, don't miss the "Double-Barreled Cannon," a whimsical piece of memorabilia that was a spectacular failure. Cast in Athens in 1862, each barrel was to be loaded with cannonballs connected to each other by an 8-foot chain. When fired, the missiles were supposed to exit together, pull the chain tight, and sweep the cannon across the battlefield like a scythe. In reality, the barrels weren't synchronized, and instead of devastating Yankees, the errant shots went in different directions, plowing up a cornfield, knocking down a tree and a log cabin chimney, and killing a cow. It was permanently retired and rests today on the City Hall grounds, pointing north, "just in case."

After a 10-minute audiovisual introduction, stroll among orchids, ferns, bamboo, bougainvillea, birds of paradise, and other lush tropical and semi-tropical plants that flourish along man-made streams and ponds. You can have lunch in the sunny indoor/outdoor *Gardenside Cafe* and browse among plants, books, and gardening paraphernalia in the gift shop. Revolving exhibits highlight botanical and horticultural paintings by regional and national artists.

Five miles of color-coded trails wind through hardwood forests and along ravines of the Middle Oconee River. As you admire azaleas, wildflowers, rhododendron, 125-year-old beech trees, and other plants and trees native to the Georgia piedmont, you might spot white-tailed deer, rabbits, foxes, opossum, and a remarkable variety of birds.

Theme gardens display roses, dahlias, mums, camellias, hollies, ornamentals, and other seasonal plants. There are plenty of spots for quiet musings. Eleven collections in the 3-acre International Garden follow the history and culture of botany back to the beginnings of civilization. Grounds are open daily from 8 a.m. to sunset. Visitors Center hours are Tues through Sat 9 a.m. to 4:30 p.m.; 11:30 a.m. to 4:30 p.m. Sun. Free admission.

UGA's contemporary vitality is a dichotomy with antebellum Athens. Stop at the *UGA Visitors Center* (Four Towers Building, 405 College Station Rd., Athens; 706-542-0842; visit.uga.edu), in a refurbished dairy barn and former College of Agriculture space on the edge of UGA's new East Campus, for information about campus landmarks and activities. Open Mon through Sat from 9 a.m. to 5 p.m. and Sun from 1 to 5 p.m.

The campus is a crazy quilt of classical and modern architecture. According to tradition, freshmen may not pass through the three-columned University Arch, which was forged in cast iron in 1857 and is the centerpiece of Georgia's Great Seal, representing wisdom, justice, and moderation. Walk under it and you're on the historic *North Campus.* Listed on the National Register of Historic Places, "Old North's" landmarks include Phi Kappa Hall, an 1836 Greek Revival building; Federal-style Waddel Hall, 1820; Palladian-style Demosthenian Hall, 1824; Greek Revival University Chapel, whose bells clamor joyously when the Bulldogs win one on the gridiron; and Old College, where Crawford W. Long, a Georgian who pioneered the use of anesthesia for surgery, was the 1832 roommate of Alexander Hamilton Stephens, who became vice president of the Confederacy.

The *Georgia Museum of Art* (10 Carlton St., Athens; 706-542-4662; georgiamuseum.org) is the official art museum of the state of Georgia and exhibits more than 7,000 paintings, sculptures, and other works by regional, national, and international artists. It hosts more than 20 annual special exhibits and educational programs and film series. Open Wed, Fri, and Sat from 12 to 5 p.m.; Thurs 10 a.m. to 9 p.m.; Sun from 1 to 5 p.m. Free admission.

With its thousands of perpetually ravenous students, finding a place to eat in Athens is no problem. Restaurants, casual cafes, coffeehouses, and snack bars line Broad Street across from the University Arch and spill over onto adjacent streets.

When it comes to music, Athens is a spawning ground for modern rock groups. The *40 Watt Club* (285 W. Washington St., Athens; 706-549-7879; 40watt.com) still lives on its reputation as the launching pad for R.E.M. and the B-52s back in the 1970s. Widespread Panic is the latest Athens group to make

Georgia's Many Symbols

From its official state bird (brown thrasher) to official state wildflower (azalea), Georgia has more than a dozen official state symbols. Some of the others are:

- butterfly (tiger swallowtail)
- fish (largemouth bass)
- fossil (shark's tooth)
- fruit (peach)
- game bird (bobwhite quail)
- gem (quartz)
- insect (honeybee)
- marine mammal (right whale)
- mineral (staurolite)

- reptile (gopher tortoise)
- seashell (knobbed whelk)
- character ("Pogo" Possum)
- tree (live oak)
- vegetable (Vidalia onion)
- two official state songs ("Our Georgia," a waltz, and "Georgia on My Mind," by Albany native Ray Charles)

the big time. Local bands and touring groups play at the early 1900s **Morton Theater** (199 W. Washington St.; 706-613-3770; mortontheatre.com). Built in 1910, the Morton was once the state's most famous black vaudeville theater. It has been restored to its former glory.

If you're at the corner of South Findley and Dearing Street and notice a rather impressive oak tree that seems to have some attitude, perhaps it is because it is "The Tree That Owns Itself." Also called the **Jackson Oak**, the tree stands on land that was once owned by Col. William Henry Jackson. Legend has it that he so enjoyed his childhood memories of the tree that in 1832, he deeded the land around the tree to the tree itself, to protect it. A plaque at its foot reads, "*FOR AND IN CONSIDERATION OF THE GREAT LOVE I BEAR THIS TREE AND THE GREAT DESIRE I HAVE FOR ITS PROTECTION FOR ALL TIME, I CONVEY ENTIRE POSSESSION OF ITSELF AND ALL LAND WITHIN EIGHT FEET OF THE TREE ON ALL SIDES—WILLIAM H. JACKSON (C. 1832).*" The original tree actually fell in 1942 but the current tree was grown from one of its acorns.

Oconee County

Knock on a farmhouse door down a rutted dirt road in the backwoods of Oconee County, or stop by a tidy house on a shady street in **Watkinsville,** the 200-year-old county seat, and don't be surprised when an artist invites you in. The rural but rapidly suburbanizing county of 40,000, just south of Athens, boasts what people here proudly claim is one of Georgia's most extraordinary congregations of creative talent. From Watkinsville (population 2,800) down pasture roads and in the woods around Farmington, Bishop, and Bogart, 100 or more virtuosos are painting, throwing pottery, and making jewelry; metal,

Gotcha Covered

There are almost 80 covered bridges across the state of Georgia, but the longest one is the **Watson Mill Bridge** near Comer. Measuring 228.6 feet long, it was built in 1885 by celebrated black bridge builder **Washington W. King**. The bridge is still in use and is at the heart of Watson Mill State Park in Oglethorpe County, just off Route 22 north of Athens. Washington King was the son of freed slave **Horace King**, also a noted bridge builder. The last remaining covered bridge in Georgia built by Horace King is **Red Oak Creek Bridge** in Meriwether County. Washington has several bridges remaining including the **Euharlee Creek Bridge** near Cartersville and the **Stone Mountain Covered Bridge**.

marble, and papier-mâché sculptures; decorative woodcraft; calligraphy; ceramics; woven rugs; forged iron; folk art; custom furniture; and blown and fused glass and fabric wall hangings that sell in shops from here to Alaska.

The **Oconee Cultural Arts Foundation** (OCAF, 34 School St.; 706-769-4565; ocaf.com) fosters many of the county's visual and performing arts programs. With the enthusiastic support of local governments and a wellspring of donated time, labor, and money, a 1902 redbrick school building has been regeared as a setting for exhibitions, plays, and educational workshops.

Works by Oconee's artists span the spectrum from representational to anarchic, folkloric to contemporary. There are Christmas ornaments that would fit in your pocket and steel and marble sculptures that would require an army to move—and a philosopher to interpret. Some artists are homegrown, but many move here initially to study in the University of Georgia's nationally respected visual arts programs.

A few artists work in close communities, but most prefer to labor alone in barns, cabins, old industrial buildings, and refitted farmhouses around the county. You can search for them by riding through the rolling piedmont countryside, a patchwork of pecan and peach orchards, cornfields, covered bridges, pine forests, and cattle farms, but many artists live and work hidden away on isolated roads, with no clue to the creative endeavors transpiring behind the trees.

The surest way to locate them is to stop first at the **Eagle Tavern Welcome Center** (21 N. Main St., Watkinsville; 706-769-5197; visitoconee.com). The tavern has been a landmark since 1820, when it was a frontier stagecoach stop. "The Oconee County Guide to the Arts," a free foldout guide, lists more than 50 artists, and the staff will point you in the right directions.

If the site of the stately Clydesdales in the Budweiser commercials makes your heart flutter, you can get up close and personal with these impressive giants in Bishop at the **Classic City Clydesdales Farm** (4190 Price Mills Rd.; 706-424-1889; classiccityclydesdales.com). You can spend the entire day on the farm if you'd like, watching the horses frolic in the fields, learning about wagon pulling and breeding, as well as even riding one. The visit itself is just $20 for adults, $10 for kids but there are hour long trail rides around the farm for $75. Classic City is not only home to 50 Clydesdales to adore, it also has a small herd of shaggy Highland cattle. Open Thurs through Sat.

Places to Stay in Northeast Georgia

ATHENS

The Colonels Bed and Breakfast
3890 Barnett Shoals Rd.
(706) 559-9595
thecolonels.net
Moderate to expensive
1860 mansion B&B with 7 bedrooms and 3 suites

Foundry Park Inn & Spa
295 E. Dougherty St.
(706) 549-7020
(800) 9ATHENS
graduateathens.com
Expensive
Boutique-style hotel with 119 deluxe guest rooms and suites; full-service restaurant, pub, spa, and conference center

CLAYTON

Beechwood Inn Bed & Breakfast
220 Beechwood Dr.
(706) 782-5485
beechwoodinn.ws
Moderate to expensive
Guest rooms and separate cabins available; on-site restaurant; full breakfast and evening reception included

CLERMONT

Ava House
6210 Dahlonega Hwy.
(678) 616-3168
theavahouse.com
Moderate to expensive
Replica 1890 farmhouse, 5 spacious rooms available; great breakfast

CRAWFORDVILLE

The Chicken Coop Bed and Breakfast
1030 Athens Rd.
(706) 743-3142
thechickencoopbedand breakfast.com
Moderate to expensive
Quaint cottage with 3 spacious guest rooms

DAHLONEGA

Cavender Creek Cabins
220 Beaver Dam Rd.
(866) 373-6307
(706) 864-7221
cavendercreek.com
Moderate to expensive
Nine 1- to 3-bedroom deluxe cabins on 25 wooded acres; stocked fishing pond; recreation lodge

Forrest Hills Mountain Resort & Conference
135 Forrest Hills Rd.
(800) 654-6313
(706) 864-6456
forresthillsresort.com
Expensive
Resort has 111 rooms, a day spa, fitness center, conference rooms, horse-drawn carriage rides, and plenty of wooded nature to explore

Lily Creek Lodge
2608 Auraria Rd.
(706) 864-6848
lilycreeklodge.com
Expensive
European-style mountain lodge with 13 guest suites; adult tree house; bocce court; outdoor pool and hot tub; full American/European breakfast included

Park Place Hotel
27 Park St.
(706) 864-0021
27onpark.com
Inexpensive to moderate
Large guest rooms and 2-room suites; complimentary Starbucks coffee and wine

GAINESVILLE

Holiday Inn Lanier Centre Hotel
400 E. E. Butler Pkwy.
(770) 531-0907
(877) 270-6397
ihg.com
Moderate to expensive
Modern motor hotel with 122 guest rooms; on-site restaurant and bar

HELEN

Helendorf Inn & Conference Center
33 Munich Strasse
(706) 878-2271
helendorf.com
Inexpensive to moderate
Hotel with riverfront rooms and suites; heated pool; on-site laundromat

Lodge at Smithgall Woods
61 Tsalaki Trail
(706) 878-3087
(800) 318-5848
gastateparks.og/
smithgallwoods
Expensive
See p. 192 for details

HIAWASSEE

Bed and Breakfast at Swan Lake
2650 Upper Bell Creek Rd.
(706) 896-1582
Moderate
B&B with 2 rooms and a cottage available; gourmet breakfast served

Henson Cove Place B&B
1137 Car Miles Rd.
(706) 896-6195
henson-cove-place.com
Moderate
Rustic farmhouse with 3 rooms; full breakfast included; separate cabin available for self-catering

The Ridges Resort & Marina
3499 US 76
(706) 896-2262
theridgesresort.com
Moderate to expensive
Lakeside resort has 66 guest rooms in the main hotel, condos and villas; full-service restaurant and bar; marina with rentals

LAKE RABUN

Lake Rabun Hotel
35 Andrea Dr.
(706) 782-4946
lakerabunhotel.com
Inexpensive
See p. 179 for details

SAUTEE

Stovall House
1526 GA-255
(706) 878-3355
stovallhousebnb.com
Moderate
See p. 190 for details

TOCCOA

Simmons-Bond Inn Bed and Breakfast
74 W. Tugalo St.
(706) 282-5183
simmons-bond.com
Moderate
Restored Queen Anne Victorian mansion offers 5 rooms with private baths; gourmet breakfast included

WATKINSVILLE

Watson Mill Bridge State Park
on GA 22, 6 miles south of Comer
(706) 783-5349
(800) 864-PARK for camping reservations
gastateparks.org/
WatsonMillBridge
Inexpensive
The site of Georgia's longest covered bridge; picnic, canoeing, and campground sites

YOUNG HARRIS

Brasstown Valley Resort
6321 US 76
(706) 379-9900
(800) 201-3205
brasstownvalley.com
Moderate to expensive
See p. 184 for details

Places to Eat in Northeast Georgia

ATHENS

Five & Ten
1653 S. Lumpkin St.
(706) 546-7300
fiveandten.com
Moderate to expensive
French, Southern

The Grit
199 Prince Ave.
(706) 543-6592
thegrit.com
Inexpensive
Vegetarian

Last Resort
184 W. Clayton St.
(706) 549-0810
lastresortgrill.com
Moderate
Southern

The National
232 W. Hancock St.
(706) 549-3450
thenationalrestaurant.com
Moderate to expensive
Mediterranean, Southern

Weaver D's
1016 E. Broad St.
(706) 353-7797
Weaverds.com
Inexpensive
Soul food, Southern

DAHLONEGA

Bourbon Street Grille
90 Public Square N.
(706) 864-0086
thebourbonstreetgrille.com
Moderate to expensive
Cajun

Casper's on the Square
84 Public Square N.
(706) 867-0070
caspersdahlonega.com
Moderate to expensive
Mediterranean

The Crimson Moon Cafe & Gallery
24 N. Park St.
(706) 864-3982
thecrimsonmoon.com
Inexpensive
Coffeehouse and bakery

Smith House
202 S. Chestatee St.
(706) 867-7000
smithhouse.com
Moderate
See p. 194 for details

Wolf Mountain Vineyards
180 Wolf Mountain Trl.
(706) 867-9862
wolfmountainvineyards.com
Moderate to expensive
Wine, American buffet

GAINESVILLE

2 Dog
317 Spring St.
(770) 287-8382
2dogrestaurant.com
Moderate
European, soul food

Luna's
200 Main St.
(770) 531-0848
lunas.com
Moderate to expensive
Fine dining, international

HELEN

Hofer's of Helen
8758 N. Main St.
(706) 878-8200
hofers.com
Moderate
See p. 191 for details

Mully's Nacoochee Grill
7277 S. Main St.
(706) 878-8020
mullysnacoocheegrill.com
Inexpensive to moderate
American

Troll Tavern
Castle Inn, Main Street
(706) 878-3181
trolltavern.com
Moderate
See p. 191 for details

JASPER

Mary Ann's Country Cooking
408 E Church St.
(706) 253-2225
woodbridgeinn.net
Moderate to expensive
Southern

HELPFUL WEBSITES

Athens Welcome Center
athenswelcomecenter.com

Dahlonega-Lumpkin County Chamber of Commerce
dahlonega.org

Helen and White County Convention & Visitors Bureau
helenga.org

State Botanical Garden of Georgia
botgarden.uga.edu

Towns County Tourism
mountaintopga.com

Union County Chamber of Commerce
blairsvillechamber.com

University of Georgia Performing Arts Center
pac.uga.edu

Index